Chronicles
of a
Liquid Society

Also by Umberto Eco

Chronicles
of a
Liquid Society

———

Umberto
Eco

Translated from the Italian by Richard Dixon

HOUGHTON MIFFLIN HARCOURT
BOSTON   NEW YORK   2017

For information about permission to reproduce selections from this book,
write to trade.permissions@hmhco.com or to Permissions, Houghton Mifflin Harcourt
Publishing Company, 3 Park Avenue, 19th Floor, New York, New York 10016.

First published in Italian as *Pape Satàn Aleppe. Cronache di una società liquida*
First published in Italy by La nave di Teseo, 2016

hmhco.com

Library of Congress Cataloging-in-Publication Data is available.
ISBN 978-0-544-97448-7

Book design by Brian Moore

Printed in the United States of America
DOC 10 9 8 7 6 5 4 3 2 1

Contents

Foreword

I began writing a regular column called "La bustina di Minerva" for the Italian weekly magazine *L'Espresso* in 1985, first every week, then every other week. Its title referred to a brand of matchbook that had two white spaces inside that were useful for brief jottings, and so I intended my articles to be short notes and digressions on ideas that came to mind. They were generally inspired by topical events, but not always, since I regarded it as topical that one evening I had decided, maybe, to reread a page of Herodotus, a Grimms' fairy tale, or a *Popeye* comic.

A number of earlier articles appeared in *How to Travel with a Salmon and Other Essays* (1994), and others, written before 2000, were published in *Turning Back the Clock: Hot Wars and Media Populism* (2007). But between 2000 and 2015 I had written more than four hundred articles—roughly twenty-six a year—and felt that some of these could be salvaged.

I think that most of the "Bustina di Minerva" pieces collected in this book can be seen as reflections on aspects of this "liquid society" of ours, about which I wrote in a more recent article, placed here at the beginning of the book.

Though many repetitions have been cut, some remain, since several topics came up with worrying regularity over those fifteen years, causing me to return and dwell on certain themes that were still disturbingly relevant.

UMBERTO ECO

The Liquid Society

The idea of "liquid" modernity or society comes from Zygmunt Bauman. Those who want to understand the various implications of this concept may find it helpful to read *State of Crisis*, where Bauman and Carlo Bordoni discuss this and other topics.

The liquid society begins to take shape with the movement known as postmodernism, an umbrella term that brings together a great variety of phenomena, from architecture to philosophy to literature, not always in a coherent fashion. Postmodernism signaled the crisis of "grand narratives," each of which had claimed that one model of order could be superimposed on the world; it devoted itself to a playful or ironic reconsideration of the past, and was woven in various ways with nihilistic tendencies. But postmodernism, according to Bordoni, is also on the way out. It was temporary in character, we have passed through it without noticing, and it will be studied one day like pre-Romanticism. It served to point out an event that was happening and represented a sort of ferry from modernity to a present that still has no name.

Among the characteristics of this nascent present Bauman includes the crisis facing the state: what freedom do nation-states retain when faced with the power of supranational entities? We are witnessing the disappearance of something that used to ensure individuals could resolve the various problems of our time in a homogeneous fashion. This crisis has led to a collapse of ideologies, and therefore of political parties, and to a general call for a sharing of values that allowed individuals to feel part of something that understood their needs.

The crisis in the concept of community gives rise to unbridled individualism: people are no longer fellow citizens, but rivals to beware of. This "subjectivism" has threatened the foundations of modernity, has made it fragile, producing a situation with no points of reference, where everything dissolves into a sort of liquidity. The certainty of the law is lost, the judiciary is regarded as an enemy, and the only solutions for individuals who have no points of reference are to make themselves conspicuous at all costs, to treat conspicuousness as a value, and to follow consumerism. Yet this is not a consumerism aimed at the possession of desirable objects that produce satisfaction, but one that immediately makes such objects obsolete. People move from one act of consumption to another in a sort of purposeless bulimia: the new cell phone is no better than the old one, but the old one has to be discarded in order to indulge in this orgy of desire.

The collapse of ideologies and political parties: it has been suggested that political parties have become like taxis taken by vote-controlling mob leaders or Mafia bosses, who choose them casually, according to what is on offer—politicians can change party allegiance without creating any scandal. It's not just people: society itself is living in an increasingly precarious condition.

What can replace this liquefaction? We don't yet know, and the interregnum will last for quite a long time. Bauman notes that a typical feature of the interregnum, once the faith in salvation from above, from the state, or from revolution is gone, is indignation. Such indignation knows what it doesn't want, but not what it does. And I'd like to mention that one of the problems the police raise in relation to Black Bloc protest movements is that they can no longer be labeled, as used to be the case with anarchists, Fascists, or the Red Brigades.

Such movements act, but no one knows when they will act, or in what direction. Not even they know.

Is there any way of coming to terms with liquidity? There is, and it involves an awareness that we live in a liquid society that, to be understood and perhaps overcome, requires new instruments. But the trouble is that politicians and a large part of the intelligentsia haven't yet understood the implications of this phenomenon. For the moment, Bauman is still a "voice of one crying in the wilderness."

2015

Turning Back the Clock

Freestyle Catholics and
sanctimonious secularists

When people refer to the great spiritual transformations that marked the end of the twentieth century, they immediately start talking about the collapse of ideologies, which is undeniable, and has blurred traditional distinctions between right and left. But the question remains whether the fall of the Berlin Wall was the cause of this collapse or just one of its consequences.

Think of science. People wanted science to be a neutral territory, ideal for progress shared by both liberals and socialists: the only difference was how this progress was to be managed and in whose favor —still exemplified by *The Communist Manifesto* of 1848, which lauded capitalist triumphs only to conclude, more or less, that "we too now want these things." A liberal was someone who believed in technological advance, whereas a reactionary preached the return to tradition and the unspoiled nature of once upon a time. The cases of "revolution back to the past," like that of the Luddites who sought to destroy machinery, were marginal—they had no real influence on the net division between the two positions.

This division began to go wrong in 1968, a time that mixed together Stalinists in love with steel, flower power, workerism (which expected automation to bring about the destruction of employment), and prophets of liberation through the drugs of Don Juan. It fell apart at a time when third-world populism became a common standard for both the far left and the far right, and now we find ourselves confronted with a movement like that of Seattle, a meeting point for neo-Luddites, radical environmentalists, ex-workerists, lumpen and spearhead workers, in the rejection of cloning, of the Big Mac, of transgenic and nuclear technologies.

A significant transformation came about in the opposition between the religious and the secular worlds. For thousands of years, the spirit of religion was associated with a distrust of progress, rejection of the world, doctrinal intransigence. The secular world, on the other hand, looked optimistically upon the transformation of nature, the flexibility of ethical principles, the fond rediscovery of "other" forms of religion and of primitive thought.

There were, of course, those believers, such as Teilhard de Chardin, who appealed to "worldly realities," to history as a march toward redemption, while there were plenty of secular doom merchants, with the negative utopias of Orwell and Huxley, or the kind of science fiction that offered us the horrors of a future dominated by hideous scientific rationality. But it was the task of religion to call to us at the final moment, and the task of secularism to sing hymns in praise of the locomotive.

The recent gathering of enthusiastic young papal groupies shows us the transformation that has taken place under the reign of Pope John Paul II. A mass of youngsters who accept the Catholic faith but, judging from the answers they recently gave in interviews, are far distant from neurotic fundamentalism, are willing to make compromises over premarital relationships, contraceptives, even drugs, and certainly when it comes to clubbing; meanwhile, the secular world moans about noise pollution and a New Age spirit that seems to unite neo-revolutionaries, followers of Monsignor Milingo, and sybarites devoted to Oriental massage.

This is just the start. We have plenty of surprises in store.

2000

Have we really invented so much?

The following advertisement probably appeared on the Internet, but I don't know where, since it arrived by email. It's a modest proposal for the sale of something entirely new, Built-in Orderly Organized Knowledge, whose initials spell out BOOK.

No wires, no battery, no electronic circuits, no switches or buttons, it is compact and portable—you can even use it while you're sitting in an armchair by the fire. It's a sequence of numbered sheets of recyclable paper, each of which contains thousands of bits of information. These sheets are held together in the correct sequence by an elegant device called a binding.

Each page is scanned optically and the information is registered directly in the brain. There is a "browse" control that allows you to pass from one page to another, either forward or back, with a single flick of the finger. By using the "index" feature you can immediately find the information you want on the exact page. You can also buy an accessory called a "BOOKmark," which enables you to return to where you left off in the previous session, even if the BOOK has been closed.

The ad ends with various details about this innovative device and also announces the availability of the Portable Erasable-Nib Cryptic Intercommunication Language Stylus (PENCILS). Not only is it a nice piece of humor, but it also provides the answer to many anxious questions about the possible demise of the book with the advance of the computer.

There are many objects that, once invented, cannot be further improved, such as the cup, the spoon, the hammer. When Philippe Starck decided to change the shape of the lemon squeezer he produced a magnificent object, but it lets the pips fall into the glass, whereas the old-fashioned squeezer holds them with the pulp. I was annoyed the other day, in class, to find I had to use an expensive new electronic machine that projects hazy images—the old luminous blackboard, or even the ancient overhead projector, does a better job.

As the twentieth century draws to a close, I wonder whether in fact we have invented so many things—so many new things—in recent years. The objects we use from day to day were all invented in the nineteenth century. Here are some of them: the train (though the steam engine dates from the eighteenth century), the car and the oil industry that came before it, propeller-driven steamships, reinforced concrete, the skyscraper, the submarine, underground railways, the dynamo, the turbine, the diesel engine, the airplane, the typewriter, the gramophone, the Dictaphone, the sewing machine, the refrigerator, canned food, pasteurized milk, the cigarette lighter and the cigarette, Yale security locks, the elevator, the washing machine, the electric iron, the fountain pen, the eraser, blotting paper, the postage stamp, the pneumatic tube, the water closet, the electric bell, the electric fan, the vacuum cleaner (1901), the safety razor, the folding bed, the barber's chair and swivel office chair, friction and safety matches, the raincoat, the zipper, the safety pin, fizzy drinks, the bicycle with inner-tube tires, wheels with steel spokes and chain transmission, the omnibus, the electric tram, the elevated railroad, cellophane, celluloid, artificial fibers, department stores to sell all this stuff, and—please note—electric lighting, telephone, telegraph, radio, photography, and cinema. Charles Babbage invented a calculating machine capable of doing sixty-six additions per minute, and we are therefore partway to the computer.

The twentieth century has, of course, brought us electronics, penicillin and many other life-prolonging drugs, plastic materials, nuclear fission, television, and space travel. Perhaps I've left something out, but it is also true that today's costliest fountain pens and wristwatches try to duplicate the classic models of a hundred years ago, and I have noted before that the Internet, the latest step forward in the field of communication, overtakes the wireless telegraphy invented by Marconi with a telegraphy that uses wires—in other words, marking the return (backward) from radio to telephone.

In the case of at least two twentieth-century inventions—plastics and nuclear fission—there are attempts to disinvent them because it's now clear they are harming the planet. Progress doesn't necessarily involve going forward at all costs. I've asked for my luminous blackboard to be returned to me.

2000

Full speed backward!

Some time ago I warned that we were witnessing an interesting technological regression. First of all, the disturbing influence of television had been put in check thanks to the remote control, enabling viewers to channel-hop and thus ushering in a phase of creative freedom. Final liberation from television came with the video recorder, which was a step toward cinematography. The remote control could also be used to mute the sound, so returning to the delights of the silent movie. In the meantime, the Internet, an eminently literate form of communication, had disposed of the dreaded Culture of the Image. At this point pictures, too, could be eliminated, inventing a sort of box that just emitted sounds and required no remote control. I thought I was joking at the time in imagining the rediscovery of radio, but I was prophesying—evidently through some supernatural inspiration—the advent of the iPod.

We reached the final stage when, after broadcasts on the airwaves, the new era of cable television arrived with pay-TV, passing from wireless telegraphy to cable telegraphy, a phase completed by the Internet, thus superseding Guglielmo Marconi and going back to Antonio Meucci and Alexander Graham Bell.

I expounded this theory about the march backward in my book *Turning Back the Clock*, where I applied these principles to political life—and, what's more, I recently noted that we are returning to the nights of 1944, with military patrols in the streets and teachers and children in school uniform.

Then something else happened. Computers become obsolete in three years. Anyone who has had to buy a new one recently will have found that computers now have Windows Vista already installed. Now, you only have to read the various Internet blogs about what users think of Vista (I won't go any further for fear of ending up in court), and hear the views of your friends who have fallen into that trap, to come to the perhaps mistaken, but absolutely firm, conclusion not to buy a computer with Vista installed. And yet, if you want an up-to-date computer of reasonable dimensions you have to put up with Vista. Or make do with a clone as large as a trailer truck, put together by an eager seller who will still install Windows XP and earlier versions. Your desk will then look like an Olivetti laboratory with the 1959 Elea computer.

I think the computer manufacturers are realizing that sales are falling significantly as customers decide not to buy a new computer so as to avoid Vista. So what then? To find out, go to the Internet and look for "Vista downgrading" or something similar. There you will learn that if you've bought a new computer with Vista, spending whatever it cost, then by paying yet more, and going through a complex procedure that I gave up trying to follow, you could go back to using Windows XP or earlier versions.

Computer users know what upgrading is. So downgrading is taking your highly advanced computer back to the happy condition of the older system—for a price. Before the Internet had invented this magnificent neologism, a normal dictionary defined the word "downgrade" as a noun meaning a downward gradient or descending slope, or a downward course or tendency in morals, religion, etc., while as a verb it means to reduce to a lower grade, rank, or level of importance. We are therefore being offered the opportunity, with much effort and for a certain amount of money, to lower the grade, rank, or level of importance of something for which we have already paid a certain sum. This would be unbelievable if it weren't for the fact that it's true: hundreds of poor computer buffs are working away madly online and paying whatever it costs to downgrade their software. Are we ever going to reach the stage when, for a reasonable sum, we can exchange our computer for an exercise book with an inkwell, pen, and Perry & Co. nib?

But the whole thing is not so paradoxical. Some technological advances cannot be bettered. A mechanical spoon cannot be invented: what was invented two thousand years ago is still fine as it is. The Concorde has been abandoned even though it flew between Paris and New York in three hours. I'm not so sure it was the right thing to do, but progress can also mean moving back a few steps, such as reverting to wind power instead of using oil, and so forth. Be prepared for the future! Full speed backward!

2008

I remember, I remember

Life is but a slow remembrance of childhood. Fine. But what sweetens this remembrance is that, looking back with nostalgia, we have a fond memory even of moments that seemed painful at the time, like the day we fell into a ditch and sprained an ankle, and had to spend a couple of weeks at home plastered in gauze soaked with egg white. I fondly remember the nights I spent in an air raid shelter. We'd be roused from our deepest sleep, dragged in our pajamas and coats into a damp, reinforced-concrete cellar lit with dim bulbs, and we'd play and run around with the dull thuds of explosions overhead, unable to tell whether they were antiaircraft guns or bombs. Our mothers shivered, cold and frightened, but for us it was a strange adventure. That's nostalgia for you. We're therefore ready to accept all that reminds us of the dreadful years of the 1940s, and it's the tribute we pay to our old age.

What were cities like at that time? Dark at night, when the blackout compelled the occasional passersby to use lamps powered not with batteries but with dynamos, much like an old bicycle lamp, which was operated by friction, by rather clumsily setting in motion a sort of hand trigger. Later on, though, a curfew was imposed and you weren't allowed onto the streets.

During the daytime the city was patrolled by military units, at least until 1943, when the Royal Italian Army was stationed there, but more heavily during the Republic of Salò, when squads and patrols of marines from the San Marco Regiment or the Black Brigades used to pass through continually, while in the villages there were more likely to be groups of partisans—both sides armed to the teeth. In this militarized city, people were not permitted to congregate at certain hours, Blackshirts and girls in Fascist uniforms swarmed about, and children in black smocks came out of school at midday. Meanwhile, mothers went off to buy what little there was in the grocery stores, and you had to pay considerable sums on the black market for any kind of bread that wasn't vile and made of sawdust. At home there was hardly any light, and the only heat was in the kitchen. At night we slept with a warm brick in the bed, and I even fondly remember the icy temperatures. Now, I'm not suggesting we are back in those times, or certainly not completely. But I'm beginning to have some sense of this. For a start, there are Fascists in the government—not just Fascists, and no longer exactly like the old Fascists, but what does it matter? We know perfectly well that history is played out first as tragedy and then as farce. There again, in the old days we used to see posters on the walls showing a drunken black American with his claw hand clasped around a white Venus de Milo. Today, on television, I see the faces of thousands of emaciated black people arriving in our countries and, frankly, the people around me are much more frightened than they were in those days.

The black smock is being brought back in schools, and I have nothing against it; better that than the tough-guy designer T-shirts, except that I sense a taste of madeleines dipped in tea. I have just read a news story that the mayor of Novara, in Piedmont—a member of the Lega Nord (Northern League)—has banned gatherings of more than three people in the park at night. I wait with a Proustian thrill for the return of the curfew. Our soldiers are fighting against rebels in various parts of East Asia. But I also see military units, well armed and wearing camouflage jackets, on the sidewalks of our cities. The army, as then, doesn't fight only at the frontiers but carries out policing operations. I seem to find myself in a scene from Rossellini's *Rome, Open City*. I read articles and hear discussions very much like those I used to read in the magazine *La Difesa della Razza* (*The Defense of the Race*), which attacked not only Jews but also Gypsies, Moroccans, and foreigners in general. Bread has become expensive. We are warned to save on oil, to stop wasting electricity, to switch shop window lights off at night. There are fewer cars, and bicycle thieves are reappearing. For a touch of originality, there will soon be water rationing. We don't yet have separate governments for southern and northern Italy, though certain politicians are working on it. I miss a leader who hugs and kisses buxom farm girls chastely on the cheek. But each to his own taste.

2008

Being Seen

Wave *ciao ciao* to the camera

As I become conscious of global warming and the disappearance of spring and fall, and find it confirmed in various authoritative writings, I wonder how my grandson, who is not yet two, will react one day when he hears mention of the word "spring" or reads poetry at school that describes the first languorous moments of autumn. How, in the future, will he react to Vivaldi's *Four Seasons*? Perhaps he will live in another world to which he is fully accustomed, and won't miss the spring, watching berries form on hot winter days. After all, as a child I had no experience of dinosaurs and yet I could imagine them. Perhaps springtime is just an old person's nostalgia, like nights spent in air raid shelters playing hide-and-seek.

And will this child of the future think it normal to live in a world where the prime virtue is being seen, a value more important now than sex or money? A world where people will be ready to do anything to be seen on television—or whatever will have replaced television by then—so as to be recognized by others and not to vegetate in a frightening and unbearable anonymity. A world where more and more respectable mothers will be ready to recount the most sordid family tales in a sob-story broadcast, so that they can be recognized the next day in the local supermarket and sign autographs. A world where young girls will say they want to be an actress, as they do today, but not to become a Dietrich or a Garbo, not to perform Shakespeare or to sing like Josephine Baker, wearing nothing but bananas on the stage of the Folies Bergère, and not even to do a graceful high kick like the dancers of a bygone time, but to become a television quiz girl, purely for show, with nothing in the way of talent.

Someone in the future will then explain to this child at school, along with lessons about the kings of Rome and the fall of Berlusconi, or films titled *Once Upon a Time There Was Fiat*, how human beings have always, from earliest antiquity, sought to be recognized by those around them. And how some would try to be good company at the local bar in the evening, others to excel at soccer or clay-pigeon shooting at local festivities, or boast how they hooked a fish this long. And how girls wanted to be noticed for the pretty bonnet they wore to church on Sunday, and grandmothers for being the best cook or seamstress in the village. And heaven forbid that it shouldn't have been so, for human beings, to become known, need to catch the eye of an Other, and the more they are recognized, or think they are recognized, the more they are loved and admired by the Other—and if instead of one Other there are a hundred or a thousand, then so much the better. They feel satisfied.

And so in an age of great and ceaseless movement, when people leave their villages and lose their sense of home, and the Other is someone with whom they communicate via the Internet, it will seem natural for human beings to seek recognition in other ways, and the village square is replaced by the global audience of the television broadcast, or whatever comes next.

But perhaps not even schoolteachers, or those who take their place, will recall that in that bygone time there was a rigid distinction between being famous and being talked about. Everyone wanted to become famous as the best archer or the finest dancer, but no one wanted to be talked about as the most cuckolded man in the village, for being impotent, or for being a whore. If anything, the whore would claim to be a dancer and the impotent man would make up stories about his gargantuan sexual exploits. In the world of the future, if it is anything like what is going on now, this distinction will be lost. People will do anything to be "seen" and "talked about." There will be no difference between the fame of the great immunologist and that of the young man who killed his mother with a hatchet, between the great lover and the man who has won the world competition for the shortest penis, between the person who has established a leper colony in central Africa and the man who has most successfully avoided paying his tax. Every little bit will help, just to be seen and recognized the next day by the grocer or the banker.

I'd like to ask anyone who thinks I'm being apocalyptic why people now position themselves behind a person being interviewed so as to be seen waving *ciao ciao* to the television audience, or why they go on a quiz show not even knowing that one swallow doesn't make a summer. What does it matter? They'll be famous just the same.

But I'm not being apocalyptic. Perhaps the child I'm referring to will become the follower of some new sect whose purpose will be concealment from the world, exile in the desert, withdrawal into the cloister, the dignity of silence. After all, this has already happened, at the end of an age when emperors began to appoint their own horse as senator.

2002

God is my witness that I'm a fool . . .

The other morning in Madrid, I was at lunch with my king. Don't misunderstand me: despite my proudly republican allegiance, two years ago I was appointed a duke of the Kingdom of Redonda with the title of Duque de la Isla del Día de Antes. I share this ducal dignity with Pedro Almodóvar, A. S. Byatt, Francis Ford Coppola, Arturo Pérez-Reverte, John Ashbery, Orhan Pamuk, Claudio Magris, Ray Bradbury, and several others, all of whom share the common quality of being liked by the king.

The island of Redonda lies in the West Indies and measures thirty square kilometers, the size of a handkerchief. It is completely uninhabited, and I don't think any of its monarchs have ever set foot on it. It was acquired in 1865 by Matthew Dowdy Shiell, a banker who had petitioned Queen Victoria to establish it as an independent realm, which she graciously did—she could see it posed no threat to the British colonial empire. Over the decades the island had been passed down to various monarchs, some of whom had sold the title several times over, causing disputes between the various pretenders. If you want to find out more about its multidynastic history, look up Redonda in Wikipedia. The last king abdicated in 1997 in favor of the Spanish writer Javier Marías, who set about appointing dukes left, right, and center.

That's the whole story, which of course has a slight whiff of pataphysical folly, though, after all, becoming a duke doesn't happen every day. The point, however, is another: in the course of our conversation, Marías said something that struck me as interesting. We were discussing how people today are prepared to go to any lengths to appear on television, even if only to be the idiot who waves *ciao ciao* behind the person being interviewed. Recently in Italy, the brother of a young woman who had been brutally murdered, after the sad privilege of a mention in the crime columns of the newspapers, approached a television celebrity asking to be hired so he could exploit the tragic notoriety—and we know of some individuals who, to catch the limelight in a news story, are prepared to declare themselves cuckolded, impotent, or fraudulent, nor is it a secret to criminal psychologists that what moves the serial killer is his desire to be discovered and hence become a celebrity.

Why this folly? we asked. Marías suggested that what is happening today stems from the fact that people no longer believe in God. At one time they were persuaded that everything they did had at least one Spectator, who knew their every thought and deed, who could sympathize with them or, if necessary, condemn them. They could be outcasts, good-for-nothings, losers scorned by their fellow men. They were people who would be forgotten as soon as they were dead, but who nourished the belief that there was at least One who knew all about them.

"God at least knows how much I've suffered," the sick grandmother abandoned by her grandchildren would say. "God knows I'm innocent," the person unjustly convicted would say in consolation. "God knows how much I've done for you," the mother would say to her ungrateful child. "God knows how much I love you," the abandoned lover would shout. "God alone knows what I've had to deal with," complained the wretch whose misfortunes everyone ignored. God was always invoked as the all-seeing eye, whose gaze brought meaning to the grayest and most senseless life.

Once this all-seeing Witness has gone, has been taken away, what remains? All that's left is the eye of society, the eye of the Other, before whom you must reveal yourself so as not to disappear into the black hole of anonymity, into the vortex of oblivion, even at the cost of choosing the role of village idiot who strips down to his underpants and dances on the pub table. Appearance on the television screen is the only substitute for transcendence, and all in all it's a satisfying substitute. People see themselves, and are seen, in a hereafter, but in return, everyone in that hereafter sees us here, and meanwhile we too are here. Think about it: to be able to enjoy all the advantages of immortality, albeit swift and ephemeral, and at the same time to have a chance of being celebrated in our own homes here, on earth, for our assumption into the Empyrean.

The trouble is that "recognition" is ambiguous. We all hope that our merits, or our sacrifices, or whatever good qualities we have, are "recognized." But when we appear on the television screen and people see us afterward at the local bar and say, "I saw you on television last night," they are merely saying "We recognize you"—in other words, we recognize your face—and that's a different proposition altogether.

2010

I tweet, therefore I am

I'm not on Twitter, not on Facebook—the Italian Constitution allows me not to be. But there is evidently a false Twitter account in my name, as there seems to be for other well-known people. I once met a woman whose eyes brimmed with gratitude as she explained how she read me all the time on Twitter and sometimes corresponded with me, reaping much intellectual benefit. I tried telling her that it was a false me, but she gazed back as though I were telling her I wasn't really who I am. If I was on Twitter, then I existed. *Twittero ergo sum.*

I wasn't too worried about trying to convince her, whatever she might have thought of me, since she was evidently pleased with what the false Eco was telling her, and this whole business was hardly going to change the history of Italy, nor that of the world—nor my own, for that matter. At one time I regularly received large dossiers from someone who stated she also sent them to the Italian president and other illustrious figures in protest against a person who was persecuting her. She was sending them to me, she said, because each week in my *L'Espresso* column, I came out in her defense. She therefore interpreted everything I wrote as relating to her personal problem. I never tried to contradict her, as it would have been pointless, and her own grave paranoia would have done nothing to solve the Middle East crisis. Eventually, because I didn't reply, she turned her attention on someone else, I've no idea who.

The opinions expressed on Twitter have no relevance, since everyone is talking—those who believe in the appearances of Our Lady of Medjugorje, those who go to fortunetellers, those who claim that September 11 was planned by the Jews, and those who believe in Dan Brown. I'm always fascinated by the Twitter messages that appear at the bottom of the screen during television shows. They say anything and everything.

Twitter is like a village or suburban bar. You hear the village idiot, the small landowner who reckons he's being persecuted by the tax authority, the local doctor who resents not getting the post of professor of comparative anatomy at a big university, the passerby who has already had too much grappa, the truck driver who talks about the beautiful women he has picked up on the highway, and occasionally there is someone with a few sensible ideas. But it all ends there. Barroom gossip has never changed international politics, and it was only the Fascists who worried about it and banned the discussion of high politics in bars. On the whole, though, what the majority of people think is reflected in the statistic that emerges at the moment when, after due reflection, they vote, at which point they ignore what's been said at the bar and vote for the views expressed by someone else.

And so the ether of the Internet is crossed by irrelevant opinions, not least because, even though great ideas can be expressed in fewer than 140 characters, such as "Love thy neighbor as thyself," rather more are needed to describe Adam Smith's *The Wealth of Nations*, and still more to explain the meaning of E=mc².

Then why is Twitter being used by leading politicians, who could simply send out a press release and be quoted in newspapers and on television, reaching also the multitude who aren't connected to the Internet? And why does the pope get a few seminarians employed by the Vatican as temps to write short summaries of what he has already said *Urbi et Orbi* in front of millions of television viewers? Frankly, I don't know. Someone must have persuaded them that it all helps to stir faith among a large number of Web users. But then, apart from politicians and the pope, why does anyone else use Twitter?

Perhaps to feel important.

2013

The loss of privacy

Privacy is one of the problems of our time—it concerns more or less everyone. Privacy means, roughly, very roughly, that we are all entitled to go about our business without the rest of the world—and, in particular, agencies linked to the organs of power—knowing what we're doing. There are of course institutions that try to protect privacy. And so it's all the more worrying that it's possible out there to discover through our credit cards what we've been buying, which hotel we've stayed at, and where we've dined. The same is true with telephone tapping, except in cases where it's essential for identifying criminals; indeed, Vodafone has recently warned that agents from every country can find out more or less secretly whom we are telephoning and what we are saying.

Privacy therefore seems a right that each of us should want to defend at all costs, to make sure that we don't find ourselves in a world of Big Brother, the real Big Brother, where the universal eye can monitor all that we do or even think.

But the question is whether people are really concerned about privacy. At one time the threat to privacy came from gossip. The fear of gossip, or the washing of dirty linen in public, came from the impact it had on our public reputation. But perhaps in the so-called liquid society, where people suffer from lack of identity and values, and have no points of reference, the only means for obtaining social recognition is through "being seen" at all costs.

And so a woman today who goes out and sells herself, who at one time would have tried to keep her vocation hidden from her family and neighbors perhaps by describing herself as an "escort," happily performs her role in public and even appears on television; the couples who once jealously guarded their differences now take part in trash broadcasts, telling everyone about their adultery and unfaithfulness, to public applause; on the train, our neighbor yells into his cell phone about what he thinks of his sister-in-law and what his tax consultant ought to be doing; those under criminal investigation, instead of withdrawing to the countryside until the wave of scandal has died down, now generally prefer to appear in public with a smile on their face, since it's better to be a dishonest celebrity than an honest nonentity.

A recent article by Zygmunt Bauman in *La Repubblica* reported that the social networks (especially Facebook), instruments for keeping an eye on other people's thoughts and emotions, are being used by the organs of power, but with the enthusiastic endorsement of those taking part. Bauman also talks about a "confessional society, promoting public self-exposure to the rank of the prime and easiest available, as well as arguably the most potent and only truly proficient proof of social existence." In other words, for the first time in the history of mankind, those who are being spied upon are helping the spies to make their work easier, and gain satisfaction from being observed as they live, even if at times they are behaving like criminals or idiots.

It is also true that, as soon as everyone is capable of knowing everything about everyone, and everyone identifies with the sum of the inhabitants of the planet, the excess of information can produce only confusion, noise, and silence. But this ought to worry the spies, whereas those being spied upon think it's a good thing that their friends, their neighbors, and perhaps their enemies know their most intimate secrets, as this is the only way they feel themselves to be a living and active part of the social body.

2014

The Old and the Young

The average lifespan

I wonder whether many Italians remember this poem by Edmondo De Amicis:

> Beauty is not always canceled out by time
> Or marred by toil and fever;
> My mother is sixty and past her prime,
> Yet more beautiful I think than ever.

It's a hymn not to female beauty but to filial devotion. A devotion that ought now to be shifted toward the bounds of ninety years, since a woman of sixty, provided she's in good health, is still lively and active—and, with a little plastic surgery, can look twenty years younger. Yet I remember asking myself as a child whether it was right to go on living beyond sixty, since it would be terrible to end up weak, dribbling, and senile in an old people's home. And thinking about the year 2000, I imagined, with Dante in mind, that I might live to seventy, and therefore till 2002, but it seemed such a remote conjecture, since rarely at that time did people reach so venerable an age.

I was reminded of this a few years ago when I met Hans-Georg Gadamer, who was then one hundred. He had traveled a long way for a conference, and was tucking into his meal with gusto. I asked him how he was, and he replied with an almost mournful smile that his legs were getting creaky. I felt like thumping him for his cheerful impudence. Indeed, he remained in excellent health for another two years.

We continue to think we are living in an age when technology is making great strides forward each day; we wonder where globalization will eventually lead us; but less often do we consider that the greatest advance achieved by humanity is in prolonging the average lifespan. After all, the idea that mankind could control nature was once vaguely understood by the troglodyte who managed to make a fire, not to mention our more advanced ancestor who had invented the wheel. Ideas about the future construction of a flying machine were put forward by Roger Bacon, Leonardo da Vinci, and Cyrano de Bergerac; the prospect of increasing the speed of travel was apparent from the invention of steam power; the advent of electricity could be foreseen back in the days of Alessandro Volta. But people for centuries had been dreaming in vain about the elixir of long life and the fount of eternal youth. In the Middle Ages there were excellent windmills, still good today for producing alternative energy, but a church was the place for pilgrims looking for the miracle of reaching the age of forty.

We landed on the Moon more than thirty years ago and cannot yet get to Mars, but at the time of the lunar landing many people of seventy had reached the end of life, whereas today, heart attack and cancer aside, it's not unreasonable to hope to reach ninety. In short, the great progress—if we want to call it progress—has been in the field of life expectancy more than in the field of the computer. Computers had been heralded by Pascal's calculating machine, and Pascal died at the age of thirty-nine, which was then a good age. There again, Alexander the Great and Catullus died at thirty-three, Mozart at thirty-six, Chopin at thirty-nine, Spinoza at forty-five, Saint Thomas Aquinas at forty-nine, Shakespeare and Fichte at fifty-two, Descartes at fifty-four, and Hegel at the ripe old age of sixty-one.

Many of the problems we face today result from the extension of the average lifespan. I'm not talking about pensions. The enormous migration from the third world to Western countries is surely due to millions of people hoping to find food, work, and all that cinema and television promise, but they are also hoping to reach a world in which people live longer—and in any event to escape from one where they die too young. And yet, though I don't have the figures at hand, I believe the amount we spend on geriatric research and preventive medicine is infinitely lower than what we spend on military technology and information. Yet we know more than enough about how to destroy a city and how to move information around cheaply, whereas we still have no exact idea about how to reconcile collective well-being, the future of young people, global overpopulation, and the prolongation of life.

Young people might think that progress is what allows them to send text messages from their phone or fly at low cost to New York. But the amazing fact, and the unresolved problem, is that they plan, if all goes well, to reach adulthood at forty, whereas their ancestors became adults at sixteen.

Certainly we have to thank the Lord, or our lucky stars, that we are living longer, but we have to regard this not just as a self-evident fact, but as one of the most dramatic problems of our time.

2003

Fair is foul, and foul is fair?

Hegel observed that only with Christianity did the artistic portrayal of pain and horror make its first appearance. "Forms of Greek beauty," he said, "cannot be used to portray Christ flagellated, crowned with thorns . . . crucified, dying." He was wrong, because the Greek world wasn't just white marble Venuses, but also the punishment of Marsyas, the anguish of Oedipus, and the murderous passion of Medea. All the same, in Christian painting and sculpture there is no shortage of faces disfigured with pain, notwithstanding the sadism of Mel Gibson. In any event, Hegel reminds us, thinking in particular of early German and Flemish painting, that deformity triumphs when Jesus's persecutors appear.

Someone recently pointed out that in a famous painting of the Passion, by Hieronymus Bosch in Ghent, two of the hideous torturers would send many of today's rock singers and their young imitators mad with envy: one with a double piercing on his chin and the other with his face pierced all over with metal gewgaws. Except that Bosch wanted in this way to produce a sort of manifestation of evil, anticipating the belief of the Italian criminologist Cesare Lombroso that those who tattooed and interfered with their bodies were innate delinquents, whereas today one might have feelings of distaste for youngsters with beads on their tongues, but it would be, if nothing else, statistically wrong to consider them genetically defective.

If we then think that many of these same young people swoon over the "classic" beauty of George Clooney or Nicole Kidman, it becomes clear that they follow their parents, who, on the one hand, buy cars and televisions designed according to the Renaissance canons of the golden ratio or crowd the Uffizi Gallery to experience Stendhal syndrome, while, on the other hand, they get their entertainment from splatter movies where walls are covered with brain matter, buy dinosaurs or other toy monsters for their children, and go to happenings where artists pierce their hands, torture their limbs, and mutilate their genitals.

Not that parents or children are rejecting all things to do with beauty in preference for what in previous centuries was considered hideous. That was perhaps what the futurists were doing when they sought to shock the bourgeoisie by proclaiming, "Let us boldly create ugliness in literature," and what Aldo Palazzeschi was doing in *Il controdolore* (1913) when he suggested giving children a healthy education in ugliness by letting them have, as toys, "puppets that are hunchbacked, blind, gangrenous, crippled, consumptive, syphilitic, that mechanically cry, shout, complain, that have attacks of epilepsy, plague, cholera, hemorrhages, hemorrhoids, discharges, madness, that faint, gasp, die." Quite simply, people today still enjoy certain kinds of classic beauty, and appreciate a good-looking child, or a fine landscape, or a Greek statue; and then, at other times, they gain pleasure from what had once been seen as intolerably ugly.

Ugliness is indeed sometimes chosen as the new model for beauty, as happens in cyborg "philosophy." In William Gibson's early novels, a human being in whom various organs had been replaced by mechanical or electrical equipment could still be seen as representing a disturbing vision of the future. Today, however, certain radical feminists propose that sexual distinctions can be overcome through the creation of neutral, postorganic, or transhuman bodies, and Donna Haraway has launched the slogan "I'd rather be a cyborg than a goddess."

According to some, this means that the postmodern world has removed all contradiction between beauty and ugliness. It's not even a matter of repeating with the witches in *Macbeth*, "Fair is foul, and foul is fair." The two values, they argue, have simply merged, losing their distinctive characteristics.

But is it true? And are certain forms of behavior among young people and artists just phenomena of marginal significance, celebrated by a minority of the world's population? On television we see children dying of hunger and reduced to skeletons with distended stomachs, we learn of women raped by intruders, we hear about human bodies tortured, while, on the other hand, constantly returning before us are the not-too-distant images of other living skeletons destined for the gas chamber. Only yesterday we saw limbs torn apart by the explosion of a skyscraper or an aircraft in flight, and we live in terror that this might also happen to us tomorrow. Each of us knows that these things are gruesome, and no awareness of the relativity of aesthetic values can persuade us to experience them as an object of pleasure.

Perhaps, then, cyborg, splatter, The Thing from Another World, and disaster movies are all superficial manifestations, hyped by the mass media, through which we exorcise a far deeper horror that besieges us, terrifies us, and which we desperately want to ignore, pretending that everything is a sham.

2006

Thirteen years misspent

The other day an interviewer asked me, as many do, which book has had the greatest influence on my life. If, over the course of my entire life, just one book had influenced me more than any other, I'd be an idiot. There are books that were crucial in my twenties and others that defined my thirties, and I impatiently await the book that will sweep me away when I reach a hundred. Another impossible question is, Who has really taught you something in your life? I never know how to answer, unless I were to say my mother and father, since at every juncture of my life someone has taught me something. They might have been those close to me or some dear departed friend, like Aristotle, Saint Thomas Aquinas, John Locke, or Charles Sanders Peirce.

In any event, I can say that, apart from books, there have been lessons that have certainly changed my life. The first came from Signorina Bellini, my wonderful junior high school teacher who, as homework for the following day, used to give us a word, such as "hen" or "steamship," that we had to use as the starting point for a thought or a story. One day, in the enthusiasm of the moment, I said I would talk there and then on any subject she chose. She looked at her desk and said "notebook." In retrospect, I could have spoken about a journalist's notebook or an explorer's travel diary, but instead I leapt boldly onto the teacher's platform and froze. Signorina Bellini taught me on that occasion never to be too sure of my own strengths.

The second lesson was that of Father Giuseppe Celi, the Salesian priest who had taught me to play a musical instrument. It is rumored he is being considered for sainthood, but not for the reason given here, which, on the contrary, could be used against him. On January 5, 1945, I bounded up to him and said, "Father Celi, I'm thirteen today." "Very misspent," he replied rather gruffly. What did he mean? That having reached such a venerable age I had to begin a serious examination of conscience? That I shouldn't expect to receive praise simply for having performed my biological duty? Perhaps it was just a normal Piedmontese manifestation of reserve, a refusal to embark on rhetoric, or perhaps these words were a fond expression of congratulations. But I think Father Celi was well aware, and was teaching me, that a master must always challenge his pupils, and not overly excite them.

After that lesson I have always been parsimonious in my praise of those who were expecting it, except in cases of superior performance. Perhaps this reluctance of mine has upset some, and if that is so, then in addition to misspending my first thirteen years, I have also misspent my first sixty-six years. But I resolved that the best way of expressing my approval was by making no criticism. No criticism means someone has done well. I have always been irritated by expressions such as "good pope" or "honest politician," which left room only for the thought that other popes were bad and other politicians dishonest. They are all simply doing what is expected of them, and it's hard to see why they should receive congratulations.

But Father Celi's reply taught me not to feel too proud of what I had done, even if I thought I'd done it well, and above all not to go around being smug. Does this mean we shouldn't aim to do better? Certainly not. But in a rather odd way Father Celi's answer reminds me of a quote I came across from Oliver Wendell Holmes Jr.: "The secret of my success is that at an early age I discovered that I was not God." It's very important to realize you're not God, always to be doubtful about what you do, and to feel you haven't spent the years of your life well enough. It's the only way of spending the remaining years better.

You might wonder why these thoughts come to mind now, at the start of an electoral campaign when candidates have to behave in a god-like fashion to win—in other words, to say of all they have done, like the Creator after the creation, that it was good, and to display a certain delusion of omnipotence in proclaiming themselves capable of doing better things, whereas God was satisfied at having created the best of all possible worlds. I don't wish to moralize: an electoral campaign demands such behavior. Can you imagine a candidate telling future voters that "up to now I've made a lot of big mistakes, I can't be sure I'll do any better in the future, and all I can promise is to have a go"? He wouldn't get elected. Therefore, I repeat, no false moralism. It's just that, listening to the televised debates, Father Celi returns to mind.

2007

Once upon a time there was Churchill

I read a short article recently in *Internazionale* about a survey in Great Britain that suggested a quarter of Britons under twenty thought

Churchill was an imaginary character, and Gandhi and Dickens too. Many of those interviewed, though the article didn't say how many, apparently put Sherlock Holmes, Robin Hood, and Eleanor Rigby among those who actually existed.

My initial response was not to take the survey too seriously. First of all, I'd be interested to know what social background that quarter of youngsters who got it wrong about Churchill and Dickens came from. If they had interviewed Londoners in the time of Dickens, or those we see in Doré's engravings of London poverty or in scenes from Hogarth, at least three quarters of those filthy, brutish, starving people would not have known who Shakespeare was. Nor am I surprised that people think Sherlock Holmes or Robin Hood really existed, because there's a Holmes industry in London that lets you visit the flat in Baker Street where he was supposed to have lived, and because the character that inspired Robin Hood did in fact exist. The only thing that makes him unreal is that in those times of feudal economy they robbed the rich to give to the poor, whereas with the arrival of the market economy they rob the poor to give to the rich. There again, as a child I thought Buffalo Bill was an imaginary character until my father told me that he had not only existed but that he, my father, had seen him when he had passed through our city with his circus: Buffalo Bill had ended up making a living from the legendary Wild West in Italy's Piedmont.

It's true that people's ideas even about the recent past are vague, and we realize this when we question the young about it. Some Italian schoolchildren, when tested, thought that Aldo Moro had been a member of the Red Brigades, that Alcide De Gasperi had been a Fascist leader, Pietro Badoglio a partisan, and so on. You could say that it was a long time ago: why should eighteen-year-olds know who was in the government fifty years before they were born? Well, at the age of ten, perhaps because the Fascist schools used to test such things, I knew that the prime minister at the time of the March on Rome twenty years before was Luigi Facta, and at eighteen I also knew who politicians like Urbano Rattazzi and Francesco Crispi had been, and that stuff went back to the nineteenth century.

Our relationship with the past has in fact changed, and probably also at school. At one time we had great interest in the past because there wasn't much news about the present. A newspaper used to report everything in eight pages. Now, with the mass media, there's a vast amount of information on the present, and just think how much news there is on the Internet about millions of things, even the most irrelevant, happening at this very moment. The past as described by the mass media—the exploits of Roman emperors, for example, or Richard the Lion-Hearted, or the First World War—is viewed, through Hollywood and similar industries, along with the flow of information on what's going on now, and it's hard for a film audience to appreciate the difference in time between Spartacus and Richard the Lion-Hearted. Likewise, the difference between imaginary and real gets blurred or at least loses its significance: tell me why any child who watches a television film should think that Spartacus actually existed and Marcus Vinicius in *Quo Vadis* didn't, that the Countess of Castiglione was a historical character and Emma Bovary wasn't, that Ivan the Terrible was real and Ming the tyrant of Mongo wasn't, seeing that each much resembles the other.

In American culture this flattening of the past onto the present is viewed casually, and you sometimes come across a professor of philosophy who tells you it's irrelevant to know what Descartes had to say about our way of thinking, seeing that what interests us is what cognitive science is discovering today. He is forgetting that, if the cognitive sciences have come as far as they have, it is because a particular discussion had begun with seventeenth-century philosophers, but above all there is a failure to use the experience of the past as a lesson for the present.

Many dismiss the old saying that "history is life's teacher" as banal, but we can be sure that if Hitler had made a careful study of Napoleon's campaign in Russia, he wouldn't have fallen into the trap that he did, and if George W. Bush had properly studied the British wars in Afghanistan in the nineteenth century, or even the most recent Soviet war against the Taliban, he would have planned his Afghan campaign differently.

You might think there's an enormous difference between the British idiot who thought Churchill was an imaginary character, and Bush, who goes to Iraq convinced he can wrap up the war in fifteen days, but there isn't. They are both examples of the same phenomenon: losing sight of history.

2008

A generation of aliens

I think Michel Serres is the finest philosophical mind in France today, and like every good philosopher, he can also turn his thoughts to current affairs. I'm making shameless use here, apart from a few comments of my own, of a wonderful article of his, published recently in *Le Monde*, where he recalls things that relate to the children of my younger readers, and for us older people, to our grandchildren.

For a start, these children or grandchildren have never seen a pig, a cow, or a hen, though I remember an American survey thirty years ago showed that most children in New York thought that milk, which they saw packaged in supermarkets, was a manufactured product, like Coca-Cola. These new human beings are no longer used to living in nature. They know only the city, and when they go on vacation they stay in "non-places," where a holiday resort looks very much like the Singapore airport, and shows them a stylized and manicured nature that is completely artificial. This is one of the greatest anthropological revolutions since the Neolithic Age. These children live in a super-populated world, their life expectancy is now close to eighty, and, due to the longevity of their parents and grandparents, if they inherit anything, they'll no longer be thirty but verging on old age.

European children haven't known war for over sixty years; with the benefit of medical advances they haven't suffered like previous generations; their parents are older than ours and most of them are divorced; they go to schools where they sit side by side with children of a different color, religion, or customs—and, asks Serres, how much longer can they continue to sing "La Marseillaise," which refers to the "impure blood" of foreigners? What literary works can they still enjoy, as they haven't known rural life, grape harvests, invasions, monuments to the dead, banners riddled with enemy gunshots, the urgent need for morale?

They have been educated by media fashioned by adults in which the length of a visual image has been reduced to seven seconds, and the time to answer questions reduced to fifteen seconds, and where nevertheless things are seen that are no longer seen in everyday life—blood-soaked corpses, destruction, devastation: "By the age of twelve, adults have already forced them to see twenty thousand killings." They learn from advertising peppered with abbreviations and foreign words that cause the native language to lose its meaning, the school is no longer a place of learning, and these children, now computer literate, live much of their lives in the virtual world. Writing with just the index finger rather than with the whole hand "no longer stimulates the same neurons or the same cortical areas," and they are forever multitasking. We adults live in a discernible and measurable space, and they live in an unreal space where proximity and distance no longer make any difference.

I won't discuss Serres's reflections on the possibility of managing the new requirements of education. His scenario, in any event, gives us the picture of a period that is comparable, in terms of its upheavals, to the invention of writing and, many centuries later, of printing. Except that today's new technologies are changing at great speed, and "at the same time the body is metamorphosing, birth and death are changing, and so too are suffering and treatment, jobs, space, habitat, being-in-the-world." Why weren't we prepared for this transformation? Serres concludes that perhaps it's the fault of philosophers, whose job it is to predict changes in knowledge and practice, but they haven't done enough because, "having been involved in everyday politics, they haven't felt the arrival of contemporaneity." I don't know that Serres is entirely right, but there's truth in what he says.

2011

Online

My email doubles

I was trying to reach an American colleague by email and found an Internet service that gave the addresses of those who are registered under a particular name. I checked my colleague's name and came up with ten different addresses, including one in Japan. Was that possible? It occurred to me to check out my own name, and I found twenty-two addresses. I recognized two, now defunct, in which my name did not appear in the address but had been given at the time I had registered. The others looked quite normal, such as umbertoeco@hotmail.com, or umberto_eco@hotmail.com, but I was struck by agartha2@hotmail.com, which had been registered using my name.

Agartha is the capital of Rex Mundi, a well-known occult legend quoted in my *Foucault's Pendulum*. It then occurred to me that those who register with an email service can, of course, call themselves whatever they like. They can take the name of a favorite writer, and can even choose Dante Alighieri if they wish. Caught by the jealous doubt that Dante might be more popular than me, I went and searched for him. Result: fifty-five addresses, including dante@satanic.org, danteSB@yahoo.com, alighieri@vergil.inferno.it, belzebius@yahoo.it, divinpoeta@yahoo.it, mostromaldido@yahoo.it.

I then tried out the name of a contemporary writer who might stir some excitement, and naturally I hit on Salman Rushdie. There are thirty-six addresses, including not only the plain and simple salman@netcom.com, salman@grex.com, salman.rushdie@safe.com, but also, far more disturbing, satan@durham.ac.uk, love@iraq.com, atheist@

wam.umd.edu, blasphem@aol.com, and sephiroth@zombieworld.com —I'd be worried about contacting anyone with addresses of that kind. But the problem is not so much these bizarre addresses as those that are seemingly normal. No one will imagine that Dante is going to answer an email, but how many gullible people might contact salman. rushdie@safe.com, perhaps receiving some ruinously compromising answer in Rushdie's name? There is obviously only one solution: not to trust email addresses. And therefore a service that the Net might usefully have provided loses all effectiveness. It would be the same as tampering with telephone directories by putting the number of a left-wing politician under the name of Berlusconi, or giving the address of a strip club as that of a well-known journalist.

The principle of caution is taken for granted by anyone who gets involved in chat rooms, since everyone knows that a young man can make amorous advances online to a certain Greta Garbo who turns out to be a retired policeman. But this principle is now officially true in all circumstances after the recent case of the ILOVEYOU virus. We must now be suspicious not only of every message whose exact provenance we don't know, but also of those from our regular correspondents, since the virus could have been passed on in their name.

A newspaper that by definition published only false news would not be worth buying except for entertainment, and we wouldn't pay a cent for a railroad timetable that told us to take a train for Milan that was in fact going to Naples. Newspapers and railroad timetables have an implicit pact with their readers, which cannot be violated without compromising every social contract. What is going to happen if the main instrument of communication in the new millennium cannot respect this pact and ensure that it is enforced?

2000

How to elect the president

First the good news: as I pointed out in a recent article, if you go to the website www.poste.it, you can register for a service that allows you to send a letter or telegram from your computer. The post office will then print and deliver it to the correct address at a cost of 1,700 lire, or 85 euro cents, thus eliminating the whole business of its being carried by train and held up in station depots. Congratulations—incredible as that may sound—to the Italian postal service.

Now the bad news: it's the story of the American elections, of course, where the vote-counting mechanism has proved less efficient than the Italian postal service. And yet there was a solution, and it was the great Isaac Asimov who provided it in the 1950s story "Franchise," which appeared in Italian in *Galaxy* magazine in December 1962. Reducing the story to its bare bones, it describes how, in what was then the far-off year 2008, in the United States, the choice was between two candidates who were so alike that the votes of the electorate were split almost fifty-fifty. The opinion polls, then carried out by extremely powerful computers, could calculate endless variables and get close to the actual result with almost mathematical precision. But to reach a scientifically exact decision, the vast Multivac computer, half a mile long at that time and the height of a three-story building—and here's an example of how science fiction failed to predict future progress—needed to take into account "various imponderable aptitudes in the human mind."

Since the story assumes that human minds in an advanced and civilized country are all very much the same, Multivac had only to carry out a few tests on a single voter. And so, at each yearly election, the computer identified one state, and one citizen in that single state, who thus became the voter, and the president of the United States was chosen on the basis of his ideas and opinions. So each election took the name of the single voter: the MacComber vote, the Muller vote, and so on.

Asimov gives a delightful description of the excitement in the family of the chosen one, who became famous, signing lucrative contracts and making a career of it, like a survivor of the reality show *Big Brother*. There's an amusing scene in which a young girl is amazed as her grandfather explains how at one time everybody used to vote, and she can't understand how a democracy could function with millions and millions of voters, a system far more fallible than Multivac.

Jean-Jacques Rousseau had already ruled out the possibility of a collective democracy, except in a small country where the citizens all knew each other and could easily meet. But a representative democracy that calls on its people to choose their representatives every four or five years is now also having a hard time. In a mass civilization dominated by electronic communication, opinions tend to level out to such an extent that the policies of the candidates become similar. The candidates are not chosen by the people but by party members, and the people have to choose between just two candidates selected by others, who are as alike as two peas in a pod. It's reminiscent of the Soviet system, but in that case the party members chose only one candidate and the voters elected him. If the Soviets had offered voters not one but two candidates, the Soviet Union would have been much the same as American democracy.

Yes, I know, in a democracy, even after the pointless ritual of elections, those who govern are controlled by the press, by pressure groups, by public opinion. But that could also be done using the system proposed by Asimov.

2000

The hacker is crucial to the system

The recent global incidents on the Internet come as no surprise. Clearly the more sophisticated technology becomes, the more it lends itself to acts of terrorism. It was easy to deal with the hijacker of a propeller aircraft with an unpressurized cabin: the door could be opened and the hijacker ejected. On an intercontinental jetliner, even a madman with a blank pistol can keep everyone on tenterhooks.

The problem here is more that technological development is accelerating. Once the Wright brothers had attempted the first flight, decades passed before Louis Blériot, Baron von Richthofen, Francesco Baracca, Charles Lindbergh, and Italo Balbo could adapt to the subsequent improvements in aircraft technology. The car I drive today does things that were unimaginable for the old Fiat 600 in which I passed my driving test, but if I had started then with the car I'm driving now, I'd have crashed it in no time. Fortunately I have grown with my cars, adapting gradually to their increased power.

With computers, on the other hand, I don't get enough time to learn all the possibilities of one machine and its software before a new machine and more complicated software appear on the market. I can't even opt to continue with the old computer, which would perhaps be adequate, because essential updates are available only on the new machines. This rate of acceleration is due first of all to commercial imperatives—the industry wants us to scrap the old and buy the new, even if we're happy as we are—but it also depends on the fact that no one can stop a researcher from inventing a more powerful computer. The same is true of cell phones, video recorders, personal organizers, and digital equipment in general.

Our reflexes would not be able to keep up with cars that increased their performance every two months. Fortunately cars are too expensive and highways are what they are. Computers cost less and less, and the highways on which their messages travel impose no restrictions. As a result, the latest version appears before we've come to grips with the full potential of the previous one. This is a problem not just for the ordinary user, but also for those who ought to be monitoring data flow, including FBI agents, banks, and the Pentagon.

Who has the time, twenty-four hours a day, to work out the new capabilities of their personal equipment? The hacker. He's a kind of stylite, a desert father, who devotes his entire day to meditation—electronic meditation. Have you seen pictures of the hacker who recently found his way into Clinton's message system? All hackers look like that: fat, clumsy, malformed people who have grown up in front of a computer screen. Having become the only complete experts in an innovation that moves at breakneck speed, they have the time to understand everything their machine and the Web do, without developing any new philosophy or studying its positive applications. So they devote themselves to the single direct action their inhuman competence allows: hijacking, interfering, destabilizing the global system.

In doing so, many of them may well believe they are acting in the "spirit of Seattle," and are thereby combating the new Moloch. In truth, they end up being the system's best collaborators, since to counteract them requires further innovation, carried out ever more swiftly. It's a vicious circle in which the hacker strengthens what he thinks he's destroying.

2000

Too much of the Internet? But in China . . .

Over the past ten days I took part in three different cultural events. One had to do with the problems of information and the other two on other matters. But there were questions and heated discussions in all three about the Internet. There again, the same would probably have happened if I'd been involved in a conference on Homer, and if you don't believe me, go to a good search engine and see how much you find, good and bad, about Homer on the Web. Any conference on Homer now needs to express judgments on the reliability of sites dedicated to the poet; otherwise, students and academics will no longer know what they can trust.

I'll list just a few of the points in the discussions. When one delegate praised the Internet as the achievement of total democracy in terms of information, another objected that a young person today could stumble across hundreds of racist sites and download *Mein Kampf* or *The Protocols of the Elders of Zion*. Reply: if you leave this building and visit the occult bookshop down the road, you'll come across a copy of the *Protocols* right away. Counter-reply: yes, but you have to want to look for it, whereas on the Web you'll find it even when you're looking for something else. Counter-counter-reply: but at the same time you'll come across a vast number of antiracist sites, therefore Web democracy self-compensates.

Final response: Hitler published and distributed *Mein Kampf* before the Internet, and perhaps that was lucky for him. With the Internet there could never be another Auschwitz, since everyone would find out about it right away, and no one could say they didn't know.

In support of this final comment, I heard a Chinese sociologist a few days later speak about what was happening with the Internet in China. Users cannot get direct access to the Web, but have to pass through state centers that screen information. So there seems to be censorship. Yet it appears that censorship of the Internet is impossible. First example: it's true that state filters allow you, let us say, to access site A but not site B, yet every good navigator knows that, having reached A, in some way or other you can get from A to B. Then there's email: once you allow this, people begin to circulate news. Lastly there are chat rooms. In the West, it seems, they are visited mostly by people who have nothing better to do and nothing to say, but in China it's different: people discuss politics there, which they couldn't do elsewhere.

But the state's impotence in relation to the network goes further. Network bureaucrats don't know what to block. Some time ago, it seems the *New York Times* telephoned to protest that its site was being screened, but that of the *Washington Post* was not. The bureaucrats said they'd check it out, and the next day they responded by saying not to worry, they'd taken steps to block the *Washington Post* as well. But these are anecdotes. The fact is that, for example, if I remember correctly, you can't access the CBS site, but you can reach ABC. I asked a Chinese friend why. There are no good reasons, he replied; bureaucrats have to show they're doing something, and they strike more or less at random. Conclusion: in the battle between the Chinese government and the Internet, the government is bound to lose.

Every so often, some good news.

2000

Here's a good game

If today a new Humbert Humbert, the celebrated character in *Lolita*, were to leave home with a young girl, we'd be able to find out all about him. The satellite navigator in his car would tell us where he is and where he's going; his credit cards would show which motel he's been at and whether he booked one or two rooms; the closed-circuit television in supermarkets would show him buying a porno magazine rather than a newspaper, and if he gets a newspaper we could discover his political leanings; if he buys a Barbie doll at the supermarket, we can assume the girl is still underage; and if he links up to a pedophile site on the Internet, we could draw our own conclusions. Even if Humbert Humbert hasn't yet committed any crime, we could decide he has dangerous inclinations and think it a good idea to have him arrested. If, then, the young girl happens to be his niece, and if this person's private fantasies didn't in fact lead to any criminal acts, no matter: it's better to have one more innocent person in prison than a dangerous loose cannon in society.

All of this can now be done. Furio Colombo, in his book *Privacy*, adds a small touch of science fiction and imagines a device that makes it possible to monitor not just behavior but also thought. Build into it a belief that prevention is the supreme good, and there you have it. By comparison, Orwell's 1984 is a fairy tale with a happy ending.

Reading Furio Colombo's book, you might wonder whether we're not already nearing the future it predicts. I'd like to use his book as a pretext for imagining a game halfway between the present reality and the future he foretells.

The game is called Brothers of Italy but can be played just as well in other countries, and is a refinement of *Big Brother*. Instead of people sitting in front of a television to watch the goings-on of a few half-wits put into an artificial situation, by extending supermarket monitoring systems to the entire urban setting, to every street and public building, perhaps even to private homes, viewers could follow hour by hour, minute by minute, the daily goings-on of other citizens as they wander the streets, do their shopping, make love, work, come to blows over some minor car accident. Great fun. It would make reality seem far more exciting than fiction. The taste for voyeurism and gossip in each of us would be given free rein.

I can't pretend that it wouldn't raise certain problems. Who is watching, and who is performing? At first, those who watch would be the ones who didn't have anything better to do, whereas the action and entertainment would come from those who did. Later it may turn out that some preferred not to be seen, but to stay at home and watch others. But the monitoring would also reveal the private lives of those watching, and sixty million viewers could end up watching sixty million viewers in real time, prying on the expressions on their faces. And most probably, since it's becoming increasingly important to be seen, everyone would perform so as to be seen. But who then would watch? They would all need a small portable viewer in which, as they perform, they could see others performing. We could be left with sixty million people behaving abnormally while they watch the others behaving abnormally as they stumble about performing while watching their tiny portable televiewer. In short, we'd have a real treat in store.

2001

The textbook as teacher

The government's idea, still in the planning stage, of replacing text-books with material taken directly from the Internet (so lightening the weight of schoolbags and pushing down the price of schoolbooks) has caused mixed reactions. Educational publishers and booksellers have two objections to this. First, they see the project as a death blow for an industry that provides work for thousands of people. While I sympathize with the publishers and booksellers, it's also true that the same arguments could have been used by carriage builders, coachmen, and grooms on the advent of the steam train, or by textile workers, as indeed happened on the introduction of the mechanical loom. If history is moving inescapably in the direction determined by the government, this labor force ought to be finding alternative work, perhaps producing material for the Internet.

Their second objection is that the proposal envisages a computer for every pupil: it's unlikely the state would saddle itself with such an expense, and if parents had to pay, the cost would be more than for the textbooks. On the other hand, if there were only one computer for each class, pupils would have little opportunity to use it for personal research, which is the intriguing aspect of this proposal. One computer per class would be about as beneficial as the government printing and distributing thousands of leaflets each morning, like handing out bread to the poor. There again, perhaps everyone will have a computer one day.

But the problem is another. The Internet is not going to replace books; it is simply a formidable complement, an incentive to read more books. The book is still the main tool for providing and transmitting knowledge (what would pupils study on a day when there's a blackout?), and textbooks are the first priceless opportunity to teach children how to use a book. Moreover, the Internet provides a fantastic store of information but offers no filters, whereas education is about not only transmitting information but also teaching the criteria for selecting it. This is the role of a teacher, but it is also the function of a schoolbook, which is an example of a selection made from the great sea of all possible information. This is true even of the worst textbook, and here the teacher must criticize its one-sidedness and provide supplementary information from a different point of view. Unless pupils are taught that culture is not accumulation but discrimination, then what they're learning is not education but mental clutter.

Some pupils when interviewed said, "Great, so we can print out only the pages we need and not carry around those we don't have to study." Wrong. I remember in my rural secondary school, which operated more or less on alternate days during the last year of World War II, the teachers, the only ones in my whole school and university career whose names I've forgotten, didn't teach me a great deal. Instead, I spent my time leafing through my poetry anthology, and that was how I first came across the poems of Giuseppe Ungaretti, Salvatore Quasimodo, and Eugenio Montale. It was a revelation; I was introduced to a new world. The value of a schoolbook is that it provides a chance to discover something the teacher has not taught, whether through idleness or lack of time, and that someone else considered fundamental.

The textbook also remains a poignant and useful past record of school years, whereas a few printed sheets for immediate use, which are continually slipping to the floor and get tossed away after a few underlinings—that's true for us academics, so it's bound to be true for pupils as well—would leave no trace on the memory. It would be a great loss.

Books could certainly be lighter and less expensive were it not for the color illustrations. It would be sufficient for a book to explain who Julius Caesar was, and then it would be interesting for anyone with their own computer to look for pictures of Julius Caesar or contemporary reconstructions of Rome, for diagrams that explain how a Roman legion was organized. Even better if the book suggested a few reliable websites and further areas of study, so that pupils could embark on a personal adventure, but the teacher would need to show them how to distinguish between serious and reliable sites and those that are cobbled together and superficial.

Lastly, though abolishing textbooks is a bad idea, the Internet could certainly replace dictionaries, which weigh down schoolbags more than anything else. Downloading a dictionary in Latin, Greek, or any other language would be useful and fast.

But everything should always revolve around the book. It's true that our prime minister, Silvio Berlusconi, once claimed he hadn't read a novel in twenty years, but schools don't have to teach pupils how to become prime minister—at any rate, not like this one.

2004

How to copy from the Internet

There's great debate in the Internet world about Wikipedia. I don't know to what extent its administrators can control the content from all its contributors, but when I've had reason to consult it on familiar topics, to check a date or a book title, I've always found it well done and well informed. But to allow collaboration from anyone whatsoever has its risks, and people have sometimes found themselves wrongly accused of certain acts or even misdemeanors. When they have protested, the entry has been corrected. At one time the page relating to me contained an inaccurate biographical detail. I corrected it and the error is no longer there. I also found an interpretation, in a summary of one of my books, that I felt was wrong: the entry suggested that I had advanced an idea about Nietzsche when in fact I disputed it. I changed "develops" to "argues against," and this correction was also accepted.

But I'm not at all happy about the situation. Somebody could interfere with this entry tomorrow and suggest the opposite of what I have said or done, perhaps as a joke, or out of malice or stupidity. There again, since it's rumored on the Internet that I am the well-known hoaxer Luther Blissett, even years after the authors of those pranks have come out and revealed their true identities, I could be scurrilous enough to go around tampering with entries on authors I don't like, accusing them of plagiarism, pedophile pasts, or links to the Daughters of Satan.

It's argued that, as well as editorial control, there's a self-correction, so that sooner or later someone will identify and correct false information. Let's hope so, but clearly there is no absolute guarantee, as we have with a wise encyclopedia editor who compiles all the entries and accepts responsibility for them.

Yet the case of Wikipedia raises little concern in comparison to another serious problem of the Internet. Along with reliable sites created by competent people, there are bogus sites, developed by blockheads, nutcases, or Nazi subversives, and not all Internet users are able to judge whether a site can be trusted.

This is of major concern for education, since many pupils and students don't bother with textbooks and encyclopedias, and they take information straight from the Internet, and to such an extent that I've been arguing for some time that the new core subject for the school syllabus ought to be techniques for selecting information online. Yet it's a skill that's hard to teach, since those who teach are often as unprepared as students.

Many educators also complain that when young people write a research paper, they copy what they find on the Internet. If they've copied from an unreliable site, it has to be assumed the teacher realizes they are writing drivel, but when it comes to specialized subjects it's difficult to establish immediately whether a student's arguments are false. What happens if a student chooses to write a paper on an author of marginal importance, about whom the teacher has only indirect knowledge, and the student claims the author wrote a particular book? Would the teacher be in a position to state that the author had never written that book, which would mean carefully checking the various sources for every essay, and he may have dozens to read?

There again, the student may present research that seems, and is, correct, but has been cut and pasted directly from a website. I tend to regard this situation as less serious, since copying well is not a simple art, and a student who knows how to copy well is entitled to a good mark. Besides, before the Internet, students could copy from a book they'd found in the library and the issue was the same, even though more physically tiring. In the end, a good teacher always notices when a text has been copied indiscriminately and will sniff out the trick. There again, if it has been copied selectively, the student deserves full credit.

But I think there's one effective way of exploiting the defects of the Internet for educational purposes. For a class exercise, homework, or university essay, give the following subject: "Find a series of unreliable arguments available on the Internet, and explain why they are unreliable." Here is research that demands critical skill and an ability to compare different sources, and that enables students to practice the art of discrimination.

2006

What's the point of having a teacher?

Among the wealth of articles about the bullying of teachers, I read one account that I wouldn't describe as bullying but at most as impertinence, though a singular impertinence. A pupil, in order to annoy a teacher, had asked, "Excuse me, but in the age of the Internet, what's the point of having you?"

What the pupil was saying had a grain of truth in it, and it's a question that has worried teachers for at least twenty years now. At one time the school certainly had to educate, but above all it had to transmit basic facts, from multiplication tables at primary school, to information about the capital of Madagascar in junior high school, to the date of the Thirty Years' War in high school. With the advent not only of the Internet, but of television before it, and also radio, and perhaps even with the arrival of cinema, children learned many of these basic facts outside the school curriculum.

My father didn't know that Hiroshima was in Japan, or that there was an island called Guadalcanal; he had a vague idea about Dresden, and knew about India only through the stories of Emilio Salgari. Back in the 1940s, I could pick these things up from the radio and from the maps in newspapers, whereas my children could watch television and see pictures of the Norwegian fjords or the Gobi Desert, how bees pollinated flowers, what a *Tyrannosaurus rex* looked like; and they know everything about the ozone layer, koala bears, Iraq, and Afghanistan. Perhaps they don't know exactly what stem cells are, but they've heard of them, though in my time it meant nothing even to the science teacher. So what's the point of having teachers?

I said that the question posed by the student had a grain of truth, because the teacher's task, above all, is formation as well as information. What transforms a class into a good class is not the facts and figures it has absorbed, but the continual dialogue, the exchange of opinions, the discussion about what is being taught in school and what is happening outside it. Television, of course, tells us what is going on in Iraq, but only the school can explain why something has been going on there since way back to the Mesopotamian civilization, and not, for example, in Greenland. It might be argued that there are experts who tell us this on current affairs programs, in which case the school must discuss what has been said on those programs.

The mass media tell us many things, and even transmit values, but schools should know how to talk about the way these values are transmitted, and to assess the tone and strength of the arguments put forward in print and on television. And then there is the investigation of information relayed by the media; for example, who but the teacher can correct the errors in English pronunciation people pick up from television?

But our pupil wasn't suggesting that he didn't need the teacher because he now had radio and television to tell him where Timbuktu is, or what has been said about cold fusion. In other words, he wasn't telling the teacher that his role had been taken over by the disjointed discussions that circulate daily in a casual and disorderly fashion in the media. The student was saying that the Internet, the Great Mother of all Encyclopedias, is where we can find Syria, cold fusion, the Thirty Years' War, and endless discussion on the largest odd number. He was telling him that the information available online is far larger and deeper than a teacher's knowledge. Yet he was ignoring one fundamental point: the Internet tells us almost everything apart from how to search, filter, select, accept, or reject that information.

Everyone is capable of storing new information, so long as they have a good memory. But deciding what is worth remembering, and what is not, is a subtle art. This marks the difference between those who have passed through formal education, however poorly, and those who are self-taught, however brilliantly.

The crucial problem is that not even teachers themselves know how to teach the art of being selective, certainly not in every branch of knowledge. But at least they know they ought to know, and if they can't give exact instructions on how to be selective, they can be the model of someone who tries to compare and judge, case by case, what the Internet has to offer. And lastly, they can strive daily to put into a proper context what the Internet transmits merely in alphabetical order when it tells us, for instance, that Tamerlane and monocotyledons exist but doesn't explain the relationship between these two notions.

Only schools can bring sense to these relationships, and if the school doesn't know how, then it must equip itself to do so. Otherwise, the teaching of the Internet at school is as pointless as the braying of a donkey that never reaches the ears of heaven.

2007

The fifth estate

At one time we were accustomed to two principles. One was encapsulated in a savory Sicilian saying, *Megghiu cumannari c'a fottiri*, which might prudishly be translated as "It's better to exercise power than to fornicate." The other was that men of power, if they wished to indulge in sexual relations, aimed for the likes of the Countess of Castiglione, Mata Hari, Sarah Bernhardt, or Marilyn Monroe.

It's surprising that many politicians and businessmen now let themselves be corrupted not so much by joint interests in the Panama Canal as by the services of professional women who are highly capable but charge no more than 1,000 euros a session, a lot for a casual worker but a great deal less than she would have charged at the time of Madame de Pompadour. If they have other tastes, they aim not for the refined Alcibiades but for a transsexual scarred by misfortunes in the narrow streets of Piraeus.

But that's not all. Many men are looking for positions of command not because they consider them to be better than sexual positions, but for the prime purpose of trying out sexual positions they've never tested before. Let's be clear: this doesn't mean the governors of bygone times were insensitive to the pleasures of the flesh. Italian postwar leaders such as Alcide De Gasperi and Enrico Berlinguer had accustomed us to another kind of austerity; the most that Palmiro Togliatti had dared was to get divorced. But Julius Caesar had it off indiscriminately with Roman centurions, noblewomen, and queens of Egypt; the Roi Soleil had a string of favorites; King Victor Emmanuel II had the beautiful Rosina; and best not mention President Kennedy. Nevertheless, these great men seemed to consider the woman, or the youth, as providing a warrior's repose. In other words, he had first to conquer Bactria, crush Vercingetorix, win victory from the Alps to the pyramids, and bring unity to Italy. Sex was a bonus, like a martini straight up at the end of a tiring day.

The powerful men of today, however, seem to aspire in the first instance to an evening of showgirls, and to hell with great enterprises —or with the Great Enterprise.

The heroes of the past obtained their excitement from reading Plutarch, whereas those of today zap around the soft-porn TV channels after midnight or get their thrills surfing online. I went on the Internet and did a search for "Padre Pio": 1,400,000 sites. Not bad. I did a search for "Jesus": 4,830,000 sites. The Nazarene is still way ahead. Then I did a search for "porn" and came up with 130,000,000—yes, one hundred and thirty million—websites. Thinking that "porn" was too generic in comparison to "Jesus," I decided to make a comparison between "porn" and "religion." "Religion" gives just over 9,000,000 sites, more than twice that of "Jesus," which seems politically correct, but minuscule compared with "porn."

What do 130,000,000 porn sites contain? Among our options, we find: Anal, Asiatic, Latino, Fetish, Orgy, Bisexual, Cunnilingus, German (*sic*), Lesbian, Masturbation, Voyeur (we spy on someone who is spying on a carnal congress), and then the various forms of incest —father and daughter, brother and sister, mother and son, father, mother, son, and daughter together, godmother and godson, but also grandson and granny, and MILF, which means Mother I'd Like to Fuck (see Wikipedia), generally containing attractive women between the ages of thirty and forty-five. Just think: Balzac gave the title *A Woman of Thirty* to a story about female decline.

Now, pornography can provide an outlet for someone who for whatever reason can't have live sex, or it can help a rather jaded couple to revive their own relationship, and in that respect it has a positive purpose. But it can stir the imagination of those who are repressed, leading them to give vent to their instincts through rape, sexual attack, and assault. Moreover, pornography persuades you that a 1,000-euro escort can do things that not even Phryne, the ancient Greek courtesan, would have imagined.

But let's not limit ourselves to the thirty percent of Italians who use the Internet; the remaining seventy percent can see pictures every day on their television screens that are ten times more enticing than those sights that only Milanese grandees could get in the 1940s, when they would pay dearly to see the saucy performances of Wanda Osiris. Normal people today are far more conscious of sex than their grandparents. Think of poor parish priests: at one time all they saw was their housekeeper, and all they read was *L'Osservatore Romano,* whereas now they see skimpily clad girls swaying their hips every evening.

Is it inconceivable that this relentless solicitation of desire is also having an effect on those in public office, causing a mutation of their kind, and changing the very purposes of their social behavior?

2010

A further note

It has been said that a sociologist is someone who, in a striptease club, studies the audience and not the stage. I have no means of studying those who look at porn sites, let alone studying the whole stage. The number of porn sites, according to Internet surveys, seems impossible to gauge. According to a 2003 Web survey, the number of such sites was said to be 260,000,000, but that seems an exaggeration—perhaps they've counted sites where Carroll Baker appears *en déshabillé* as being pornography. Choosing just one of them, perhaps the most visited, I saw 71 categories, each containing on average thousands of videos. Considering that the site is updated daily, though it's possible to view previous material, we can reckon it contains 170,000 videos. From here we can gain access to another 21 sites, so I arrived at a figure of 3,570,000, taking into account repetitions, and that some sites are not large. This doesn't get me to 260,000,000, and perhaps 3,000,000 is on the low side, but this is presumably the extent of the phenomenon.

Not having had the opportunity to visit 3,000,000 sites—*ars longa, vita brevis*—I went by an almost random sample and have made an observation that I cannot claim has scientific validity but which I myself find persuasive. Making it clear that I lingered only on the female faces —those of the men are irrelevant, since with men the camera tends to dwell on their reproductive equipment—I noted that most of the girls involved in these erotic games display a poor set of teeth when they open their mouth, which they do often, and not just to smile or groan with satisfaction. Generally the incisors are all right, but the canines are crooked and small, not to mention the irregular molars and the unsightly fillings on display.

The first thing Hollywood does when it launches a new actress is to get her teeth fixed. But the work costs a lot of money, as anyone going to a dentist in Bucharest is also aware. So a large proportion of the girls taking part in porn videos, who are often beautiful or at least attractive, come from a poor social background and don't have the money for a dentist. I think they have little hope of making much from their services, since the statistics tell us that supply is high, so the money they earn cannot be astronomical: the Web tells me once again that the more popular girls can make up to $10,000 a month, though the season isn't long and the real stars can be counted on the fingers of two hands. Perhaps they hope that by appearing on the computer screen some Hollywood magnate will notice them and take the trouble to fix their teeth. Or do they perhaps realize they won't get to Hollywood with bad teeth and are resigned to playing erotic games in the minor leagues.

This tells us that the immense army of full-time fornicators comes from the sexual proletariat, and therefore the business of porn production is nothing other than a form of white slavery and an exploitation of casual labor without hope.

It's important that this be said, since visitors to porn sites often get aroused at the thought that the girls taking part do what they do out of brazenness, impudence, enjoyment, or shamelessness, making them seem more desirable. Instead, they do it out of desperation, knowing that with those teeth there is no future, only an underpaid now.

2015

Dogmatism and fallibilism

In an article that appeared in last Sunday's *Corriere della Sera,* Angelo Panebianco wrote about possible examples of dogmatism in science. I basically agree with him and would like to highlight just one aspect of the question.

In short, Panebianco says that science is by definition antidogmatic because it consciously proceeds by trial and error, and because (in agreement, I would add, with Charles Sanders Peirce, who inspired Karl Popper) its implied principle is that of "fallibilism," which means science is always ready to correct its own errors. It becomes dogmatic in its disastrous journalistic simplifications, which transform what had been a cautious research hypothesis into a miraculous discovery and firm truth. But it also risks becoming dogma when it accepts one inevitable criterion: that the culture of an age is dominated by a "paradigm," such as that not only of Darwin or Einstein, but also of Copernicus, to which every scientist adheres so as to eradicate the follies that move outside it, including those of madmen who still claim the Sun revolves around the Earth. How do we reconcile this with the fact that innovation occurs at the precise moment when some doubt is cast on the dominant paradigm? Isn't science acting dogmatically when it holds rigidly to a certain paradigm, perhaps to defend acquired positions of power, dismissing those who doubt the paradigm as madmen or heretics?

The question is crucial. Should paradigms always be defended or always contested? A culture, by which I mean a system of knowledge, opinions, beliefs, customs, and the historical legacy shared by a particular human group, is not just an accumulation of facts but also the result of their filtration. Culture can also throw away what is not useful or necessary. The story of culture and civilization consists of tons of information that has become buried. What is true of culture is also true of our individual lives. Borges, in his story "Funes the Memorious," describes a character who remembers everything—every leaf he has seen on every tree, every word he has heard throughout his life, every gust of wind he has felt, every flavor he has tasted, every phrase he has read. And yet, because of this, Funes is a complete idiot, a man blocked by his inability to select and discard. Our unconscious works because it eliminates. Then, if some snag arises, we go to the psychoanalyst to recover the little that was useful to us and which we have mistakenly discarded. But all the rest has fortunately been eliminated, and our mind is the precise product of the continuity of this selective memory. If we had the mind of Funes, we would be people with no mind.

What culture and its body of paradigms does is therefore the result of a shared encyclopedia, comprising not only what has been conserved but also, so to speak, the taboo on that which is eliminated. On the basis of this shared encyclopedia there is then discussion. But for a discussion to be comprehensible to everyone, it needs to start from existing paradigms, if only to demonstrate that these paradigms no longer hold. Copernicus's discourse would have remained incomprehensible without his negation of Ptolemy's paradigm, which formed the background.

The Internet is like Funes. As a totality of content available in a disordered, unfiltered, unorganized manner, it enables anyone to construct their own encyclopedia, or rather their own free system of beliefs, ideas, and values, which may contain, as happens inside the heads of many human beings, the idea that water is H_2O at the same time as the idea that the Sun revolves around the Earth. In theory, we could therefore arrive at the existence of seven billion encyclopedias, and human society would be reduced to a fractured dialogue among seven billion people who each speak a different language that only the person speaking can understand.

Fortunately this supposition is only theoretical, but that's because the scientific community ensures that shared languages circulate, knowing that to overturn a paradigm there has to be a paradigm to overturn. Defending paradigms certainly produces the risk of dogmatism, but it is on this contradiction that the development of knowledge is based. In order to avoid rash conclusions, I agree with what was said by the scientist quoted at the end of Panebianco's article: "I don't know, it's a complex phenomenon, I need to think about it."

2010

Marina, Marina, Marina

I received the following email: "You are the one I want to know well. Ciao. My nominative is Marina, 30 years me. I saw you profile and decided to produce to you. How you are doing? I have a marvelous state of mind. I am looking for an individual for serious relation, what type of link that you are searching? I am very interested to know you, but believe it be better if you and me corrispond by email. If you are stimulated to do the comprehension with me, here my email address:

abhojiku@nokiamail.com. Or me email your email address I will write you circular. One cannot start I hope without the attention and the epistle you write me. I would be very please to collect your opinion. I wait the hour your missive in the mail. Your Marina."

The photo attached shows a creature worthy of Miss Universe, ready to be invited to an elegant dinner by a prime minister, so the question is why a young girl as attractive as Marina is reduced to looking for a "serious" relationship on the Internet. Maybe the photo has been taken from some online site and hidden behind Marina is a character who might interest Roberto Saviano, though who knows? Yet since there are plenty of gullible people around, I'm leaving her address in the message so that anyone who wishes can hasten into an affectionate correspondence with her. Needless to say, I accept no responsibility for the consequences. Judging by the number of people watching teleshopping or horoscope channels and the many voters in the previous elections, Marina can hope for a great many virtual followers.

As for the virtual world, it is widely known, since the news has spread across the Internet, that one of my false Twitter accounts recently announced the death of Dan Brown, while my own death was announced on another. Although all organs of information have established that this was a hoax, I see that some people then assumed that, since everyone knows I'm a notorious prankster, I had sent a "false" message from a "real" address. In short, the gods are ready to amaze all those who wish to lose themselves on the Web, and I hope there's someone out there who will get in touch with Marina and start up a beautiful friendship.

Teachers who want to show young people how not to trust the Internet can find websites that expose online hoaxes. Fortunately, as well as hosting bogus sites, the Internet has ways of unmasking them. All you need to know is how to navigate properly.

But Web idolatry has its victims. Take the news that appeared last week. In Rome, a boy straddled over the parapet of his bedroom window on the ninth floor of an apartment block with a knife to his stomach threatens to kill himself. Family, police, fire brigade, inflatable mattress stretched out on the ground below. No one can persuade him to climb down. Until the boy shouts out that he wants to appear on a reality show, and wants to be taken there in a limousine. The police remember there's a limousine parked nearby, used the previous day for a publicity shoot. They have it brought there, and the boy gets down.

Moral of the story: the only "real" thing that can dissuade someone from suicide is the promise of virtual reality. It's easy to say the boy was disturbed, but this is no comfort to us, since it's reasonable to imagine that all those who believe in reality shows (or who reply to Marina, or who seriously believe those sites that suggest the attack on the Twin Towers was carried out by Bush and by the Jews) would easily pass a psychiatric test. Therefore, apart from exceptional cases, the problem of the virtual world doesn't relate to the sick but to the sane.

2013

I urge you to be brief

At a time when everyone is going mad over Twitter, when even the pope is tweeting, and a universal tweet ought to replace representative democracy, two contrasting views continually emerge. The first is that Twitter leads people to express themselves in a moralistic but superficial manner, since, as is well known, it requires more than 140 characters to write the *Critique of Pure Reason*. The second is that Twitter encourages brevity and succinctness.

Allow me to temper both positions. It is said that text messages also make our children understand and use only telegraphic language such as "Luv u 4ever," forgetting that the first telegram was sent by Samuel Morse back in 1844, and despite years and years of "mother ill come now" or "fond wishes Katerina," many people still write like Proust. Humanity has learned to send messages of few words, but that didn't stop a certain politician from speaking for eighteen hours in the Italian Chamber of Deputies in 1981.

As for the notion that Twitter encourages brevity, I think that's going too far. Even with 140 characters there's a risk of rambling. Certainly this news: "In the beginning God created the heavens and the earth. And the earth was without form and void; and darkness was upon the face of the deep" is worthy of the Pulitzer Prize, since it says in just under 140 characters, including spaces, exactly what the reader would like to know. But there are much shorter ways of saying things of great wit—"To lose one parent may be regarded as a misfortune, to lose both looks like carelessness," "A good poet is made, as well as born"—or of great profoundness, such as "Blessed are the poor in spirit, for theirs is the kingdom of heaven," "But let your communication be, Yea, yea; Nay, nay: for whatsoever is more than these cometh of evil," "Man is a rational, mortal animal," "Power is not taken, it is found," "To be or not to be, that is the question," "Whereof one cannot speak, thereof one must be silent," "All that is real is rational," "All Gaul is divided into three parts." Or phrases or ideas that have marked the history of humanity, such as *"Veni vidi vici," "Non possumus,"* "Italy, or death!"

To paraphrase Ugo Foscolo: Twitter users, I urge you to be brief.

2013

On Cell Phones

More thoughts on the cell phone

I wrote a fairly irate article in the early 1990s when cell phones were in the hands of just a few people, but a few who were making train journeys hell. I said, in short, that cell phones should be allowed only for organ transplanters, plumbers, and adulterers. For everyone else, especially in cases where otherwise unremarkable people were blabbing away in trains or airports about stocks and shares, metal section beams, or bank loans, it was more than anything a sign of social inferiority. Those in real power don't have cell phones but twenty secretaries who screen their calls and messages, whereas those who need them are middle managers who have to answer to the CEO at any moment, or small businessmen whose banks need to tell them their account is overdrawn.

As for adulterers, the situation has changed twice since that article appeared. Initially they had to forgo this very personal means of communication, since its acquisition gave rise to justifiable suspicion in the minds of their spouses. Then the situation changed: everyone had one, so it was no longer cast-iron evidence of an adulterous relationship. Lovers can now use them, unless they're having affairs with persons who are to some degree in the public eye, in which case their conversations will certainly be tapped. No change with regard to social inferiority—there are still no photos of Bush with his ear to a cell phone—but it's a fact that the cell phone has become an instrument for communication, and excessive communication, between mothers and children, for cheating on exams, and for photomania.

Younger generations are abandoning their wristwatches because they can check the time on their cell phones. Add to this the birth of text messages, of up-to-the-minute news information, of the opportunity to connect to the Internet and receive wireless emails. In their more sophisticated forms, cell phones can function as pocket computers, so that we're now in the presence of a phenomenon that is socially and technologically essential.

Can we still live without a cell phone? Given that "living with a cell phone" means a total acceptance of the here-and-now and a frenzy of contact that deprives us of a single moment of solitary thought, anyone who cherishes their own inner and outer freedom can exploit the very many services it offers, apart from its use as a telephone. At most it can be switched on just to call a taxi or tell those at home that the train is three hours late, but not for being called—all you have to do is keep it switched off. When anyone complains about this practice of mine, I reply with a rather somber argument. When my father died over forty years ago, and therefore long before cell phones, I was on a journey and it was many hours before I could be reached. Well, those hours of delay had changed nothing. The situation would have been no different had I been called within ten minutes. This all means that instant communication provided by the cell phone has little to do with the great questions of life and death, it's of no use to someone who is studying Aristotle, nor to someone struggling over the existence of God.

Does that mean a philosopher would have no interest in a cell phone, apart from its allowing him to carry in his pocket a list of three thousand books on Malebranche? On the contrary. Certain technological innovations have changed human life to such an extent as to become a topic for philosophical discussion—just think of the invention of writing, from Plato to Derrida, or the advent of mechanical looms (see Marx). Curiously there has been little philosophical reflection on other technological changes that seem so important to us, such as the car or the airplane, though there has been on the changing concept of speed. But we use the car and the airplane only at particular times, unless we're a taxi or truck driver or a pilot, whereas writing and the mechanization of most of our daily activities have had a radical impact on every second of our lives.

Maurizio Ferraris has written about the philosophy of the cell phone in *Where Are You? An Ontology of the Cell Phone.* Perhaps the title raises a hint of light amusement, but Ferraris draws a number of serious reflections from his subject, and involves us in a rather intriguing philosophical game. Cell phones are radically changing our way of life and have therefore become "philosophically interesting." Having also taken on the role of pocket diary and minicomputer with a Web connection, the cell phone is less and less an oral instrument and more and more an instrument for reading and writing. As such, it has become an all-inclusive tool for recording, and we can see how words like "writing," "recording," and "inscription" might make a confederate of Derrida prick up his ears.

The first hundred pages on the "anthropology" of the cell phone are fascinating even for the nonspecialist. There's a substantial difference between talking on a telephone and talking on a cell phone. On the telephone we could ask whether a certain person was at home, whereas on the cell phone, unless it's stolen, we always know who is answering, and whether he or she is there, which also changes the quality of intimacy. But with a landline we know where we are calling. Now, with the cell phone, there's the problem of where the person is. There again, if he or she replies "I'm right behind you" but has an account with a cell phone company in a different country, the answer may be traveling halfway around the world. Nonetheless, we don't know where the other person is, whereas the telephone company knows where we both are, so that while we can avoid letting the other person know our precise whereabouts, our movements are totally transparent when it comes to Orwell's Big Brother.

We can see various pessimistic and paradoxical, though credible, aspects of the new *Homo cellularis*. For example, it changes the very dynamic of face-to-face interaction between A and B, which is no longer a one-to-one relationship because the conversation can be interrupted by a cell phone call from C, and the interaction between A and B continues intermittently or stops altogether. And so the prime instrument of connection, my being continually available to others and they to me, becomes at the same time the instrument of disconnection: A is connected to everyone except B. Among those reasons for optimism I like to recall the tragedy of Dr. Zhivago, who after many years sees Lara on a tram. He cannot alight in time to reach her, and dies. If both had had mobile phones, how would their tragic story have ended? Ferraris's analysis wavers, rightly, between the possibilities opened up by the cell phone and the way in which it cuts through our lives, above all in our loss of solitude, of silent personal reflection, and being condemned to a constant presence of the present. Change doesn't always equate with liberation.

But one third of the way through the book, Ferraris passes from the cell phone to a discussion of questions that have increasingly interested him in recent years, including arguments against his early influences, from Heidegger to Gadamer and Vattimo, against philosophical postmodernism, against the idea that there are no facts but only interpretations, up to what is now a full defense of knowledge as *adaequatio*—that is, *pace* Richard Rorty, as a "Mirror of Nature." This, of course, has to be taken with many pinches of salt, and I'm sorry I can't follow step by step the foundation of realism that Ferraris calls "weak textualism."

How do we get from the cell phone to the problem of Truth? Through a distinction between physical objects such as a chair or a mountain, ideal objects such as Pythagoras's theorem, and social objects such as the Italian Constitution or our duty to pay for what we order at a bar. The first two types of object also exist independently of our decisions, whereas the third becomes operative, so to speak, only after a recording or an inscription. Once it is said that Ferraris also attempts to provide some kind of "natural" basis for these social recordings, it is here that the cell phone appears as the absolute instrument for every act of recording.

It would be interesting to discuss many parts of the book. For example, the pages devoted to the differences between types of recording, which include a bank statement, a law, any collection of personal data, and communication. Ferraris's ideas about recording are intriguing, whereas his ideas about communication have always been somewhat generic. To use the metaphor from one of his earlier papers against him, they seem to have been purchased at IKEA. But this is not the place for deep philosophical debate.

Some readers will ask if it was really necessary to start from the cell phone to reach conclusions that could also have been reached from concepts of writing and "signature." Certainly the philosopher can also start off from a reflection on a worm to draw an entire metaphysics, but perhaps the most interesting aspect of the book is not that the cell phone has allowed Ferraris to develop an ontology, but that his ontology has allowed him to understand, and help us to understand, the cell phone.

2005

Swallowing the cell phone

Last week, I read this extraordinary newspaper headline: "Cell Phone Swallowing Moroccan in Rome Saved by Police." As the police pass by late one evening, they see someone on the ground spitting blood, surrounded by a few countrymen, so they pull him up and take him to the hospital, where a Nokia is extracted from his throat.

Now, it seems impossible to me, unless it's a publicity stunt for Nokia, that a human being, however deranged, could swallow a cell phone. The newspaper suggested the incident had happened during a settling of scores between drug dealers, and it is therefore likely the cell phone had been forced down his throat, not as a tasty morsel but as an act of retaliation. Perhaps the person punished had been calling someone he shouldn't have.

A stone in the mouth is an insult of Mafia origin: it is stuck between the jaws of the corpse of whoever has divulged secrets to outsiders. Giuseppe Ferrara made a film about it in 1969, and it's no surprise that the practice has been passed on to other ethnic groups. There again, the Mafia is such an international phenomenon that several years ago in Moscow, my Russian translator was asked how you say "Mafia" in Italian.

But this time it wasn't a stone but a cell phone, and it seemed highly symbolic to me. The new criminal gangs are no longer rural but urban and technological; it is natural that they no longer settle scores with killings by ligature strangulation but instead, let us say, by "incyborga-tion." Moreover, thrusting a cell phone into someone's mouth is like a kick in the testicles: the cell phone is the most intimate and personal thing he possesses, the natural complement to his physical being, an extension of his ear, his eye, and also of his penis. Suffocating someone with his cell phone is like strangling him with his own entrails. There's a message for you.

2008

On photography

Some time ago, during a speech I was giving at the Spanish Academy in Rome, a photographer kept dazzling me with a light to get a picture with her film camera so that I couldn't read my notes. I reacted with irritation, saying, as I tend to do on such occasions with tactless photographers, that division of labor requires that when I'm working they must stop. So the person with the camera switched off her light, but behaved as if she'd been unfairly treated. Only last week, in the Apennine hill town of San Leo, at the start of a marvelous public event on the rediscovery of landscapes in the Montefeltro area that appear in the paintings of Piero della Francesca, three individuals were blinding me with their flashes, and once again I had to remind them about the rules of good behavior.

It should be noted that in both cases the dazzlers were not of the *Big Brother* kind, but presumably intelligent people who had come of their own free will to listen to discussions of a certain depth. Yet evidently the syndrome of the electronic eye had made them sink from the human level. With practically no interest in what was being said, all they wanted was to record the event, perhaps to put it on You-Tube. They preferred not to follow what was being said so they could record on their cell phone what they could have seen with their own eyes.

This dominance of a mechanical eye to the detriment of the brain therefore seems to have affected the minds of otherwise civilized people. They'd have come out of whatever event they had attended with a few pictures—and they'd have been well justified had I been a striptease artist—but with no idea what they had heard. And if, as I imagine, they go around the world photographing everything they see, they are evidently condemned to forget the next day what they have recorded the day before.

I have described on previous occasions how in 1960, after a tour of French cathedrals, taking photographs like a madman, I gave up photography. When I got home I found myself with a series of mediocre photos and couldn't remember what I had seen. I threw the camera away and recorded only mentally what I saw on my travels. For future reference, more for other people than for myself, I would buy a few good postcards.

Once, when I was eleven, my attention was caught by some odd noises on the highway just outside the city where I had been evacuated. Some distance away I saw that a truck had crashed into a horse-drawn cart driven by a farmer. His wife, who'd been sitting beside him, had been thrown to the ground, her head split open, and she was lying in a pool of blood and brain matter. I still recall the sight with horror, while her husband clung to her, howling in desperation.

I was terrified and didn't get too close. Not only was it the first time I'd seen brain matter strewn across the asphalt, and fortunately it was also the last, but it was the first time I'd come face-to-face with Death. And Suffering, and Despair.

What would have happened if I'd had a cell phone with a camera in it, as every child has today? Perhaps I'd have recorded it to show my friends I was there, and then I'd have loaded my visual gem onto YouTube to give pleasure to other disciples of schadenfreude. And then, who knows, by continuing to record other tragedies I might have grown indifferent to the suffering of others.

Instead, I have stored all of it in my memory, and that picture, after seventy years, continues to obsess me and to teach me, yes, to make me a non-indifferent participant in the suffering of others. I don't know whether children of today will still have these possibilities of becoming adults. Adults, with their eyes glued to their cell phones, are now lost forever.

2012

Evolution: all with just one hand

The other day, five people of both sexes walked past me on the street: two were telephoning, two frantically texting and in danger of tripping over, one was walking along holding the object, ready to answer any sound that promised human contact.

One cultured and eminent friend of mine has thrown away his Rolex because, he says, he can now check the time on his BlackBerry. Technology had invented the wristwatch so human beings didn't have to carry a pendulum clock around their neck or pull a pocket watch out of their waistcoat pocket every few minutes, and now my friend has to walk around, whatever he's doing, with one hand perennially busy. Humanity is losing the use of one of its limbs, and yet we know how much two hands with opposable thumbs have contributed to the evolution of the species.

It occurred to me that when people wrote with a goose quill they needed just one hand, but with the computer keyboard we need two, and so the telephone addict cannot use a telephone and PC at the same time. But then, I thought, cell phone addicts don't need their PC, which today is prehistoric, since the cell phone can connect to the Internet and send text messages, nor do they have to send emails when they can talk directly to the person they wish to pester or by whom they wish to be pestered. It's true that their consultations of Wikipedia will be more difficult and therefore more rapid and superficial, their written messages will be more telegraphic—whereas with email they can even write *The Screwtape Letters*—but telephone addicts no longer have the time to gather encyclopedic information nor to express themselves clearly because they're too busy in conversations. These are conversations about whose syntactical consistency we learn a great deal from those much-criticized instances of telephone interception, from which it can be deduced that phone addicts, spurning moreover all concerns about secrecy, express their plans with ellipses and a few such Neanderthal interpolations as "shit" and "fucking hell."

This reminds me of the film *Love Is Eternal While It Lasts*, directed by Carlo Verdone, in which a pert young woman transforms sexual intercourse into a nightmare: as she rides on the stomach of her partner she's forever answering urgent messages. In an interview I gave to a Spanish journalist, who seemed otherwise bright and intelligent, he commented with amazement that I hadn't interrupted our conversation once to answer my cell phone, concluding therefore that I was most courteous. He couldn't imagine that either I had no cell phone or I kept it switched off because I didn't want it for unsolicited messages, only for checking my diary.

2013

The cell phone and the queen in "Snow White"

I was walking along the sidewalk and saw a woman approaching me. She was glued to her cell phone and wasn't looking where she was going. Unless I stepped aside we would have bumped into each other. I have a hidden wicked streak, and so I stopped and turned and she collided with my back. I had braced myself for the impact and remained firm, but she was taken aback, dropped her cell phone, realized she had hit someone who couldn't see her. She muttered a few words of apology while I, in an affable tone, said, "Not to worry, such things happen these days."

I only hope her cell phone broke when it fell, and I advise anyone in a similar situation to do as I did. Cell phone addicts should be dealt with when they are young, but since a Herod doesn't turn up every day, it's better to punish them at least as adults, even if they'll never understand into what chasm they have fallen, and will carry on regardless.

I'm well aware that dozens of books have been written on the cell phone syndrome and that there's nothing more to add, but if we think for a moment, it seems inexplicable that the bulk of humanity is made up of people caught in the same frenzy, people who no longer talk face-to-face, no longer look at the countryside, no longer reflect on life and death, and instead talk obsessively, invariably with nothing urgent to say.

We are living in an era in which humanity, for the first time, can fulfill one of the three wishes that magic has been trying to satisfy for centuries. The first is the desire to fly, but by levitating with our body, flapping our arms, not climbing into an aircraft; the second is being able to influence our enemy or the person we love by pronouncing arcane words or pricking a clay figure; the third is communicating at a great distance, passing over oceans and mountain ranges, having a genie or miraculous object that will take us from Frosinone to Pamir, from Innisfree to Timbuktu, from Baghdad to Poughkeepsie, communicating instantly with those who are thousands of miles away. Communicating directly, personally, not as still happens with television, which is dependent on someone else's will, and where things don't always happen live.

What is it that has inclined people for centuries toward magical practices? Impatience. Magic promised the chance of short-circuiting from a cause to an effect, with no intermediate steps: utter a magic formula and transform iron into gold, summon angels and get them to send a message. Faith in magic didn't disappear with the advent of experimental science, since the dream of simultaneity between cause and effect has been transferred to technology. Technology today provides everything immediately; you press a button on your cell phone and talk to Sydney, whereas science moves cautiously and its prudence doesn't satisfy us because we want the universal remedy against cancer now, not tomorrow—which leads us to trust the doctor-guru who instantly promises the miraculous potion.

There is a close relationship between technological enthusiasm and magical thought, and it is linked to the religious faith in the lightning action of the miracle. Theological thought spoke, and speaks, to us about mysteries, but used, and still uses, arguments to show that they are conceivable, yet unfathomable. Whereas faith in the miracle shows us the numinous, the sacred, the divine, which appears and operates without delay.

Can there be a link between someone who promises an immediate cure for cancer, Padre Pio, the cell phone, and the queen in "Snow White"? In a certain sense there is. That's why the woman on the sidewalk in my story was living in a fairy-tale world, bound by the spell of an ear rather than a magic mirror.

2015

On Conspiracies

Where's the deep throat?

It's widely known that there are many conspiracy theories around September 11. There are extreme theories found on Arab fundamentalist and neo-Nazi sites that claim the conspiracy was organized by the Jews, and that all Jews working in the Twin Towers had been warned the previous day not to turn up for work, despite the fact that around four hundred Israeli or Jewish American citizens were among the victims; there are the anti-Bush theories claiming the attack had been organized so that Afghanistan and Iraq could be invaded; there are those who point the finger at more or less deviant American secret services; there's the theory that it was an Arab fundamentalist plot and the American government knew the details in advance, but they let things go their own way, to provide a pretext for invading Afghanistan and Iraq, rather like the suggestion that Roosevelt knew Pearl Harbor was about to be attacked but did nothing to save the fleet because he needed a pretext for declaring war on Japan; and lastly, there's the theory that the attack was orchestrated by bin Laden's fundamentalists, but the authorities responsible for the defense of America reacted wrongly and late, demonstrating their incompetence. The supporters of one or another of these conspiracies claim the official reconstruction of events is false, fraudulent, and puerile.

Anyone wanting to find out about the conspiracy theories can read *Zero: Perché la versione ufficiale sull'11/9 è un falso* (*Zero: Why the Official Version of 9/11 Is False*), edited by Giulietto Chiesa and Roberto Vignoli, which includes interviews with such eminent figures as Franco

Cardini, Gianni Vattimo, Gore Vidal, Lidia Ravera, and many foreign contributors.

But anyone wanting to consider a different view can thank the same publisher, who, with admirable fairness, and proving its ability to capture two opposing sectors of the market, published in the same year a book against conspiracy theories, 11/9: *La cospirazione impossibile* (*9/11: The Impossible Conspiracy*), edited by Massimo Polidoro, with equally eminent contributors including Piergiorgio Odifreddi and James Randi. The fact that I am also in the book should be neither to my credit nor to my detriment, since the editor simply asked to republish a previously printed article that wasn't so much about September 11 as about the eternal conspiracy syndrome. Nevertheless, since I believe that our world was created by chance, I have no difficulty believing that most of the events that have racked it over the course of thousands of years, from the Trojan War to the present day, have happened by chance or through the concurrence of a series of human follies, and I am by nature, out of skepticism, out of caution, always inclined to doubt any conspiracy, since I believe my fellow human beings are incapable of dreaming up a perfect one. All this despite the fact that —for reasons certainly of temperament, but also of irrepressible impulse—I'm inclined to regard Bush and his administration as capable of anything.

For reasons of space, I won't go through the details of the arguments used by the supporters of both positions, which may all seem persuasive, but I appeal only to what I would describe as the "test of silence." One example of the test of silence can be used against those who allege that the American landing on the Moon was a television sham. If the American spaceship hadn't arrived on the Moon, then there must have been someone in a position to check this out, and who had an interest in revealing it, and this was the Soviets. And if the Soviets have kept silent, this is proof that the Americans actually got to the Moon. And that's the end of it.

As regards conspiracies and secrets: experience, as well as history, tells us, first, that if there's a secret, even if only one person knows about it, this person, perhaps in bed with his lover, will reveal it sooner or later. Only naïve Freemasons and followers of bogus Templar rituals believe in a secret that remains unbroken. Second, if there's a secret, there's always a price at which someone will be prepared to reveal it. A few hundred thousand dollars in publishing rights was enough to persuade a British army officer to recount all he'd done in bed with Princess Diana, and if he'd done it with the princess's mother-in-law, it would have been worth double the sum. Now, to organize a false attack on the Twin Towers, to mine them, to warn the air force not to intervene, to hide embarrassing evidence, and so forth, would have involved the collaboration of hundreds, if not thousands, of people. Generally speaking, the people used for such undertakings are never gentlemen, and it's inconceivable that at least one of them, for a sufficient sum, wouldn't have spoken. In short, what's lacking in this story is the "deep throat."

2007

Conspiracies and plots

The conspiracy syndrome is as old as the world, and its philosophy has been superbly described by Karl Popper in an essay on the conspiracy theory of society in *Conjectures and Refutations*: "This theory, which is more primitive than most forms of theism, is akin to Homer's theory of society. Homer conceived the power of the gods in such a way that whatever happened on the plain before Troy was only a reflection of the various conspiracies on Olympus. The conspiracy theory of society is just a version of this theism, of a belief in gods whose whims and wills rule everything. It comes from abandoning God and then asking: 'Who is in his place?' His place is then filled by various powerful men and groups—sinister pressure groups, who are to be blamed for having planned the great depression and all the evils from which we suffer . . . Only when conspiracy theoreticians come into power does it become something like a theory which accounts for things that actually happen. For example, when Hitler came into power, believing in the conspiracy myth of the Learned Elders of Zion, he tried to outdo their conspiracy with his own counter-conspiracy."

The psychology of the conspiracy is spawned by dissatisfaction with the obvious explanations for many disturbing occurrences. Think of the theory about the "Grand Old Man" who was supposedly behind the kidnapping and murder of Italy's prime minister, Aldo Moro, in 1978: how is it possible, people asked, that such a perfect operation could have been devised by a group of thirty-year-olds? There had to be sharper brains behind it. Not taking into account that other thirty-year-olds at that time were running companies, piloting jumbo jets, or inventing new electronic equipment, and therefore the crucial point was not how a group of thirty-year-olds managed to kidnap Moro in the center of Rome, but that those thirty-year-olds were the offspring of someone who had dreamed up the story of the Grand Old Man.

Such a suspicion absolves us from our own responsibility, since it leads us to think that hidden behind what concerns us is a secret, and that the concealment of that secret amounts to a conspiracy against us. Belief in the conspiracy is rather like believing one has been cured by a miracle, except that in this latter case one is trying to explain not a threat but a mysterious stroke of fortune. (See Popper: the origin is always in turning to the intrigues of the gods.)

The irony is that in daily life, nothing is more transparent than the conspiracy and the secret. The conspiracy, when effective, sooner or later has its own repercussions and comes to light. And the same can be said about the secret. Not only is the secret usually revealed by a series of "deep throats," but, whatever it relates to, provided it's important enough (whether it's the formula for a miraculous substance or a political maneuver), it will sooner or later come out in the open. Conspiracies and secrets, if they don't rise to the surface, are either lame conspiracies or empty secrets. The power of someone letting on they have a secret is not in hiding something; it's in making people believe there is a secret. In that sense, a secret and a conspiracy can be effective weapons in the hands of someone who doesn't believe them.

Georg Simmel, in his celebrated essay "The Sociology of Secrecy and of Secret Societies," recalled that "secrecy gives the person enshrouded by it an exceptional position . . . It is in principle quite independent of its casual content, but is naturally heightened in the degree in which the exclusively possessed secret is significant and comprehensive . . . The natural impulse to idealization, and the natural timidity of men, operate to one and the same end in the presence of secrecy; viz., to heighten it by fantasy, and to distinguish it by a degree of attention that published reality could not command."

A paradoxical consequence: hidden behind every false conspiracy there's perhaps a conspiracy by someone who stands to gain from presenting it as true.

2007

Fine company

Every time I return to the subject of the conspiracy syndrome I receive letters from indignant people who remind me that conspiracies actually exist. Of course they do. Every coup d'état was a conspiracy, people conspire to take over a company by gradually buying up shares, or they conspire to plant a bomb on the subway. There have always been conspiracies: some have failed without anyone knowing about them, others have succeeded, but what they have in common is that they are limited in their purposes and scope. When people refer to conspiracy syndrome, however, they are talking about the idea of a universal conspiracy, in certain theologies even of a cosmic dimension, so that all or almost all the events of history are moved by a single and mysterious power that operates in the shadows.

I'm sufficiently clearheaded to suspect at times that by complaining about conspiracy syndromes, I'm showing signs of paranoia, in that I'm displaying a syndrome in which I believe there are conspiracy theories everywhere. But to set my mind at rest, all it takes is a brief look at the Internet, where conspirators are legion and at times they reach the heights of subtle and unwitting humor. The other day I came across a site containing a long piece called *Le monde malade des jésuites* by Joël Labruyère. As the title suggests, it's a broad survey of world events, not just recent events, brought about by the universal conspiracy of the Jesuits.

Nineteenth-century Jesuits were among the main instigators of the Jewish-Masonic conspiracy, from Abbé Augustin Barruel to the creation of the Jesuit magazine *La Civiltà Cattolica* and the novels of Father Antonio Bresciani, and it was fitting that they should be repaid in the same way by Italian liberals, Mazzinians, Freemasons, and anticlerical movements, with the theory of a Jesuit conspiracy popularized to some extent by satirical pamphlets or such famous books as Pascal's *Lettres provinciales,* Vincenzo Gioberti's *Il gesuita moderno,* or the writings of Jules Michelet and Edgar Quinet, but much more by two novels of Eugène Sue, *Le Juif errant* and *Les Mystères du peuple.*

Nothing new, therefore, but Labruyère's site raises the Jesuit obsession to fever pitch. My list is just a bird's-eye glimpse, since space here is limited, whereas Labruyère's conspiratorial fantasy is Homeric. And so, according to him, the Jesuits had always intended to establish a world government, controlling the pope as well as the various European monarchies. Through the notorious Bavarian Illuminati, whom the Jesuits themselves had created before condemning them as Communists, they sought to bring down those monarchies that had outlawed the Company of Jesus. It was the Jesuits, he says, who had sunk the *Titanic,* because from that disaster they could set up the Federal Reserve Bank through the mediation of the Knights of Malta, whom they control, and it is no coincidence that three of the world's richest Jews, John Jacob Astor, Benjamin Guggenheim, and Isidor Straus, who opposed the founding of the bank, were drowned on the *Titanic.* Along with the Federal Reserve Bank, the Jesuits funded the two world wars, which have clearly brought advantage only to the Vatican. As for the assassination of John F. Kennedy (and Oliver Stone has clearly been manipulated by the Jesuits), if we remember that the CIA was also created as a Jesuit program inspired by the spiritual exercises of Ignatius of Loyola, and that the Jesuits controlled it through the Soviet KGB, then it's clear, Labruyère concludes, that Kennedy was killed by those who had conspired to sink the *Titanic.*

Naturally, all neo-Nazi and anti-Semitic groups are of Jesuit inspiration. There were Jesuits behind Presidents Nixon and Clinton; the Jesuits brought about the Oklahoma City bombing; and the Jesuits inspired Cardinal Francis Spellman, who fomented the Vietnam War, which brought $220 million to the Jesuit Federal Bank. Nor, of course, can we forget the role of Opus Dei, which the Jesuits control through the Knights of Malta.

I have to pass over many other conspiracies. But you no longer need to ask why people read Dan Brown.

2008

Don't believe in coincidences

Someone has said that Berlusconi had, and still has, two kinds of enemies — Communists and investigating magistrates — and has pointed out that the recent administrative elections have been won by a (former) Communist and a (former) investigating magistrate. Others have noted that in 1991, when the prime minister, Bettino Craxi, on the day of the referendum on electoral reform, invited Italians to go to the beach rather than going to vote, the referendum had remarkable success and marked the beginning of Craxi's political decline. One could go on: Berlusconi gets into power in March 1994 and in November the rivers Po, Tanaro, and many other tributaries burst their banks and flood the provinces of Cuneo, Asti, and Alessandria; Berlusconi returns to power in May 2008 and within a year Aquila is struck by an earthquake.

All are amusing coincidences but have absolutely no value, except for the parallel between Berlusconi and Craxi. The game of coincidences has fascinated paranoiacs and schemers from time immemorial, but you can do anything you want with coincidences, and especially with dates.

A host of coincidences has been identified in relation to the attack on the Twin Towers, and a few years ago, in *Scienza e Paranormale,* Paolo Attivissimo cited a series of numerological speculations based on September 11. To quote a few: New York City has 11 letters; Afghanistan has 11 letters; Ramsin Yuseb, the terrorist who had threatened to destroy the towers, has 11 letters; George W. Bush has 11 letters; the Twin Towers form an 11; New York was the eleventh state to join the United States; the first aircraft to crash into the towers was Flight 11, which carried 92 passengers, and 9+2 = 11; Flight 77, which also crashed into the towers, carried 65 passengers, and 6+5 = 11; the date 9/11 is the same as the American emergency telephone number, 911, whose constituent numbers add up to 11. The total number of victims in all aircraft was 254, whose constituent numbers add up to 11; September 11 is the 254th day of the year, whose constituent numbers add up to 11.

Unfortunately, New York has 11 letters only if we add City; Afghanistan has 11 letters, yet the hijackers came not from there but from Saudi Arabia, which also has 11 letters, as well as Egypt, Lebanon, and the Arab Emirates, which don't; Ramsin Yuseb has 11 letters, but if, instead of Yuseb, it is transliterated Yussef, the game wouldn't have worked; George W. Bush has 11 letters only if we add the middle initial; the towers formed an 11 but also a 2 in roman numerals; Flight 77 didn't crash into the towers but into the Pentagon, and it carried not 65 but 59 passengers; the total number of victims wasn't 254 but 265. And so on.

Other coincidences circulating on the Internet? Lincoln was elected to Congress in 1846, Kennedy was elected in 1946. Lincoln was elected president in 1860, Kennedy in 1960. Both had wives who lost a child while they were resident at the White House. Both were struck in the head by a southerner on a Friday. Lincoln's secretary was called

Kennedy, and Kennedy's was called Lincoln. Lincoln's successor was Johnson (born in 1808), while Kennedy's successor, Lyndon Johnson, was born in 1908.

John Wilkes Booth, who assassinated Lincoln, was born in 1838, and Lee Harvey Oswald in 1939. Lincoln was shot at Ford's Theatre; Kennedy was shot in a Lincoln automobile manufactured by Ford.

Lincoln was shot in a theater and his assassin went to hide in a depository; Kennedy's assassin shot from a depository and went to hide in a theater. Both Booth and Oswald were killed before they could be brought to trial.

2011

The conspiracy on conspiracies

Massimo Polidoro, one of the more active members of CICAP (the Italian Committee for the Investigation of Claims of the Pseudosciences) and of the quarterly magazine *Query*, has published a book titled *Rivelazioni: Il libro dei segreti e dei complotti* (*Revelations: The Book of Secrets and Conspiracies*). It is one of many books he's written about the hoaxes that circulate around the mass media and even in the heads of people whom we generally regard as responsible. I imagine that with such an intriguing title, Polidoro hopes to attract those with a love for every kind of secret, people about whom John Chadwick, the man who deciphered the Mycenaean script called Linear B, said: "The urge to discover secrets is deeply ingrained in human nature: even the least curious mind is roused by the promise of sharing knowledge withheld from others."

There is, of course, a certain difference between deciphering a script that had a meaning for someone in the past and imagining that the Americans didn't land on the Moon, that September 11 was a plot by Bush and indeed the Jews, or that a Da Vinci Code exists. But it's for the followers of this second sect that Polidoro is writing. His short chapters, with their affable tone, start off most promisingly, though in the end they tell us that the conspiracy behind the Kennedy assassination, that Hitler's true end, that the secrets of Rennes-le-Château, and that Jesus's marriage to Mary Magdalene are or were no more than hoaxes.

Why do hoaxes work? Because they promise a knowledge that others don't have, and for other reasons that Polidoro draws from Karl Popper's famous essay on the conspiracy theory of society. And he cites the studies of Richard Hofstadter, according to whom the taste for conspiracies has to be interpreted by applying the categories of psychiatry to social thought. They are two aspects of paranoia. Except that someone suffering from psychiatric paranoia sees the whole world as conspiring against him, whereas the social paranoiac thinks that the persecution by hidden powers is directed against his own group or nation or religion. The social paranoiac is, I would say, more dangerous than the psychiatrically paranoid because he sees his obsessions shared by millions of other people and believes he is acting in a disinterested manner against the conspiracy. This explains much that is happening in the world today, as well as in the past.

And Polidoro also quotes Pier Paolo Pasolini, who thought conspiracy excites because it frees us from the burden of having to face the truth. Now, we might feel indifferent about the world being full of conspiracy theorists: if anyone thinks the Americans didn't land on the Moon, then too bad for them. But recent studies by Daniel Jolley and Karen Douglas conclude that "exposure to information supporting conspiracy theories reduced participants' intentions to engage in politics, relative to participants who were given information refuting conspiracy theories." If people are convinced that world history is managed by secret societies, that the Bilderberg Group are Illuminati, that they are establishing a new world order, then what can I do? Give up, and despair. And so every conspiracy theory directs the public imagination to perceived dangers, distracting it from the real threats. As Noam Chomsky once suggested, imagining almost a conspiracy of conspiracy theories, those who reap the greater benefit from imaginings about a supposed conspiracy are the very institutions that the conspiracy theory seeks to damage. That is to say, by imagining it was Bush who caused the collapse of the Twin Towers to justify his intervention in Iraq, we become involved in hallucinations and stop analyzing the true methods and reasons for Bush's intervention in Iraq, and the influence the neocons had on him and on his policies.

Which might lead us to suspect that it was George W. Bush himself who spread the news about the Bush conspiracy against the Twin Towers. But let us not be so conspiratorial.

2014

On Mass Media

Radiophonic hypnosis

In a recent article, I described my feelings as a young boy of an evening during World War II, listening on the radio to songs, to Radio London, to messages for the partisans. Those memories became impressed upon my mind, and remain vivid and magical. Will a child of today retain such memories of television newscasts of the Gulf War, or of Kosovo?

I asked myself these questions last week when, during the Prix Italia, we listened again to excerpts from radio broadcasts over the past seventy years. The answer came from a famous distinction made by Marshall McLuhan, anticipated by many who had written about radio, including Bertolt Brecht, Walter Benjamin, Gaston Bachelard, and Rudolf Arnheim. The distinction was between hot and cold media. A hot medium occupies a single sense, and leaves no space for interaction: it has a hypnotic grip. A cold medium occupies different senses, but reaches you in fragmentary fashion, and requires your conscious involvement in order to fill in, connect up, elaborate what you receive. And so, according to McLuhan, a conference or a film, which you follow seated and passive, is hot; a debate or an evening watching television is cold; a high-definition photograph is hot, whereas a comic strip, which represents reality in a series of sketches, is cold.

When one of the very first radio plays was broadcast, the audience at home was invited to listen to it in the dark. And I recall some evening broadcasts of the weekly comedy, when my father would sit in an armchair, lights dimmed, his ear glued to the loudspeaker, and listen in silence for two hours. I sat curled up on his knee and, though I didn't understand much of what was going on, was a part of the ritual. This was the power of radio.

Theodor Adorno was among the first to complain that music, arriving in abundance through the radio, was losing its almost liturgical role, becoming a mere commodity. But Adorno was thinking how the music lover's taste can be corrupted, not how an adolescent first experiences music. I remember my intense pleasure when, thanks to radio, I discovered classical music and, checking the programs in the radio magazine, would tune in to one of those short interludes when a Chopin polonaise was listed, or a single movement of a symphony.

Is radio like this today, and will it be like this tomorrow? Radio is used increasingly as a background noise, comedy is watched on television, music is downloaded via the Internet. Radio no longer has a hypnotic effect on drivers who listen to it on the highway—and that's a good thing, otherwise they'd collide with a truck. Instead, they hop from channel to channel as the signal fades and they have to search for another station. And you have to follow the prattle of Jessica from Piacenza or Salvatore from Messina.

Fortunately radios cost less by the day, and are more beautiful, looking like samurai. It's true they're used more for playing records or cassettes than for searching out stations in mysterious cities called Tallinn, Riga, and Hilversum, as we used to do on our shortwave radios. But the history of mass media doesn't allow prophecies. Perhaps unforeseen technological innovations will bring radio back to the core of our experiences, and who knows if these fascinating ornaments hold in store new forms of "heat."

2000

There are two Big Brothers

At an international conference on privacy held recently in Venice, there were several mentions of the television program *Big Brother*, though Stefano Rodotà, president of the Italian Personal Data Protection Authority, suggested from the outset that this program didn't in itself violate anyone's privacy.

There's no doubt that it tickles the voyeuristic fancy of the viewer, who enjoys watching several individuals put into the unnatural situation of pretending they like each other, though in fact they're at each other's throats. People are heartless and always have been: they enjoyed the sight of Christians being torn apart by lions, or gladiators walking into the arena knowing their survival depended on the death of their companion; people paid to gape at the deformity of fat women at a carnival, to see dwarfs being kicked around by a circus clown, and watch a condemned man being executed in the public square. All things being equal, *Big Brother* is more respectable, and not just because nobody dies. The only risk to participants is psychological disturbance—no worse than what led them to take part in the broadcast. The fact is that Christians would have preferred to remain praying in the catacombs, the gladiator would have been happier if he'd been a Roman patrician, the dwarf if he'd had the physique of Rambo, the fat woman if she'd been Brigitte Bardot, the convict if he'd been pardoned. Yet the contestants on *Big Brother* take part voluntarily and would be willing to pay for what they regard as the paramount value, namely, public exposure and celebrity.

The morally harmful aspect of *Big Brother* lies elsewhere, in the very title that someone has dreamed up for the game. Many viewers may have failed to understand that Big Brother is an allegory invented by George Orwell in his novel 1984. Big Brother was a dictator (his name evokes the Little Father—in other words, Stalin) who, alone or with a few close comrades, could spy on all his subjects minute by minute, wherever they were. An appalling situation, reminiscent of Jeremy Bentham's Panopticon, where prison guards could spy on inmates without their knowing.

With Orwell's Big Brother, just a few people could spy on everyone. Whereas in the television version, it's everyone who can spy on just a few people. And so we'll get used to thinking of *Big Brother* as something democratic and entertaining. Yet in doing so we'll forget that behind us, while we are watching the program, there is the real Big Brother, the one about whom conferences on privacy are focused. The real Big Brother is made up of the various organs of power that are watching when we click on an Internet site, when we pay by credit card in a hotel, when we buy something by mail order, when we are diagnosed with an illness in a hospital, and even when we wander around a supermarket monitored by closed-circuit television. We know that unless these practices are strictly controlled, a staggering quantity of information about us will be gathered, making us entirely transparent and depriving us of all privacy and confidentiality.

As we watch *Big Brother* on television, we are like a spouse innocently flirting in a bar unaware that the other spouse is involved in a seriously adulterous affair. The title *Big Brother* therefore helps us not to notice, or to forget, that someone at that very moment is laughing behind our backs.

2000

Roberta

Roberta and the ruling classes

To get some idea about *Big Brother*, it's enough to watch it for two or three Thursday evenings, as I did. These are the days of reckoning. I tried connecting up via the Internet and saw in low definition a tattooed female in underpants, frying an egg. I held on for a while, then found something better to do. But every so often you catch glimpses of the average Italian mind, which might be of interest, at least sociologically. Take the case of the infamous Roberta, who, loudmouthed and extroverted, had been rejected by a united Italy, reducing the house to a morgue.

In her desperate attempts to make herself hateful, Roberta dared suggest she was a cut above her companions, most of them butchers, since she regularly dined with art dealers. In response, not only her companions in misadventure but also television viewers decided she belonged to the ruling classes and was therefore to be castigated. Nobody paused to think that members of the ruling classes do not dine with art dealers, unless she was referring to the president of Christie's. Rather, they summon art dealers to their homes to examine a 1.8-meter-high Raphael or a ninth-century Russian icon.

Why we are happy to let artists take drugs

Someone recently wrote a letter to *Corriere della Sera* asking why we are scandalized if a cyclist or soccer player shoots up with some stimulant, whereas we've always been fascinated by great artists who smoked opium or sought inspiration through LSD or cocaine. At first sight the question is reasonable: if we regard an athlete's victory as unmerited, then why should we admire a poem that comes not from the poet's genius but from a substance taken perhaps intravenously?

Yet the difference between sporting rigor and artistic broad-mindedness conceals a deep truth, and this instinctive public attitude tells us much more than any theory of aesthetics. What stirs our admiration for sporting achievement is not a ball that goes into the goal or a bicycle that crosses the finish line before another, since both are phenomena that physics can explain perfectly well. What we find interesting and admirable is a human being who does something better than we ever could. If soccer balls were fired into the goal by a cannon, soccer would lose all interest.

In art, on the other hand, we admire the work first, and the physical and mental state of the person who has created it is only secondary. So much so that we find great beauty in works by someone of low morality, we are touched by Achilles and Ulysses even if we don't know whether Homer actually existed, and *The Divine Comedy* would still be miraculous if we were told that a monkey had chanced to type it on a computer. We even look upon certain objects produced by nature or accident as being works of art, and we are moved by ruins, which, as such, have not been created by any exceptional human being. When confronted by the magic of the work, we are prepared to ignore the way in which the artist arrived at it.

And we allow Baudelaire all his artificial paradises, provided he gives us *Les fleurs du mal*.

2000

The mission of the crime story

Bernard Benstock was a fine American expert on James Joyce. After his early death, his wife gave his Joyce collection to the Scuola Superiore Interpreti e Traduttori at Forlì. This year another of his collections has been donated: nearly seven hundred volumes devoted to crime fiction. Last week, while we were commemorating him, someone asked why so many thinkers, critics, and scholars in general cultivate a passion for the detective story. Of course, those who have to read serious literature like to sit back in the evening with something more relaxing. But why do they often do so with such devotion? There are, I think, three reasons.

One is purely philosophical. The essence of the crime story is eminently metaphysical, and it's no coincidence that the English call this kind of story a whodunit, which was the question that the pre-Socratics posed, and which we haven't stopped asking. The five ways to demonstrate the existence of God, studied in the writing of Saint Thomas Aquinas, were also a masterpiece of crime investigation: with his nose to the ground like a truffle hound, he works from the evidence we find in the world of our existence back to the first beginning of the chain of causes and effects, or to the prime mover of all movements . . .

Except that we now know, from Kant on, that if working back from an effect to a cause is acceptable in the world of experience, the procedure becomes doubtful when working back from the world to something that is outside the world. And here comes the great metaphysical consolation provided by the crime story, where even the ultimate cause, and the hidden mover of all movements, is not outside the world of the story, but inside, and is part of it. And so, each evening, the crime story offers the consolation that we are denied by metaphysics, or much of it.

The second reason is scientific. Many people have shown that the investigation procedures used by Sherlock Holmes and his descendants are similar to those used in research, in both the natural and human sciences, where the quest is for the secret key to a text or the original forebear of a series of manuscripts. Holmes, who was notoriously ignorant about almost everything, wrongly described this activity, divinatory in appearance only, as "deduction," while Charles Sanders Peirce called it "abduction," and this, with a few differences, was also the logic of Karl Popper's explanation.

Lastly, a literary reason. Ideally every text should be read twice, first to know what is said, second to appreciate how it is said, and from there to obtain the full aesthetic enjoyment. The crime story is a limited but exacting model of a text that, once you have discovered who the killer is, invites you implicitly or explicitly to look back, either to understand how the author has led you to build up false ideas, or to decide that after all he hadn't hidden anything, only that you had failed to observe with the keen eye of the detective.

It's a reading experience that entertains and at the same time offers metaphysical consolation, stimulates research, and provides a model for questioning far more impenetrable mysteries, and is therefore of valuable assistance in the Mission of the Scholar.

2001

Bin Laden's allies

The debate regarding not so much censorship as caution by the mass media is troubling the Western world. To what extent can the broadcasting of news items favor propaganda actions or even help in spreading coded messages sent out by terrorists?

The Pentagon urges newspapers and television stations to be cautious, and this is natural, since no army at war likes to have its plans, or appeals from the enemy, broadcast. The mass media are now accustomed to absolute freedom and cannot adapt to wartime strictures: in times gone by, anyone spreading news against national security ended up before a firing squad. It's difficult to unravel this knot. In a communication-dense society that now also has the Internet, there is no confidentiality.

The problem, in any event, is more complex than this. It's an old story: every act of terrorism is carried out to send a message, a message that itself spreads terror, or at the very least anxiety and instability. It was ever the same, even in those bygone times when terrorists, who now seem like amateurs, limited themselves to killing a single person or planting a bomb on a street corner. If the victim is relatively unknown, the terrorist message brings insecurity even if the impact is minimal. But it brings greater insecurity if the victim is well known and is some kind of symbol.

The qualitative leap can be seen with the Red Brigades when, after the killing of journalists or political advisers who were relatively unknown to the public at large, they moved on to the capture, traumatic detention, and murder of Prime Minister Aldo Moro.

Now, what is Osama bin Laden's purpose in attacking the Twin Towers? To create "the greatest spectacle on earth," something never imagined in disaster movies, to give the visual impression of striking at the very symbols of Western power, and showing that the greatest sanctums of this power could be violated. Bin Laden wasn't aiming to cause a particular number of deaths, which, from his point of view, brought added value. He was prepared to make do with half the number of victims provided the towers were hit, and all the better if they collapsed. He wasn't waging a war that counted the enemy casualties, he was launching a message of terror, and what mattered was the image.

If bin Laden's aim was to strike at world public opinion with that image, what has happened? The mass media had to broadcast the news, which is obvious. Likewise, they had to report news of the aftermath: the rescues, the excavations, the mutilated Manhattan skyline.

Did they really have to repeat this news every day and for at least a month, with photos, films, endlessly recycled eyewitness accounts, repeatedly bringing the image of that trauma before everyone's eyes? It's difficult to say. Newspapers boosted their sales with the photos, television channels boosted their ratings with those repeated film clips, the public itself was demanding to rewatch those horrific scenes, perhaps to fuel their personal indignation, perhaps at times through some unconscious sadistic impulse. Perhaps it was impossible to do otherwise. The emotion of the days following September 11 prevented the world's television stations and newspapers from reaching some form of agreement to limit coverage. None of them alone could remain silent without losing their position in the ratings.

In this way the mass media have handed bin Laden billions of dollars of free publicity, inasmuch as each day they have shown the pictures that he himself had created, and precisely so that everyone would see them, to stir feelings of disorientation in the West, to stir pride among his fundamentalist followers.

There again, the process continues and bin Laden can still reap advantage at little expense, considering that anthrax attacks are producing a negligible number of victims compared with those of the Twin Towers, but are terrorizing many more, since everyone feels threatened, even those who don't fly in airplanes and don't live near symbols of power.

And so the mass media, while they condemn bin Laden, have been his best allies, and in this way he has won the first round.

Yet as consolation for the bewilderment caused by this apparently irresolvable situation, we should remember that when the Red Brigades raised their game with the capture and killing of Aldo Moro, the message was so devastating that it backfired on its own perpetrators: instead of causing political turmoil, it produced an alliance between the parties, popular condemnation, and for the Red Brigades terrorists it marked the beginning of their decline.

Only time will tell whether the spectacle created by bin Laden has unleashed a process that will lead to his ruin, for the very reason that he went too far, beyond what was tolerable. In that case, the media will have won.

2001

Going to the same place

We're always saying it: much of our time is spent in virtual reality. We know the world through television, which often doesn't portray the world as it is, but reconstructs it. Television reconstructed the Gulf War using archive footage, and it constructs the world *ex novo*, as in *Big Brother*. We see more and more shadows of reality.

Yet people are traveling more than ever these days. People whose parents had never been farther from home than a nearby city tell me they've seen places that I, a compulsive and professional traveler, still only dream about. No exotic beach, no lost city, lies beyond the reach of most; they spend Christmas in Kolkata and August in Polynesia. Should we therefore regard this passion for tourism as a way of escaping from virtual reality to see "the real thing"?

It's true that tourism, however superficial, is a way of learning about the world. Except that travel at one time was a special experience, and people would come back changed, but all you meet now are seasoned travelers who have not been affected at all by the bustle of Elsewhere. They come back, and think only of the next holiday. They have no life-changing experiences to tell you about.

Perhaps this happens because the places of real pilgrimage now strive to look like places of virtual pilgrimage. An expert once told me that in a circus a whole day is spent cleaning and smartening up the elephant, a naturally messy and disorderly animal, so that in the evening it looks like the elephants previously seen at the cinema or in photographs. Likewise, the tourist resort strives only to resemble its glossy media image. Naturally, tourists have to be taken to the places that fit the virtual image and don't see the rest, so they visit temples and markets but not the leper colonies, they visit ruins made to look like new rather than those pillaged by tomb robbers. Sometimes the place of pilgrimage is created *ex novo*, as seen on television, so that people can pay Sunday visits to the rustic water mill exactly like the one seen on the biscuit commercial, not to mention Disneyland, or Venice as reconstructed in Las Vegas.

But all places are now beginning to look like each other, and this, for once, is the real effect of globalization. I'm thinking of several magical districts of Paris such as Saint-Germain, where the old restaurants, dusky bookshops, and old craft workshops are gradually disappearing, to be replaced by the shops of international designers. They are identical to those you find on Fifth Avenue in New York, or in London or Milan. The main streets of major cities now resemble one another, with exactly the same shops.

Yes, great cities may look alike, but they still retain their own particular features: the Eiffel Tower, the Tower of London, Milan Cathedral, or St. Peter's. This is true, but even so, there's a tendency to illuminate towers, churches, and castles with bright multicolored lights that obliterate their architectural features beneath an electric glare, so that great monuments are in danger of looking the same, at least in the eyes of the tourist, and have become a mere backdrop for international-style light shows.

When everything comes to resemble everything else, tourism will no longer be about exploring the real world. Wherever we go, we will always find what we've already seen, and what we could have seen from home, sitting in front of our television.

2001

Mandrake, an Italian hero?

Art Spiegelman has been to Milan to present his magnificent collection of *New Yorker* covers. Spiegelman became famous with his extraordinary graphic novel *Maus*, in which he demonstrated that comics could talk about the Holocaust with the force of a great saga. But he continues to be topical, commenting on the events of our time with stories that can bring together current affairs and serious argument, with affectionate references back to the earliest comics. In short, I consider him a genius.

He came to my home for drinks, and I showed him my collection of comic books from long ago, some that are dog-eared originals and others good reprints, and he was amazed to see the covers of old Nerbini albums of *The Phantom, Mandrake, Tim Tyler's Luck,* and *Flash Gordon,* amazed not so much at *Flash Gordon,* who is still legendary on the other side of the Atlantic, but at the other three. If you look at an American history of comics you'll find references to *The Phantom* and others, but it's apparent, even on the Internet, that the great remakes are more interested in *Superman,* the brigade of superheroes such as *Spider Man,* and postmodern updates of *Batman,* or they rediscover the origins of the oldest superhero, *Plastic Man,* as Spiegelman has also done in a magnificent book. Try looking for *Tim Tyler's Luck:* you'll find plenty of references to a bad film or a television series made from it, in the same way that a terrible TV series was made out of *Flash Gordon,* which now has trash cult status, but there's very little mention of the original comics.

Spiegelman told me that *The Phantom, Mandrake,* and the rest still seem more popular in Italy than in America. He wondered why, and I gave him my explanation, which is that of a historical witness who saw their emergence and first publication in improbable and ungrammatical Italian translations very soon after they appeared in America. Among other things, the covers of some of the Nerbini albums bore the title *Mandrache,* perhaps to make it seem Italian. In Italy, we had Fascist comics like *Dick Fulmine (Dick Lightning), Romano il legionario (Romano the Legionary),* and the adolescents of *Corriere dei piccoli,* who were taking civilization to Abyssinia or performing astounding feats with the Falangists against cruel Red militiamen. But then *Flash Gordon* came along to show Italian children that they could fight for freedom on planet Mongo against a ruthless and bloodthirsty autocrat like Ming, that the Phantom was fighting not against colored people but with them to put down white mercenaries, that a vast Africa existed where the Patrol roamed around arresting ivory smugglers, that there were heroes who didn't wander about in black shirts but in tailcoats and wore what the Fascist leader Achille Starace called "stovepipes," ending with the revelation of press freedom through the adventures of Mickey Mouse the journalist, even before Humphrey Bogart arrived on our screens, though this was after the war, saying, over the telephone: "That's the press, baby. The press! And there's nothing you can do about it." Such memories bring tears to the eyes—Oh, for the return of Mickey Mouse the television reporter!

In this way, during those dark years, the American comics taught us something and had an influence on us, even on our adult lives. And while we're on the subject, let me make a forecast and give some advice to newspapers, magazines, and television programs. Every year we celebrate an anniversary, an author, a book, a remarkable event. Well, let's get ready to celebrate the seventieth anniversary of that fabulous year 1934.

In January, the first *Flash Gordon* adventure appeared in America, as well as *Jungle Jim*, also created by Alex Raymond. Two weeks later, by the same cartoonist, *Secret Agent X-9* with text by Dashiell Hammett! The first *Flash Gordon* adventure would appear in Italy in October, in *L'Avventuroso*, except that the hero was depicted not as a polo player, which was too bourgeois, but as a police chief. Leaving aside March, when *Red Barry* and *Radio Patrol* first appeared, in June we have the arrival of *Mandrake* by Lee Falk and Phil Davis, and in August *Li'l Abner* by Al Capp, which didn't reach Italy until after World War II. In September Walt Disney made his debut with *Donald Duck*—do you realize Donald Duck is now seventy years old? In October it was *Terry and the Pirates* by Milton Caniff, which made its tentative debut in Italy over the next few years in installments of *Albi Juventus,* under the title *Sui mari della Cina* (*On the China Seas*). And in the same year, *Le Journal de Mickey* appeared in France with the stories of Mickey Mouse.

Now tell me if that year doesn't offer us enough nostalgic interest.

2002

Are viewers bad for television?

A call came from Madrid, from my colleague and friend Jorge Lozano, who teaches semiotics and communication theory at Complutense University: "Have you seen what's happening here? It confirms all you wrote decades ago. I'm getting my students to read that paper you gave with Paolo Fabbri, Pier Paolo Giglioli, and others at Perugia in 1965, the paper you gave in New York in 1957 on semiological guerrilla warfare, and your 1973 essay 'Does the Audience Have Bad Effects on Television?' It had all been predicted."

It's very nice to be heralded as a prophet, but I pointed out that we hadn't been making prophecies; we were highlighting the trends that already existed. All right, all right, says Jorge, but the only people not to have read those things were the politicians. Who knows.

Here is what happened. In the 1960s and early '70s, people were saying that television and the mass media in general were a powerful instrument for controlling what were at that time called "messages," and that by analyzing those messages it was evident that they could influence viewers and shape the way they responded. But it was clear that what the messages intended was not necessarily how viewers read them. Two obvious examples: the picture of a procession of cows is interpreted differently by a European butcher and an Indian Brahmin, and the advertisement for a Jaguar car stirs a feeling of desire in a wealthy viewer and one of frustration in someone who is poor. In short, a message seeks to produce certain effects but can conflict with local contexts, with other psychological propensities, desires, and fears, and can have a boomerang effect.

This is what happened in Spain. The government messages sought to say, "Trust us, the train bombings were the work of ETA," but, for the very reason those messages were so insistent and dogmatic, the majority of viewers read them as, "I'm afraid to say it was Al Qaeda." And here another phenomenon came in, which was known at the time as "semiological guerrilla warfare." This said: if someone is controlling the television networks, then there's no way you can occupy the prime seat in front of the television cameras, but you can occupy the prime seat in front of every television set.

In other words, semiological guerrilla warfare had to consist of a series of interventions not where the message is sent from, but where it arrives, causing viewers to discuss it, criticize it, not receive it passively. In the 1960s, this "guerrilla warfare" was still perceived in an old-fashioned way, as a leafleting operation, as the organization of television forums on the model of the cinema forum, as flying visits to bars where most people still congregated around the district's only television set. But in Spain, what made a difference in the tone and effectiveness of this guerrilla warfare is that we live in the age of the Internet and cell phones. And so the guerrilla warfare was not organized by elite groups or activists or a "spearhead," but grew spontaneously, like a bush telegraph, spread from mouth to mouth, from citizen to citizen.

What caused the Aznar government crisis, Lozano tells me, is a whirl, a relentless flow of private communications that have assumed the dimension of a collective phenomenon: the people have taken action, they were watching television and reading newspapers, but at the same time they were communicating with each other and questioning whether what was being said was true. The Internet enabled them to read the foreign press, to compare and discuss the news. In a matter of hours public opinion had formed that was not thinking or saying what television wanted them to think. It was a momentous experience, Lozano stressed; the public really can be bad for television. Perhaps he was hinting, *¡No pasarán!* They shall not pass!

I wasn't joking when, a few weeks ago, I suggested in a debate that if television is controlled by a single proprietor, an electoral campaign can be carried out by people parading the streets with sandwich boards that tell us what television is not saying. I was thinking of the countless alternatives the world of communication offers us: controlled information can also be contested through text messages, instead of just texting "I luv u."

In response to my friend's enthusiasm, I replied that in Italy, alternative means of communication are perhaps not yet as well developed, that politics here consists of occupying a soccer stadium and interrupting a match (since, tragically, this is politics), and that in Italy the possible authors of semiological guerrilla warfare are engaged in harming each other rather than harming television. But what has happened in Spain is a lesson on which to meditate.

2004

Give us today our daily crime

I reckon that if the hurricane that destroyed New Orleans hadn't found a landscape so heavily excavated, leveled, dredged, deforested, and plundered, its effects might have been less catastrophic. I think everyone agrees. But the point where the debate begins is whether a hurricane here and a tsunami there are due to global warming. Let me make it clear: though I have no specific scientific knowledge, I'm convinced that changes in environmental conditions are producing phenomena that wouldn't have happened if we were more concerned about the fate of the planet, and I'm therefore in favor of the Kyoto Protocol. But there have always been tornadoes, cyclones, and typhoons—otherwise we wouldn't have Joseph Conrad's magnificent descriptions, or those famous disaster movies.

There have been many cataclysms in past centuries that have killed tens of thousands of people, perhaps happening as close together as the tsunami in Southeast Asia and Hurricane Katrina in America. A few have been described in writing, such as the earthquakes in Pompeii and Lisbon, while vague and terrifying news circulated about others, such as the eruption of Krakatoa. But all in all, I think it's fair to say that hundreds of other cataclysms have wiped out coastlines and populations while we were otherwise occupied. In the globalized world, the speed of information is such that we hear immediately about every tragic event in the remotest corner of the globe, and we are under the impression that there are now many more cataclysms than there used to be.

For example, I think the average television viewer must wonder whether some mysterious virus is causing mothers to murder their children. And here it's difficult to blame the hole in the ozone layer. There has to be something else beneath it. Indeed, there is something else, but it's as plain as can be, and there's nothing secret about it. Quite simply, infanticide has existed throughout history, and it was fairly widely practiced. Thousands of years back, the ancient Greeks went to the theater to cry over Medea, who as we know killed her children to spite her husband. We should nevertheless be comforted by the fact that out of seven billion inhabitants on the planet, the percentage of killer mothers has many zeros before it, and so we shouldn't look suspiciously on every mother who passes us with a stroller.

Yet anyone watching the television news has the impression that we live in one of the circles of hell where not only do mothers kill a baby a day, but fourteen-year-olds are going around shooting, foreigners raping, shepherds cutting off ears, fathers exterminating their families, sadists injecting bleach into mineral water bottles, and fond nephews slicing up their uncles and aunts. It's all true, of course, and within the statistical norm, and no one chooses to remember those serial killers in the halcyon years following World War II: the Soapmaker of Correggio who boiled her neighbors, Rina Fort who smashed the heads of her lover's children with a flatiron, and Countess Pia Bellentani who disrupted the dinners of VIPs with gunfire.

Now, while it's "almost" normal that a mother kills her child from time to time, it's less normal for so many Americans and Iraqis to be blown up every day. And yet we know all about the children who are killed but very little about the number of dead adults. Serious newspapers devote several pages to political problems, economics, and culture, and others to the stock market, classified ads, and those death notices our grandparents used to read so avidly—and then, apart from exceptional cases, the papers devote just a few inside pages to crime stories. Indeed, at one time they gave more summary coverage than today, so that bloodthirsty readers had to buy specialty crime magazines, in the same way, let's not forget, that they left television gossip for the illustrated weeklies found in hairdressing salons.

Today, however, after the right amount of news coverage on wars, mass killings, terrorist attacks, and suchlike, after a few judicious revelations on political affairs, but without unduly disturbing viewers, our television news bulletins move on to a sequence of crimes, matri-sorori-uxori-fratri-infanticides, robberies, kidnappings, shootings, and, for good measure, each day it seems heaven's cataracts have opened wide upon our regions and the rain has poured as never before, in comparison to which the Great Flood was a minor plumbing incident.

And there's something beneath this, or above it. The editors of our television bulletins, not wanting to compromise themselves too much with politically and economically dangerous news, prefer to stick to crime stories. A fine sequence of heads split open with a hatchet keeps the public satisfied, doesn't put bad ideas into their minds.

2005

Maybe Agamemnon was worse than Bush

I'm sitting on a train reading the newspaper when the man next to me starts up a conversation:

"You see what times we're living in? You'll have read today about the man who's killed his pregnant wife. And those two who killed their neighbors a few months ago because their radio was a little too loud? And the Romanian prostitute who sticks an umbrella into a girl's eye during an argument over nothing? And how many mothers recently have killed their children? And the one who killed his daughter—a foreigner, I need hardly add, and Muslim to boot—to stop her from marrying a Christian? And that girl not so long ago who killed her mother and little brother? And those who kidnapped their neighbor's child and killed him because he was crying? What is the world coming to?"

I point out to him that he clearly hasn't heard it all. If he'd read carefully what I had read, perhaps on the Internet, then he'd realize the list didn't stop there.

Had he read that story from Piacenza? To curry favor with the person who has to ensure the success of his venture, a certain Mennino lets him have his daughter, knowing full well that the man is unscrupulous and will abuse her. Then he heads off, happy as a lord, on his business trip. While he's away, one Egido, a hopeful gigolo, sets about consoling Mennino's wife, becomes her lover, makes himself at home, and when Mennino gets back from his trip, Egido kills him, with the wife's help. They blame it all on someone else, are seen grieving at the funeral, but Mennino's son returns from abroad, where he's been on a university scholarship, kills Egido, and, not satisfied with that, kills his mother as well. And what's more, his sister tries to save him by giving false information to the investigators. "How terrible, how terrible," sighs the man on the train.

And what about Signora Meda from Molfetta? Her husband deserts her, and since she knows that he adores his children, she kills them in revenge. "Really, nothing's sacred these days. This woman kills her own flesh and blood to spite her husband," groans my neighbor. "What sort of mothers are they? I tell you, it's the influence of television and those violent programs made by Communists."

I press on. Perhaps you haven't heard the story of Crono of Saturnia, who—I can't remember why, something to do with a legacy —chops off his father's testicles. Then, since he doesn't want children, and perhaps understandably, considering his own experience as a child, Crono makes his wife abort and eats the dead fetus. "Maybe he was part of some satanic sect," the man suggests. "Perhaps as a child he dropped rocks onto passing cars from highway overpasses, and perhaps the people where he grew up all thought he was respectable. Hardly surprising, since that same newspaper you're reading now champions abortion and marriage between transvestites."

Look, I tell him, most sex crimes today are committed within the family. You'll have heard of Lai, the man from Battipaglia, who is killed by his son. Then he, the son, sets himself up with his mother until she can bear it no more and kills herself. And in a town not far away, two brothers called Tiesti first kill their stepbrother for personal gain, then one starts an affair with the other's wife, and the other, for revenge, kills his brother's sons, has them cooked on the grill, and serves them up, and the brother feasts on them without knowing what he's eating.

Jesus, Jesus, sighs my interlocutor, but were they Italians or foreigners? Well, I admit, I've slightly changed the names and places. But they were all Greeks, and they aren't stories I've read in the newspaper but in a dictionary of mythology. Signor Mennino was Agamemnon, who sacrifices his daughter to the gods to win victory on his expedition to Troy, the young Egido who then kills him was Aegisthus, and the faithless wife was Clytemnestra, who is then killed by her son Orestes. Signora Meda was Medea. Signor Crono was Cronus, whom the Romans called Saturnus. Signor Lai was Laius, killed by Oedipus, and the wife who commits incest was Jocasta. And the Tiesti brothers were Thyestes, who eats his children, and his brother was Atreus. The founding myths of our civilization are these, and not just the marriage of Cadmus and Harmony.

Such stories were used every now and then to write a tragedy or an epic poem, and newspapers today are on the lookout for any act of violence that will fill two or three pages. If we reckon that now there are seven billion of us, whereas the population of the known world at that time was just a few tens of millions, then, keeping everything in proportion, more people were killed then than now, at least in everyday life, wars excluded. And maybe Agamemnon was even worse than Bush.

2007

High medium low

In the culture supplement of last Saturday's *La Repubblica*, Angelo Aquaro and Marc Augé wrote about the Italian publication of *Mainstream* by Frédéric Martel. They went on to look at new forms of cultural globalization and returned to a question that reemerges every so often, though always from a different perspective, namely, the dividing line between high culture and low culture.

Though the distinction may seem strange to young people who listen just as much to Mozart as to world music, I should point out that this was a live issue in the mid-twentieth century, and that in the 1960s Dwight Macdonald, in "Masscult and Midcult," a magnificent and stylish essay, identified not two but three levels. High culture, just to be clear, was represented by Joyce, Proust, and Picasso, while what he called Masscult included the whole of popular trash, including the covers of the *Saturday Evening Post* and rock music. Macdonald was one of those intellectuals who never had a television in the house, while those more open to modernity had one in the kitchen.

But Macdonald identified a third level, the Midcult, a middle culture represented by entertainment products that borrowed stylistic elements from the avant-garde but were fundamentally kitsch. Among Midcult products, Macdonald named, from the past, Lawrence Alma-Tadema and Edmond Rostand, and from his own time, Somerset Maugham, late Hemingway, and Thornton Wilder, and he would probably have added many books published successfully in Italian by Adelphi, which alongside examples of highbrow culture has brought together such names as Somerset Maugham, Sándor Márai, and the sublime Simenon—Macdonald would have classified Simenon's non-Maigrets as Midcult and his Maigret stories as Masscult.

Yet the division between popular culture and aristocratic culture is not as old as we might imagine. Marc Augé quotes the case of Victor Hugo's funeral, attended by hundreds of thousands of people. Was Hugo Midcult or high culture? Even the fishmongers of Piraeus went to Sophocles's tragedies. Alessandro Manzoni's *The Betrothed*, when first published in the 1840s, had an impressive number of pirated editions, an indication of its popularity. And let's not forget the story of the blacksmith who mangled the words of Dante's verse, angering the poet but demonstrating at the same time that his poetry was known to illiterates.

It's true that Romans abandoned the performance of a comedy by Terence to go and watch bearbaiting, but today too many highly cultured intellectuals are prepared to forgo a concert so they can watch a soccer match. The distinction between two or three cultures becomes clearly defined only when historical avant-garde movements set about provoking the bourgeoisie; then they choose illegibility, or the rejection of representational forms, as their value.

Has this rift survived up to our own time? No, because musicians like Luciano Berio and Henri Pousseur took rock music seriously, and many rock singers are more familiar with classical music than we might imagine. Pop art has broken cultural boundaries; the prize for illegibility today goes to many sophisticated comics; much music from spaghetti westerns is remade into concert music. One look at a late-night television auction will reveal how clearly unsophisticated viewers—anyone buying a picture via television auction is not a member of the cultural elite—are buying abstract canvases their parents would have attributed to the tail of a donkey, and, Augé says, "between high culture and mass culture there is a covert interaction, and often the second feeds on the richness of the first." I would add to that: "And vice versa."

Cultural levels today are perhaps distinguished not so much by their content or their artistic form as by the way in which they are enjoyed. In other words, the difference no longer depends on whether it's Beethoven or "Jingle Bells." A piece of Beethoven that becomes a cell phone ringtone, or airport or elevator music, is enjoyed absentmindedly, as Walter Benjamin would have said, and therefore, for anyone using it in such a way, comes to resemble an advertising jingle. On the other hand, a tune created for a detergent commercial can become the subject of critical attention, appreciated for its rhythmic, melodic, or harmonic inspiration. It is not so much the object that changes but the way it is perceived. There's attentive perception and inattentive perception, and an example of inattentive perception is the use of Wagner as the theme tune for the Italian television version of *Survivor.* In the meantime, the more cultured listener will go off and appreciate an old vinyl recording of "Tea for Two."

2010

"Intellectually speaking"

One evening last week in Jerusalem, an Italian journalist told me it was reported at that morning's press conference that I had said Berlusconi was like Hitler, and some leading Italian politicians declared my statement "insane" and offensive to the entire Jewish community (*sic*). But the press conference clearly dealt with different matters altogether, since the Israeli newspapers next morning gave it wide coverage. The *Jerusalem Post* did a lead article on the front page and almost the whole of page three, with no mention of Hitler, reporting instead the real questions discussed.

No reasonable person, however critical of Berlusconi, would think of comparing him with Hitler, given that Berlusconi did not spark a world war with fifty million dead, or massacre six million Jews, or close down the parliament of the Weimar Republic, or set up squads of Brownshirts and the SS, and so forth. So what had been said that morning?

Many Italians still don't realize how poorly our prime minister is viewed abroad, so that when questioned by foreigners one sometimes feels a certain patriotic need to defend him. One tiresome individual wanted me to say that, since Berlusconi, Mubarak, and Gaddafi were or had been reluctant to leave office, Berlusconi was the Italian Gaddafi. I replied that Gaddafi was a cruel tyrant who was gunning down his fellow countrymen and rose to power through a coup, whereas Berlusconi had been duly elected by a significant portion of Italians—and I added the word "unfortunately." So that, I said jokingly, if an analogy had to be made at all costs, then one might compare Berlusconi with Hitler, since both had been duly elected. Having reduced this rash supposition *ad absurdum*, we went back to talking about serious matters.

When my Italian colleague told me about the news agency piece, he added: "Journalists, you know, have to pull out the news, even if it's hidden." I don't agree. Journalists have to report news that really exists, not create it. But this is also a sign of Italy's provincialism. The Italian media have no interest in talks held in Kolkata on the future of the planet unless somebody in Kolkata has said something for or against Berlusconi.

A curious aspect of the whole business, as I saw when I returned home, is that in every Italian newspaper that covered the story, my alleged statements, placed in quotation marks, all came from the original news agency piece, where I was supposed to have described my brief comment about Hitler as "an intellectual paradox," or to have made the parallel "intellectually speaking." Now, I might possibly, after a few drinks, compare Berlusconi to Hitler, but never in the worst state of drunkenness would I ever use meaningless expressions like "intellectual paradox" or "intellectually speaking." What is the intellectual paradox opposed to? To the manual, the sensorial, the rural paradox? Not everyone can be expected to have perfect knowledge of the terminology of rhetoric or logic, but certainly "intellectual paradox" is the language of an illiterate, and anyone who claims that others say things "intellectually speaking" is a dimwit. This means that the quotation marks in the original piece were the effect of a crude manipulation by someone else.

Such shoddy material gave rise to a virtuous campaign of indignation to discredit, as usual, someone who has no love for our prime minister and wears turquoise socks. Yet no one thought to point out that Berlusconi could not be compared to Hitler, since, as everyone knows, Hitler was monogamous.

2011

Suspects behaving badly

I once wrote an article complaining about the disturbing practice in movies and television series of showing couples in bed who, before going to sleep, (i) have sex, (ii) argue, (iii) she says she has a headache, and (iv) they turn away from each other reluctantly and go to sleep. Never, I repeat never, does either of them read a book. And then we complain that people, whose behavior is modeled on television, never read.

But worse than that: what happens if detectives or police officers arrive at your house and start questioning you, perhaps about something not necessarily compromising? If you're an inveterate criminal who has been unmasked, or a known member of the Mafia, or a pathological serial killer, you might react with scorn and laughter or fall to the ground with a fake epileptic seizure. But if you're a normal person with nothing to hide, you'll invite them to sit down, answer their questions, perhaps feeling a certain concern but looking at them politely. If, then, you have some tinge of guilt, you'll take all the more care not to upset them.

But what happens in television crime stories? Let me admit, so as not to be taken for a condescending moralist: I always watch them with interest, especially those French and German series where, except for *Alarm für Cobra 11*, there is no excess of violence or tetranitratoxycarbon explosions. In television crime stories it always—note, always—happens that when police officers go into a building and start questioning someone, this person carries on just the same: he gazes out the window, finishes cooking his eggs and bacon, tidies the room, brushes his teeth, even looks as though he's about to use the toilet, sits at the table signing papers, or rushes to the telephone. In other words, he hops about like a squirrel, ignoring the officers as much as possible, before rudely telling them after a while that they have to leave since he has things to do.

But is this how to behave? Why do directors of TV crime stories insist on creating an idea in the minds of their viewers that police officers are to be treated like importunate vacuum cleaner salesmen? You'll say that bad behavior by the suspect triggers an urge for comeuppance on the part of the viewer, who will then be pleased when the humiliated detective wins, and this is true. But what happens if less sophisticated viewers treat the police like that on their first encounter, thinking that's the way to behave? Perhaps those who watch the series aren't too worried about this, since certain real-life personalities, far more illustrious than the petty crooks investigated by police officer Siska, have taught us that it's not even necessary to turn up in court.

In truth, when the interview lasts more than a few seconds, the TV director knows that two actors can't be kept staring into each other's faces, and there has to be some kind of movement in the scene. And to create movement, the suspect has to be moved about. And why can't the director sustain, or make the viewer sustain, a few minutes in which two people look at each other, especially if they're talking about something of great dramatic interest? Because to do so requires a director at least as great as Orson Welles, and the actors have to be Anna Magnani, or Emil Jannings in *The Blue Angel*, or Jack Nicholson in *The Shining*, people who are comfortable in the foreground and close-up, and can express their mood with their eyes, with a twist of the mouth. In *Casablanca*, Ingrid Bergman and Humphrey Bogart could talk for several minutes without Michael Curtiz, who was no Eisenstein, allowing himself even a medium-full shot, but if every week you have to film an episode, and sometimes two, the producer can't allow himself a director like Curtiz. And as for the actors, so much the better if, as happens in German police dramas, they give their best performance when they're munching *würstel* sandwiches between one computer search and another.

2012

Shaken or stirred?

In a recent Italian translation of *Live and Let Die*, James Bond is described as ordering a martini cocktail with "red" Martini. It is heresy to talk of a martini with sweet vermouth, and a previous Italian translation referred to gin and Martini & Rossi, which is something else. According to various early chronicles, the first martini cocktails, invented in America in the 1800s, were said to have been made with two ounces of Italian "Martini and Rosso," one ounce of Old Tom gin, plus maraschino and other ingredients that cause every well-educated person to shudder with horror. But even though Martini Rosso appeared in 1863, according to other experts the martini cocktail was first known in its present form using not Martini vermouth but Noilly Prat, and the name Martini became associated with the original cocktail either from a California town called Martinez or from a barman named Martinez. In short, for its whole intricate history, see Lowell Edmunds's indispensable *Martini, Straight Up*.

So what does James Bond drink? In reality, he drinks anything he can get his hands on. In the opening lines of *Goldfinger*, Ian Fleming, who was a master of style, wrote: "James Bond, with two double bourbons inside him, sat in the final departure lounge of Miami Airport and thought about life and death." And the first martini that 007 drinks, in *Casino Royale*, is what would pass into history as a Vesper martini: "Three measures of Gordon's, one of vodka, half a measure of Kina Lillet. Shake it very well until it's ice-cold, then add a large thin slice of lemon peel." The Kina Lillet is another and rarer type of dry vermouth, and Bond would also be seen drinking a Vesper martini in *Quantum of Solace*.

In fact, Bond usually drinks a martini as we know it, but when he orders one he specifies that it's to be shaken, not stirred—in other words, the ingredients are to be put into a shaker (as happens with other cocktails) but not mixed in a mixer. The problem is rather that, from Hemingway on, to make a good martini, a measure of dry vermouth is poured into a mixer already full of ice, the gin is added, it is mixed, and the liquid is strained into the classic triangular glass into which the olive is then dropped. But experts argue that, having poured in the vermouth and mixed it well, a grid should be placed over the mixer and the vermouth thrown away, leaving just a patina that flavors the ice cubes, after which the gin is poured in, and the chilled gin flavored with the trace of dry vermouth is then filtered out. The ratio between gin and vermouth varies from expert to expert, including the version according to which only a ray of light should be allowed to pass through the vermouth bottle until it touches the ice, and no more. In the version that Americans call a gin martini on the rocks, the ice is also poured into the glass, to the disdain of connoisseurs.

Why does an expert like Bond want his martini shaken and not stirred? Some suggest that if the martini is shaken, it introduces more air into the mixture—called bruising the drink—thus improving the flavor. But personally, I don't believe a gentleman like James Bond wants his martini shaken. In fact, some Internet sites claim that the phrase, though it appears in the films, never appears in the novels (just as "Elementary, my dear Watson" never appears in Conan Doyle), except perhaps in relation to the much-debated vodka martini. But I confess that if I'd checked the complete works of Fleming, who knows when this article would have been written.

2013

Too many dates for Nero Wolfe

For purely temperamental reasons, I spent the two months up to Christmas rereading, or reading for the first time, the eighty Nero Wolfe stories. On immersing myself in that amiable universe, I was confronted by some problems that have obsessed fans of Rex Stout.

First of all, what is or was the number of the famous brownstone on West 35th Street? In 1966, the Wolfe Pack, an association of fans of the Nero Wolfe stories, persuaded New York City to place a commemorative plaque at no. 454, but Stout referred to different numbers in his stories—no. 506 in *Over My Dead Body,* no. 618 in *Too Many Clients,* no. 902 in *Murder by the Book,* no. 914 in *Prisoner's Base,* no. 918 in *The Red Box,* no. 922 in *The Silent Speaker,* no. 939 in *Death of a Doxy,* etc.

But this is by no means the only uncertainty in the saga. We are told, for example, that Wolfe came from Montenegro—he'd been born in Trenton, then moved to Montenegro as a child. But several times Wolfe mentions becoming a naturalized American citizen fairly late, so he couldn't have been born in New Jersey. He was probably born in 1892 or 1893. But if that's the case, he'd have been eighty-three in his last story, which is set in 1975, whereas in fact he comes across just as young as in the first story, which is set in 1934. The same is true of Stout's narrator, Archie Goodwin, who, judging from a number of clues, appears to have been born in 1910 or 1912, yet in the stories that clearly take place at the time of the Vietnam War and after, he ought to be close to sixty, though he still appears as a thirty-year-old playboy able to charm attractive women in their twenties and to knock down characters much stronger than himself with a straight masterful punch.

In short, could an author who from book to book gave flawless descriptions of the layout of Wolfe's house, the food he ate, and the ten thousand orchids he cultivated, species by species, have failed to keep a general, biographically accurate record of his characters? There must be another explanation.

In many popular sagas the characters are ageless; they never grow old. Superman has no age, nor does Little Orphan Annie, on whose eternal childhood many parodies are based, nor did the Phantom, who was engaged to Diana Palmer for around fifty years. This allowed their creators to make them act in an eternal present. The same was true of Wolfe and Goodwin, who were forever young. But at the same time Stout's stories also reflect a careful attention to detail and the historical background. When Nero and Archie act as government agents during World War II or become involved in McCarthyism, Stout describes in obsessive detail particular roads, street corners, shops, taxi routes, and so forth. How did he give an eternal immovability to stories that needed continual reference to moments in history and to specific settings? By confusing the reader.

As Stout whirled before the readers' eyes dates that didn't fit and anachronisms that would be unconscionable to anyone with a computer, he feigned an exaggerated realism, wanted us to live in an almost dreamlike state. In other words, he had his own far-from-simple idea about literary fiction. It's no coincidence that he began his writing career, though with little success, as an almost experimental narrator, in *How Like a God*. And he understood the ways in which books are received. He didn't imagine his readers would, like me, read his complete works one after another, but knew instead that they would come back to his books at yearly intervals, and therefore after their memories were reasonably vague about chronology. He played on the faithful and much-anticipated recollection of recurring situations— Wolfe's habits, late-evening routines, moments in the kitchen—but left out major events. And in fact we can read these stories again and again with the pleasure of finding the same unchanging features, but having forgotten the most important thing, namely, who the murderer was.

2014

Unhappy is the land

The press and television reported with satisfaction the aftermath of the recent fire on the *Norman Atlantic* ferry carrying passengers from Greece to Italy. Some passengers died or went missing, but overall the rescue operations were carried out efficiently. The media made particular mention of Captain Argilio Giacomazzi, who stayed on board to oversee the evacuation and was the last person to leave the ship. This was impressive, particularly after the abominable behavior of another captain who had jumped ship during a recent disaster, yet the word "hero" appeared in a number of reports.

There's no doubt that Captain Giacomazzi's behavior was most proper, even if it were later to emerge that he shared some responsibility for causing the incident, and we hope all captains will behave like him in the future. But he is not a hero; he is a man who has performed his duty honestly and without shirking. The rules require a captain to be the last to leave his ship, and this exposes him to danger.

What is a hero? If we accept Thomas Carlyle's theory, a hero is a great man endowed with great charisma who has left his mark on history. In this sense Shakespeare and Napoleon are both heroes, even if they may have been timid men. But Carlyle's idea was given short shrift by Tolstoy and, later, by social historians, who placed less emphasis on great events and more on economic and social structures. And yet, if we look at dictionaries and encyclopedias, a hero is someone who has done an exceptional deed he was not duty bound to carry out, risking his own life to the benefit of others. Salvo D'Acquisto was a hero when he saved twenty-two civilians from being executed by Nazi soldiers in 1943. No one expected him to assume a responsibility that was not his, to go before a firing squad and save the inhabitants of his village, but in doing so D'Acquisto went beyond the call of duty and was killed. You don't have to be a soldier or a military leader to be a hero: a hero risks his life to save a drowning child or a fellow mine worker, or gives up the quiet routine of a local hospital to face the hazards of living in Africa among Ebola sufferers. When interviewed on his return, Captain Giacomazzi said, "Heroes are no use: my only thought is for those no longer with us." A wise way to avoid being sanctified by the media.

Why talk about heroes when people, however courageous and cool-headed, are simply doing their duty? Brecht reminds us in his play *Galileo*: "Unhappy is the land that needs heroes." Why unhappy? Because it lacks people who do their duty honestly, responsibly, and "with professionalism." That's when a country searches desperately for a heroic figure, and awards gold medals left, right, and center.

An unhappy land, then, is one whose citizens no longer know where duty lies, and seek a charismatic leader who tells them what to do. Which, if I remember correctly, is what Hitler promulgated in *Mein Kampf*.

2015

Time and history

A recent television program dealt with how Italian children and young adults were educated under the Fascist regime of the 1920s and '30s. One of the questions raised was whether the totalitarian education of a generation had a profound effect in shaping the Italian character. Pier Paolo Pasolini remarked that Italy's national character has been modified more by postwar neocapitalism than by the years of dictatorship.

Aside from neo-Fascist extremism, something of the Fascist legacy lingers in the national character, and continually reemerges—in racism, homophobia, male chauvinism, and anticommunism—yet these attitudes could also be found in provincial pre-Fascist Italy. Pasolini was right: the national character has been more deeply influenced by consumerism, by notions of free trade, by television.

What did fascism require of Italians and force upon them? To believe, obey, and fight; to practice the cult of war, indeed to glorify death; to jump through hoops of fire; to produce as many children as possible; to regard politics as the primary purpose of existence; to think of Italians as the chosen ones. Have these traits remained in the Italian character? Not at all. Curiously, they have resurfaced in Islamic fundamentalism, as Hamed Abdel-Samad recently observed in *L'Espresso*. That's where the fanatical cult resides—the glorification of the hero and *"viva la muerte,"* the submission of women, the sense of a permanent state of war. Very few Italians absorbed these ideas apart from right- and left-wing terrorists of the 1960s and '70s, though even they were more prepared to kill others than sacrifice themselves.

What has neocapitalism in its various guises had to offer, up to *Berlusconismo*? It has offered the right to acquire, perhaps on the installment plan, a car, a refrigerator, a washing machine, and a television; to regard tax evasion as a basic human right; to spend evenings devoted to entertainment, contemplating half-naked dancers or, at the furthest extreme, watching hard-core pornography at the click of a mouse; not to worry too much about politics or even about voting; to avoid financial hardship by not producing too many children—in short, to live comfortably without making sacrifices. Most of Italian society has enthusiastically endorsed this model. And those who dedicate their lives to helping desperate people in third-world countries remain a slender minority.

2015

Forms of Racism

Women philosophers

The old philosophical claim that men are capable of pondering the infinite while women give sense to the finite can be read in many ways. For example, since men cannot produce babies, they console themselves with Zeno's paradoxes. But such ideas have led to the common notion that history, at least up to the twentieth century, has brought us great female poets and writers, and women in various branches of science, but no women philosophers or mathematicians.

Such biases fostered the long-held view that women had no gift for painting, except for the likes of Rosalba Carriera or Artemisia Gentileschi. Since painting originally meant frescoing churches, it is natural that climbing on scaffolding wearing a skirt was not considered respectable, nor was it a woman's job to run a workshop with thirty apprentices, but as soon as painting could be done on easels, women painters began to appear. It's rather like saying the Jews were great at many arts except for painting, until Chagall. It's fair to say that Jewish culture was primarily auditory rather than visual, and that divinity was not to be represented through images, but there's a visual content of undoubted interest in many Jewish manuscripts. Yet during the centuries when figurative art was in the hands of the Catholic Church, it was unlikely that a Jew would be encouraged to paint Madonnas and crucifixions—it's rather like being surprised that no Jew had ever become pope.

The chronicles of Bologna University mention women professors like Bettisia Gozzadini and Novella d'Andrea, who were so beautiful that they had to give their lectures behind a veil so as not to distract the students, but they didn't teach philosophy. In the textbooks on philosophy we don't come across women who teach dialectics or theology. Eloise, Abelard's brilliant and unhappy student, had to make do with becoming an abbess.

But the position of abbess is not to be underrated, and a woman philosopher of our own time, Maria Teresa Fumagalli, has written extensively about them. An abbess was a spiritual, administrative, and political authority and carried out important intellectual functions in medieval society. A good textbook on philosophy must include among the leading figures of the history of thought such great mystics as Catherine of Siena, not to mention Hildegard of Bingen, who, in terms of metaphysical visions and perspectives on infinity, give us plenty to chew over to this day.

The argument that mysticism isn't philosophy doesn't hold. After all, histories of philosophy reserve space for great mystics like Henry Suso, Johannes Tauler, and Meister Eckhart. And to suggest that much of female mysticism placed more emphasis on the body than on abstract ideas would be like saying that someone like Maurice Merleau-Ponty should disappear from philosophy textbooks.

For some time, the chosen heroine of some feminists has been Hypatia, who taught Platonic philosophy and early mathematics in fifth-century Alexandria. Hypatia became a symbol, but unfortunately all that remains of her is the legend, since her works were lost, and so was she, literally hacked to pieces by a frenzied mob of Christians at the instigation, according to some historians, of Cyril of Alexandria, who was later canonized, though not on this account. But was Hypatia the only one?

A small book has recently been published in France called *Histoire des femmes philosophes*. Anyone curious about its author, Gilles Ménage, will discover that he lived in the seventeenth century, was Latin tutor to Madame de Sévigné and Madame de Lafayette, and that his book had been published in 1690 under the title *Historia mulierum philosopharum*. Hypatia was not alone: Ménage's book, though devoted chiefly to the classical period, presents a series of fascinating figures, including Diotima the Socratic, Arete of Cyrene, Nicarete of Megara, Hipparchia the Cynic, Theodora the Peripatetic (in the philosophical sense of the word), Leontia the Epicurean, and Themistoclea the Pythagorean. Leafing through ancient texts and works by the fathers of the Church, Ménage found sixty-five references to women philosophers, though he interpreted the concept of philosophy fairly widely. Given that in Greek society the woman was kept at home, that male philosophers preferred to entertain themselves with young boys rather than girls, and that a woman had to become a courtesan if she wanted to enjoy public celebrity, we can see to what lengths these women thinkers had to go to make a name for themselves. Aspasia, on the other hand, is still remembered as a courtesan, but a high-class one; what is forgotten is that she was skilled in rhetoric and philosophy, and that, according to Plutarch, Socrates followed her with interest.

I checked at least three modern philosophy encyclopedias and, apart from Hypatia, found no trace of these names. It's not that women philosophers didn't exist. The fact is that male philosophers have chosen to ignore them, after first borrowing their ideas.

2003

Where do you find anti-Semitism?

A series of recent events, not just terrorist attacks but also disturbing opinion polls, have brought anti-Semitism back into the headlines. It's not easy to distinguish opposition to Ariel Sharon's policies—an opposition shared by many Jewish people—from anti-Israeli sentiment, and in turn from anti-Semitism, but there is a tendency for public opinion and the mass media to bundle them together. Moreover, it seems that Western public opinion rests on two consoling thoughts: that anti-Semitism is largely an Arab question, and that it's limited in Europe to a small number of neo-Nazi skinheads.

Europe has never managed to distinguish between religious, popular, and "scientific" anti-Semitism. Religious anti-Semitism was certainly responsible for popular anti-Semitism: the claim that the Jews were a God-killing people has justified many pogroms, and a further justification was the difficulty in assimilating exiled Jews determined to keep their own traditions. As followers of a cult of the Book, therefore of reading in an illiterate world, they seemed like dangerous intellectuals speaking an unknown language. But by "scientific" anti-Semitism I mean the historic and anthropological ideas that purported to uphold the superiority of the Aryan race over the Jewish race, and the political doctrine of the Jewish conspiracy for the conquest of the Christian world, most clearly expressed in *The Protocols of the Elders of Zion*, also a product of the European secular intelligentsia.

Theological anti-Semitism doesn't exist in the Arab world, since the Koran recognizes the great patriarchs of the Bible, from Abraham to Jesus. During the period of their expansion, Muslims were fairly tolerant toward Jews and Christians: though regarded as second-class citizens, they could follow their religion and develop their business activities as long as they paid their taxes. Islamic anti-Semitism, not being religious, is today exclusively ethnopolitical—religious motivations give it support rather than being a foundation. If nineteenth-century Zionists had established the new state of Israel in Utah, the Arabs wouldn't be anti-Semitic. I don't want to be misunderstood:

for historic and religious reasons the Jews had every right to head for Palestine—they settled peacefully over the course of a century—and have every right to remain there. But Arab anti-Semitism is territorial, not theological.

More serious, however, is Europe's responsibility. Popular anti-Semitism supported by religious anti-Semitism led to massacres, though localized and unprogrammed. Real "scientific" anti-Semitism began in the late eighteenth and nineteenth centuries, and not in Germany but in Legitimist France and to some extent in Italy. It is in France that racist theories, namely of the ethnic roots of civilization, were developed, and it is between France and Italy that the theory of the Jewish conspiracy evolved, a conspiracy that was responsible first for the horrors of the French Revolution and then for a plot to subjugate Christian civilization. History has shown that *The Protocols of the Elders of Zion* was put together by Jesuit Legitimists and the French and Russian secret services, and only later was it accepted wholesale by tsarist reactionaries and by the Nazis. On the Internet, most anti-Semitic Arab websites are also based on European "scientific" anti-Semitism.

In Italy, the right-wing leader Gianfranco Fini is doing his best to detach his party from its anti-Semitic past, something he should be recognized for. But go to any specialty bookshop and, along with occult books on the Holy Grail, you'll find the speeches of Mussolini and *The Protocols of the Elders of Zion*—a strange blend that needed a homegrown right-wing ideologue like Julius Evola, whose works can also be found in such bookshops.

There are also terrorist organizations that ignore mainstream politics and declare themselves "Communists." But the Italian left, through the deaths of its own members, has earned the right to distance itself from these extremist fringes, supporting the state against the drift toward terrorism. The one person who doesn't worry too much about such matters is Berlusconi, though he is hardly a reliable authority, however politically effective he might be. Has the Italian right done the same thing? Is it prepared to say that Evola, when he wasn't being a genial nutcase, scientifically suspect but pleasantly readable, was a wild anti-Semite, and continued to be after World War II? Who is going to take responsibility, in the schools and in adult education, for dismantling the follies of "scientific" anti-Semitism with which certain members of the Italian right were associated in the frenzied rhetoric of magazines such as *La Difesa della Razza* (*The Defense of the Race*)?

It is our duty to defend ourselves against Arab terrorism. At the same time, however, we must use education as a weapon to fight the enemies at home who are fomenting Arab anti-Semitism.

2003

Who told women to veil themselves?

There has been much debate over the question of the veil. I think the position expressed by our prime minister, Romano Prodi, is sensible: if by veil we mean a headscarf that leaves the face uncovered, then anyone can wear one if they wish. If my own unbiased aesthetic judgment doesn't sound irreverent, it adds a refinement to the woman's face and makes her look like all those Virgin Marys painted by Antonello da Messina. Any other form of veil that prevents identification is another matter: Italian law doesn't allow it. This prohibition could of course lead to other arguments, since even carnival masks would be banned, and if you remember *A Clockwork Orange*, a comic mask can be used to commit appalling crimes. But let us say these are marginal problems.

If we can identify a sign in all those cases where something represents something else in some respect or capacity, then the Muslim veil is a semiotic phenomenon. The same is true of uniforms, whose primary function is not to protect the body in bad weather, and of a nun's wimple, which is elegant. This is why the veil stirs so much argument —and yet we never argued about those large headscarves that farm women once wore, which had no symbolic value.

The veil is criticized because it is worn as a declaration of identity. But there's nothing wrong with displaying an identity or affiliation, and people do so when they wear the badge of a party, the cowl of a monk, or an orange robe and shave their heads. One interesting question is whether Muslim girls must wear a veil because the Koran requires it. Now comes the publication of *Islam,* by Gabriele Mandel Khan, Italian leader of the Sufi Jerrahi Halveti order, which seems to me an excellent introduction to the history, theology, practices, and customs of the Muslim world. He says that the use of the veil to cover the face and hair is a pre-Islamic custom related to climate. But it is not prescribed by sura 24 of the Koran, the passage always quoted on this question, which advises covering only the breasts.

Fearing that Mandel's interpretation was perhaps too modernist or moderate, I looked up on the Net the Italian translation of the Koran by Hamza Piccardo, carried out under the doctrinal control of the Union of Islamic Communities and Organizations in Italy. There I found the whole passage: "And say to the believing women that they should lower their gaze and be chaste and that they should not show their ornaments, except that which appears; that they should draw their veil over their bosoms and not display their beauty to others except to their husbands, to their fathers, to their husband's fathers, to their sons, to their husband's sons, to their brothers, to their brothers' sons, to their sisters' sons, to their women, to the slaves they own, to the male servants that have no desire, to children below the age of puberty who have no interest in the hidden parts of women." Finally, out of scruple I consulted the Koran in the classic translation of the great Iranian scholar Alessandro Bausani, and there I found, with few lexicographical variations, the requirement that "they cover their breasts with a veil."

For someone like me who doesn't know Arabic, three witnesses of such different provenance are enough. The Koran is simply encouraging modesty, and if it were written today in the West, it would also be encouraging the covering of the navel, since nowadays in the West the belly dance is practiced in the streets.

Who then was asking women to veil themselves? Mandel takes a certain satisfaction in revealing that it was Saint Paul, in his First Epistle to the Corinthians, though Paul limited this duty to women who preach and prophesy. Yet here, once again before the Koran, is Tertullian—who, though a heterodox Montanist, was nevertheless a Christian—in his text *On the Ornaments of Women:* "You must please only your husbands. And the more you please them, the less you will worry about pleasing others. Do not worry, O blessed ones, no woman is ugly to her husband . . . Every husband demands the duty of chastity, but does not desire beauty, if he is Christian . . . I do not tell you this to suggest to you a totally coarse and wild outer appearance, nor do I want to persuade you that it is permissible to be untidy and dirty, but (I advise you) the measure and the proper limit in caring for the body . . . Indeed they sin against Him those women who torment the skin with spiced embellishments, who mark their cheeks with red and lengthen their eyes with soot . . . God commands you to veil yourselves, so that, I think, the heads of each of you are not seen." And this is why, throughout the history of art, the Virgin Mary and pious women appear veiled, like so many charming Muslim women.

2006

Husbands of unknown wives

An Italian encyclopedia of women (www.enciclopediadelledonne.it) records a great number of women, from Catherine of Siena to Tina Pica, including many who have been unjustly forgotten. Yet back in 1690, Gilles Ménage wrote, in his history of women philosophers, about Diotima the Socratic, Arete of Cyrene, Nicarete of Megara, Hipparchia the Cynic, Theodora the Peripatetic (in the philosophical sense of the word), Leontia the Epicurean, and Themistoclea the Pythagorean, about whom we know very little. It is right that many of these have now been rescued from oblivion.

What's lacking is an encyclopedia of wives. It is said that behind every great man is a great woman, starting from Justinian and Theodora and arriving, if you wish, at Obama and Michelle. It's curious that it isn't true the other way around—witness the two Elizabeths of England—but wives are generally not mentioned. From antiquity onward, mistresses counted more than wives. Clara Schumann and Alma Mahler became known for their extra- or postmarital activities. In the end, the only woman always referred to as a wife is Xanthippe, wife of Socrates, and then only to be maligned.

I happened to come across a piece by the journalist and novelist who wrote under the pseudonym Pitigrilli. He crammed his stories with erudite quotes, often getting the names wrong, writing "Yung" instead of "Jung," and using anecdotes he had picked up from who knows what periodicals. Here he recalls the advice of Saint Paul: *Melius nubere quam uri,* "Get married if you can't hold out any longer" —which is my advice to pedophile priests—though he observes that most great men, such as Plato, Lucretius, Virgil, and Horace, were bachelors. This isn't true, however, or at least not entirely true.

As far as Plato is concerned, we know from Diogenes Laërtius that he wrote epigrams only for pretty boys, though his disciples included two women, Lasthenia of Mantinea and Axiothea of Phlius, and though he also declared that the virtuous man should take a wife. We can see that Socrates's unsuccessful marriage had an effect on Plato. Aristotle had first married Pythias, and after her death became attached to Herpyllis, whether as wife or concubine is not clear, and he lived with her *more uxorio,* and remembered her affectionately in his will. She also bore him a son, Nicomachus, who later lent his name to one of the *Ethics.*

Horace had neither wife nor children, but I suspect, considering what he wrote, that he allowed himself the occasional fling, and it seems Virgil was so timid that he didn't dare propose, though it was rumored he had a relationship with the wife of Lucius Varius Rufus. Ovid, however, married three times. As for Lucretius, the ancient sources tell us almost nothing; a remark by Saint Jerome suggests that he had committed suicide because a love potion had driven him mad (though Jerome had every motive for declaring a dangerous atheist mad). Later on, medieval and humanist tradition embroidered the story of a mysterious Lucilia, a wife or a mistress, enchantress or woman in love, who had asked a sorceress for the potion. It is also said that Lucretius had procured the potion himself, but in any event Lucilia doesn't make a favorable impression. That is, unless Pomponio Leto was right, according to whom Lucretius had killed himself because of his unrequited love for a boy called Astericon.

Moving ahead through the centuries, Dante continued to dream about Beatrice, but was married to Gemma Donati, though he never wrote about her. Everyone thinks Descartes was a bachelor, having lived a busy life and dying too young, but in fact he had a daughter, Francine, who died when she was just five. Her mother was a servant,

Helena Jans van der Strom, whom Descartes had known in Holland and kept as a companion for several years, acknowledging her only as a domestic. Contrary to certain false accusations, however, he had recognized the daughter, and it seems also had other affairs.

In short, assuming that members of the clergy were celibate, along with those who more or less admitted their homosexuality, such as Cyrano de Bergerac and Wittgenstein, the only great bachelor we can be sure about was Kant. One might not think it, but even Hegel was married—indeed was something of a womanizer—and had a natural daughter as well as a passion for food. Marx was married too, and devoted to his wife, Jenny von Westphalen.

One problem remains: what was the influence of Gemma on Dante, of Helena on Descartes, not to mention the many other wives about whom history remains silent? And might Aristotle's works have been by Herpyllis? We will never know. History, written by husbands, condemns wives to anonymity.

2010

Proust and the Boche

These are harsh times for anyone who believes in the European Union: with Cameron, who is asking his compatriots to decide whether they still want it, or ever wanted it; with Berlusconi, who one day declares himself pro-European but the next day, when he's not making some visceral appeal to the old Fascists, appeals to those who think it better to return to the lira; to the Northern League and its hypo-European provincialism. In short, the bones of the founding fathers of Europe must be rattling in their graves.

And yet we should all remember that forty-one million Europeans died massacring each other during World War II (and that's just Europeans, not including Americans and Asians). Since then, apart from the tragic episode in the Balkans, Europe has witnessed sixty-eight —yes, sixty-eight—years of peace. And if we tell young people that the French today might dig trenches along the Maginot Line to hold back the Germans, that the Italians might want to smash Greece, that Belgium might be invaded, or that the British might bomb Milan, these young people (who are perhaps going off to spend a year in some other European country on a university scholarship, and perhaps at the end of this experience will meet a kindred spirit who speaks a language other than their own and their children will grow up bilingual) would think we're inventing a science-fiction story. Nor do adults realize that the borders they now cross without a passport had been crossed by their fathers and grandfathers carrying guns.

But is it true that Europeans have failed to be seduced by the idea of Europe? Bernard-Henri Lévy recently launched a passionate manifesto for the rediscovery of a European identity, *Europe ou chaos?*, which starts off with a disturbing warning: "Europe is not in crisis, it is dying. Not Europe as a territory, of course, but Europe as an Idea. Europe as a dream and as a plan." The manifesto was signed by António Lobo Antunes, Vassilis Alexakis, Juan Luis Cebrián, Fernando Savater, Peter Schneider, Hans Christoph Buch, Julia Kristeva, Claudio Magris, Gÿorgy Konrád, and Salman Rushdie, who isn't European but found his first place of refuge in Europe at the beginning of his persecution. Since I too have signed, I found myself with some of my co-signatories at the Théâtre du Rond-Point in Paris for a debate on these questions. A theme that immediately emerged, and with which I broadly agree, is that there is an awareness of European identity, and I happened to quote several passages from Proust's *À la recherche du temps perdu*. It is

World War I, we are in Paris, the city fears night attacks from German zeppelins, and public opinion accuses the hated Boche of every kind of cruelty. And yet, in the pages of Proust one breathes a Germanophile air, which emerges in the conversations of his characters. Charlus is a Germanophile, though his admiration for the Germans seems to depend not so much on cultural identity as on his sexual preferences: "'Our admiration for the French must not allow us to underestimate our enemies, that diminishes ourselves. And you don't know what a German soldier is, you've never seen them as I have, on parade doing the goose-step in Unter den Linden.' In returning to the ideal of virility he had touched on at Balbec . . . 'You see,' he said, 'that superb fellow, the German soldier, is a strong, healthy being, who only thinks of the greatness of his country, "Deutschland über Alles."'"

Let's move on from Charlus, even if his philo-Teutonic discourses stir literary reminiscences, and talk instead about Robert de Saint-Loup, a brave soldier who would die in battle. "To make me grasp contrasts of shade and light which had been 'the enchantment of the morning,' [Saint-Loup] alluded to a page of Romain Rolland or of Nietzsche with the independence of those at the front who unlike those at the rear, were not afraid to utter a German name . . . Saint-Loup, when he spoke to me of a melody of Schumann gave it its German title and made no circumlocution to tell me, when he had heard the first warble at the edge of a forest, that he had been intoxicated as though the bird of that 'sublime Siegfried' which he hoped to hear again after the war, had sung to him."

Or further on: "I had learnt, in fact, of the death of Robert Saint-Loup, killed, protecting the retreat of his men, on the day following his return to the front. No man less than he, felt hatred towards a people . . . The last words I heard him utter six days before, were those at the beginning of a Schumann song which he hummed to me in German on my staircase; indeed on account of neighbors I had to ask him to keep quiet."

And Proust hastened to add that French culture made no prohibition on studying German culture, even in those days, though with some precaution: "A professor wrote a remarkable book on Schiller of which the papers took notice. But before mentioning the author, the publishers inscribed the volume with a statement like a printing license, to the effect that he had been at the Marne and at Verdun, that he had had five mentions, and two sons killed. Upon that, there was loud praise of the lucidity and depth of the author's work upon Schiller, who could be qualified as great as long as he was alluded to as a great Boche and not as a great German."

What lies at the base of the European cultural identity is a long dialogue among literatures, philosophies, and musical and theatrical works. Nothing that can be canceled out in spite of war, and this is the core identity of a community that holds out against the greatest of barriers, that of language.

Although this sense of European identity is strong among intellectual elites, is it the same with everyone else? I found myself thinking that, even today, every European country, in schools and in public commemorations, celebrates its own heroes, all people who have valiantly slaughtered other Europeans, beginning with Arminius, who exterminated the Roman legions of Publius Quinctilius Varus in AD 9, then Joan of Arc, El Cid (the Muslims against whom he fought had been Europeans for centuries), and the Italian and Hungarian heroes of the nineteenth century, including those Italian soldiers who fell to the Austrian enemy. Has anyone talked about a European hero? Have there never been any? And who were the Byrons or Santorre Santarosas who fought for Greek independence, or the many Schindlers who saved the lives of thousands of Jews regardless of what nation they belonged to, or the heroes who were not warriors, such as Alcide De Gasperi, Jean Monnet, Robert Schuman, Konrad Adenauer, and Altiero Spinelli? And by searching in the recesses of history we could find others to tell our children about.

2013

From *Maus* to *Charlie*

I consider my friend Art Spiegelman to be a genius. His graphic novel *Maus,* though a comic, is one of the most important pieces of literature on the Holocaust. But this time I disagree with him. Spiegelman was asked to do a cover illustration for the *New Statesman* on freedom of thought. The cover he delivered is of a woman brutally gagged. It has been published in other magazines, and is magnificent. But Spiegelman had asked the *New Statesman* to publish one of his caricatures of Muhammad as well, and the magazine said no. So he withdrew the cover.

There has been much confusion over the business of *Charlie Hebdo.* I haven't written about it since I gave two interviews immediately after the tragedy, and I was deeply upset by it, not least because Georges Wolinski, who was killed in the massacre, was a friend. He had done an amusing caricature of me when we were on the editorial team of *linus,* the Italian comic-strip magazine, and used to meet at a neighborhood bar.

I'll now get to the point. I believe that two rights and two duties were involved. Bear in mind Pope Francis, who worried many when he said that if anyone had insulted his mother he would have punched them. He didn't say he would have killed them. He knew there was a commandment against killing and therefore he could only condemn the actions of terrorists, who, with their cutthroat allies of ISIS, represent a new form of Nazism—racism, elimination of other ethnic groups, a plan to conquer the world. People had to condemn the massacre and had to march, as they did, to defend freedom of expression.

Voltaire teaches us that we have to defend the freedom of thought even of those who don't think as we do. But if the journalists of *Charlie Hebdo* hadn't suffered the atrocious revenge attack, and if the massacre hadn't taken place, anyone would have had the right to criticize their cartoons, not only of Muhammad, but of Jesus and the Virgin Mary, which are similar to those nineteenth-century cartoons by Leo Taxil representing Mary pregnant with a dove and Joseph cuckolded.

It is a moral principle that the religious sensibilities of others should not be offended, which is why those who swear in their own home should not swear in church. People mustn't stop drawing cartoons of Muhammad for fear of retaliation, but because—and I regret if the expression sounds too delicate—it is "uncivil." And people shouldn't draw cartoons of the Holy Virgin, even if Catholics are against the idea, as they are, at least today, of slaughtering those who do it. There again, I have searched the Internet and have observed that none of the sites condemning the censorship of the *New Statesman* have reproduced Spiegelman's picture. Why? Out of respect for others or out of fear?

With the *Charlie Hebdo* affair, two basic principles came into play, but because we were confronted by the slaughter, it was difficult to see them separately. And so it was legitimate to defend the right of expression, even in an uncivil manner, by declaring, *Je suis Charlie*. But if I were Charlie, I wouldn't go fooling around with Muslim sensibilities, nor Christian sensibilities, nor Buddhist ones.

If Catholics are upset when you offend the Blessed Virgin, respect their feelings, and if necessary write a judicious historical essay that casts doubt on the Incarnation. If Catholics shoot at those who offend the Blessed Virgin, oppose them.

Nazis and anti-Semites of every kind have circulated hideous caricatures of the "vile Jews," but Western culture in the end has accepted these insults, respecting the freedom of those who circulated them. Yet when caricature is transformed into massacre, people have rebelled. In other words, they respected the freedom of Édouard Drumont, in the nineteenth century, to be ferociously anti-Semitic, but they hanged the Nazi murderers at Nuremberg.

2015

On Hatred and Death

On hatred and on love

Over the past few months I have written on racism, on inventing the enemy, and on the political role of hatred toward "others" or toward those who are "different." I thought I had said everything, but a friend in a recent discussion raised considerations that were new to me, and it's one of those cases in which you no longer remember who said what, though the conclusions were the same.

With a rather pre-Socratic thoughtlessness we tend to think of hatred and love as opposites that face each other symmetrically, as though whatever we don't like we hate, and vice versa. And yet between the two poles there are countless shades. Even if we use these two terms metaphorically, the fact that I love pizza but am not mad about sushi doesn't mean I hate sushi. I like it less than pizza. And taking the two words in their proper sense, that I love one person doesn't mean I hate everyone else. The opposite of love can perfectly well be indifference: I love my children and was indifferent to the taxi driver who gave me a lift two hours ago.

But the real point is that love isolates. If I'm madly in love with a woman, I expect her to love me and no one else, at least not in the same way. A mother passionately loves her children and wants them to feel a special love for her (they have only one mother), and she would never love the children of another with the same intensity. Love, in its own way, is therefore selfish, possessive, selective.

Of course, the commandment tells us to love our neighbor as ourselves, all seven billion neighbors, but this commandment asks us in practice not to hate anyone, and it doesn't expect us to love an unknown Eskimo in the same way as we do our father or our grandchild. Love will always favor my grandchild over a seal hunter.

On the other hand, hatred can be collective, and in totalitarian regimes it must be so. When I was a child, the Fascist school required me to hate "all" sons of Albion, and every evening on the radio Mario Appelius proclaimed, "May God damn the English." The same is true of dictatorships and populist regimes, and fundamentalist religions too, since hatred for the enemy unites peoples in their rage. Love moves the heart toward few people, while hatred moves my heart, and the hearts of those on my side, against millions of people, or a nation, or an ethnic group, or people of a different color or language. The Italian racist hates all Albanians or Romanians or Gypsies. Certain members of the Northern League hate all southerners, then draw their salaries from taxes paid also by southerners, a true masterstroke of malevolence where the pleasure of insult and mockery is united with hatred. Berlusconi hates all judges and demands that we do likewise, and that we hate all Communists, even at the risk of seeing them where they no longer exist.

Hatred is therefore not individualistic but generous, philanthropic, and holds vast multitudes in a single embrace. Only in stories are we told that it is beautiful to die for love, but in the newspapers, at least when I was a child, the death of the hero as he hurled a bomb against the hated enemy was portrayed as something beautiful.

This is why the history of our species has been marked chiefly by hatred, and by wars and massacres, and not by acts of love, which are less comfortable and often wearing when extended beyond the circle of our egoism.

2011

Where has death gone?

In France, *Le Magazine Littéraire* has devoted its November issue to "what literature knows about death." I looked at a number of articles with interest, but was disappointed to find that, apart from some things I didn't know, they were in the end restating a familiar concept: that literature has always been preoccupied with death—along, of course, with love. The articles deal eloquently with the presence of death in twentieth-century narrative as well as in pre-Romantic Gothic literature. But they could just as easily have described the death of Hector, or the grief of Andromache, or the suffering of martyrs in many medieval texts. To say nothing of the history of philosophy, which begins with the most common example of a major premise in a syllogism: "All men are mortal."

But I think the problem lies elsewhere, and perhaps has to do with the simple fact that people today read fewer books. We have become incapable of dealing with death. Religions, myths, and ancient rituals made us familiar with death, however daunting it remained. We became familiar with it through funeral celebrations, the wailing of mourners, the great requiem masses. We were prepared for death by sermons on hell, and while still a child I was encouraged to read pages on death from *The Companion of Youth* by Don Bosco, who was not only a jolly priest who encouraged children to play, but had a fiery and visionary imagination. He reminded us that we cannot know where death will surprise us—whether in our bed, at work, in the street, through a burst vein, catarrh, a rush of blood, a fever, a sore, an earthquake, a thunderbolt, "perhaps just as you finish reading this consideration." At that moment we will feel our head darken, our eyes fill with pain, our tongue burn, jaws closed, chest heavy, blood chilled, flesh consumed, heart pierced. From here comes the need to practice the Exercise for a Good Death: "When my motionless feet warn me that my career in this world is about to end . . . When my numb and tremulous hands can no longer grasp you, my blessed Crucifix, and against my will I let you fall onto the bed of my suffering . . . When my eyes, dimmed and stricken with horror at imminent death . . . When my cold and trembling glances . . . When my pale and leaden cheeks inspire compassion and terror in those around me, and my hair soaked with the sweat of death, rising up on my head announce that my end is near . . . When my imagination, agitated by terrible and fearsome ghosts is immersed in mortal sorrow . . . When I lose the use of all senses . . . merciful Jesus, have pity on me."

Pure sadism, it might be said. But what do we teach our young people today? That death takes place far away from us in a hospital, that people usually don't walk behind the coffin to the cemetery, that we no longer see the dead. We no longer see them? We see them constantly blown up, crashed on the sidewalk, dropped into the sea with their feet in a cube of cement, their heads left rolling on the cobbles, their brains splattered over the windows of taxis. But they are not us, and they are not our loved ones; they are actors. Death is entertainment, even when the media reports about the girl actually raped or the victim of a serial killer. We don't see the mutilated body that would remind us of death. The news bulletins let us see grieving friends who bring flowers to the scene of the crime or, far worse sadism, reporters ring the mother's doorbell and ask, "What did you feel when they killed your daughter?" Rather than death, they show us friendship and maternal grief, which affect us less violently.

And so the disappearance of death from our immediate experience will terrify us more when the moment approaches—the event that is part of us from birth, and to which every wise person grows accustomed throughout life.

2012

Our Paris

On the night of the Paris massacre I stayed glued to the television, like so many others. Familiar with the streets of Paris, I was trying to understand where the events were taking place and to work out whether they were close to the homes of friends, how far they were from my publisher's office, or from the restaurant where I regularly eat. I felt reassured by the thought that they were far away, on the Right Bank, whereas my own Parisian world is on the Left Bank.

This did nothing to diminish the shock and horror, yet it was like knowing one had missed boarding the aircraft that had just crashed who knows where. No one that night had yet absorbed that this could possibly have happened in one of our own cities.

But I began to feel a vague unease when I realized that Bataclan was a familiar name. Finally I remembered. It was there, around ten years ago, that one of my novels had been presented, with a magnificent concert by Gianni Coscia and Renato Sellani. So it was a place I had been to, and where I could have returned. Then—no, not then, but almost immediately—I recognized the name Boulevard Richard Lenoir: it was where Inspector Maigret used to live!

You'll tell me it's not right to introduce something imaginary into the scene when such frighteningly "real" events were happening. And yet this explains why the Paris massacre affected everyone so deeply, even though terrible massacres had happened in other cities around the world. Paris is a place that many of us think of as home, because real cities and fictional cities merge in our memory, as if both were a part of us, or as if we had lived in both.

There is a Paris that is just as real as Café de Flore—the Paris, perhaps, of Henry IV and Ravaillac, of Louis XVI's beheading, of Felice Orsini's assassination attempt on Napoleon III, of the entry of General Leclerc's troops in 1944. But let's be honest. What do we remember most, the event itself, not having been there, or its portrayal in books and movies?

We saw the liberation of Paris on the screen with *Is Paris Burning?*, just as we saw nineteenth-century Paris in Marcel Carné's *Les enfants du Paradis*, just as the real experience of entering Place des Vosges at night gives us the thrill we'd felt only in the cinema, just as we relive the world of Edith Piaf even though we never knew her, and we know all about Rue Lepic because Yves Montand sang about it.

We can actually walk along the Seine, pausing at the stalls of the *bouquinistes*, but there, too, we are reliving so many romantic walks we have read about, and on seeing Notre-Dame from a distance, we cannot help thinking of Quasimodo and Esmeralda. We remember the Paris of the musketeers dueling at the monastery of the Barefoot Carmelites, the Paris of Balzac's courtesans, the Paris of Lucien de Rubempré and Eugène de Rastignac, of Bel Ami, of Frédéric Moreau and Madame Arnoux, of Gavroche on the barricades, of Swann and Odette de Crécy.

Our "real" Paris is Montmartre, the one we can now only imagine, in the time of Picasso and Modigliani, or Maurice Chevalier, and let's also include Gershwin's *An American in Paris* and its saccharine yet memorable reinterpretation with Gene Kelly and Leslie Caron, and even that of Fantômas escaping through the sewers and, naturally, that of Inspector Maigret, whose cases we have followed through all the fogs, all the bistros, all the nights of Quai des Orfèvres.

We have to acknowledge that much of what we have understood about life and society, about love and death, we have learned from this imaginary, fictional, yet very real Paris. And so a blow has been struck against our own home, a home in which we have lived much longer than the houses we actually live in. But all these memories nevertheless give us hope, because "*la Seine roule roule*," the Seine flows on.

2015

Religion and Philosophy

Seers see what they know

When I read Sister Lúcia's letter about the third secret of Fátima, now made public for the first time, it struck me as being familiar. Then I realized: the good sister's text, written not in 1917 when she was an illiterate child but in 1944 as a grown-up nun, is interwoven with immediately recognizable references to the book of Revelation.

Lúcia sees an angel with a flaming sword that appears as though it will set the world on fire. The book of Revelation speaks of angels that spread fire in the world, as in chapter 8, verse 8, with reference to the angel of the second trumpet. It's true this angel doesn't have a flaming sword, but we shall see later where this sword might have come from, although traditional iconography has a fair number of archangels with flaming swords.

Then Lúcia sees the divine light as in a mirror. Here the idea comes not from Revelation but from Saint Paul's First Epistle to the Corinthians: heavenly things we now see "through a glass," and only later will we see them face-to-face.

After which comes the bishop dressed in white. There is just one, whereas in various parts of Revelation (6:11, 7:9, and 7:14) there are several servants of the Lord in white robes, elected to martyrdom.

Then bishops and priests are seen going up a steep mountain, and we are now at Revelation 6:15, where the powerful men of the world hide in the dens and rocks of the mountains. Then the Holy Father arrives in a city "half in ruins" and encounters the souls of corpses along the way. The city, along with the corpses, is mentioned in Revelation

11:8, while it falls into ruins in 11:13 and again, in the form of Babylon, in 18:19.

We continue on. The bishop and many other followers are killed by soldiers with arrows and guns, and though Sister Lúcia brings matters up to date by introducing guns, massacres are carried out in 9:7, at the sound of the fifth trumpet, by breastplated locusts with spiked weapons.

Finally, two angels appear who sprinkle blood from a crystal watering jug (in Portuguese, a *regador*). Now, there are many angels in Revelation who sprinkle blood, but in 8:5 they do it with a censer, in 14:20 the blood comes out of a winepress, in 16:3 it is poured from a vial.

Why a watering jug? It occurred to me that Fátima is not far from the Asturias region where those splendid Mozarabic miniatures were created in the Middle Ages. And in them angels appear pouring jets of blood from cups that are difficult to identify, as though watering the world. That Lúcia may have been remembering the iconographical tradition is suggested by the angel with the flaming sword mentioned earlier, since the trumpets held by the angels in those miniatures sometimes look like scarlet blades.

It is interesting that if we go beyond the brief newspaper reports and read the full theological commentary by Cardinal Ratzinger, we can see that this man, while he stresses that a private vision is not a matter of faith, and that an allegory is not a prophecy to be taken literally, specifically notes similarities with the book of Revelation.

Furthermore, he states that a person sees things in a vision "insofar as he is able, in the modes of representation and consciousness available to him," so that "he can arrive at the image only within the bounds of his capacities and possibilities." By which, in rather more secular terms, though Ratzinger heads the section "The Anthropological Structure of Private Revelations," he means that, if Jungian archetypes don't exist, every seer sees what his culture has taught him to see.

2000

European roots

This summer the newspapers have been livened up by the debate as to whether it is acceptable for the European Constitution to make reference to Europe's Christian origins. Those in favor argue the obvious fact that Europe was born under a Christian culture before the fall of the Roman Empire, from at least the time of Emperor Constantine's edict in 313. Just as the Eastern world cannot be conceived without Buddhism, Europe cannot be conceived without recognizing the role played by the Catholic Church, by the devoutly Christian kings, by scholastic theology, and by the actions and example of its great saints.

Those who argue against such a reference invoke the secular principles on which modern democracies are based. Those in favor suggest that secularism is a recent development in Europe, a legacy of the French Revolution, nothing to do with the origins that are rooted in the monastic or Franciscan tradition. Those against it think above all about the Europe of tomorrow, which is destined to become a multiethnic continent, and where an explicit reference to Christian roots could halt the process of integration for newcomers and reduce other traditions and beliefs, some of considerable size, to the status of minority cultures and cults that are merely tolerated.

It is therefore not just a war of religion; it relates to a political project, an anthropological vision, and the decision about whether the physiognomy of Europe should be drawn on the strength of its population's past or on the strength of its people's future.

Let us look at the past. Has Europe developed solely on the basis of Christian culture? I'm not thinking about the benefits European culture has reaped over the centuries, starting with Indian mathematics, Arabic medicine, or contacts farther east that predate Marco Polo and go back as far as Alexander the Great. Every culture absorbs elements from cultures near and far, but then develops its own character. It's not enough to say that we have to be grateful to the Indians or the Arabs for the number zero if it was Europe that first came up with the idea that nature is written in mathematical notation. The fact is that we're forgetting Greco-Roman culture.

Europe absorbed Greco-Roman culture in terms of its law, its philosophical thought, and even its popular beliefs. Christianity incorporated pagan rituals and myths, often casually, and forms of polytheism can still be found in popular religion. It wasn't only the Renaissance world that was populated with Venuses and Apollos and went on to explore the classical world, its ruins, and its manuscripts. Medieval Christianity built its theology on the thought of Aristotle, rediscovered through the Arabs, and if it ignored much of Plato it didn't ignore Neo-Platonism, which greatly influenced the fathers of the Church. Nor could Augustine, the greatest of Christian thinkers, be imagined without the impact of Platonic thought. The very notion of empire, over which there has been a thousand-year conflict between European states, and between states and Church, is of Roman origin. Christian Europe chose the Latin of Rome as the language of its sacred rituals, its religious thought, its law, and its university disputations.

There again, a Christian tradition is inconceivable without Jewish monotheism. The text on which European culture is based, the first text that the first printer thought to print, the text whose translation by Luther practically established the German language, the principal text of the Protestant world, is the Bible. Christian Europe was born and grew up singing the psalms, quoting the prophets, meditating on Job and on Abraham. Jewish monotheism was indeed the bridge that allowed dialogue between Christian monotheism and Islamic monotheism.

But it doesn't end there. Indeed, Greek culture, at least from the time of Pythagoras, would have been inconceivable without the influence of Egyptian culture, and one of the most significant phenomena of European culture, namely the Renaissance, was inspired by the teachings of the Egyptians and the Chaldeans, while the European image, from the first attempts to decipher the obelisks up until Champollion, from the Empire style to the modern and very Western imaginings of the New Age, were inspired by Nefertiti, the mysteries of the pyramids, the pharaoh's curse, and the golden scarab.

So I don't think it out of place in a constitution to make reference to the Greco-Roman and Judeo-Christian roots of our continent. Likewise, just as Rome opened its own pantheon to gods of every race and put men with black skin on the imperial throne—and we shouldn't forget that Saint Augustine was born in Africa—Europe should declare itself ready, by virtue of these very roots, to include every other cultural and ethnic contribution, since openness is one of its most distinguished cultural features.

2003

The lotus and the cross

I've followed with a great deal of interest the discussion begun by Cardinal Ratzinger over allowing Catholic clergy to use Eastern corporeal techniques as an aid to meditation and religious discipline. Certainly, leaving aside the breathing techniques practiced by Hesychasts in early Christian times, the prayers of modern-day devotees take account of the role bodily rhythms and postures play in setting the mind to meditation. The techniques of Eastern meditation tend, however, to use the body to bring about a sort of annulment of sensibility and of will, in which the body, and with it the pain and miseries of our material nature, are forgotten. In this respect they come close to that search for suppression of anxiety and pain that characterized classical and pagan ataraxia.

On this point one can agree with Cardinal Ratzinger. Christianity is based on the idea of a son of God who, as son of man, points the way to redemption from evil through the cross. For Christianity, pain cannot be forgotten; indeed, it is a fundamental instrument of spiritual growth.

I don't wish to be misunderstood: what I am referring to here has nothing to do with a recent controversy that has erupted at a high level over whether or not Christians should be reducing pain in the world. From reading just a few pages of the Gospels it is clear that Christians have a duty to alleviate the pain of others. But they must know how to deal with their own pain. Christians must make sacrifices so others do not suffer, and must do what is possible to reduce the pain that afflicts the world. So they must also reduce their own pain, if this can be done without harming others. Medicine is therefore welcome if it alleviates our sufferings; suicide and masochism are sinful. But since some degree of pain, through original sin or through the imperfections of this sublunary world, is impossible to eliminate, Christians must draw the maximum moral and ascetic benefit from the pain that awaits them.

Ideally no one should suffer, to the extent that it depends on you.

But since even with the best of intentions you cannot eliminate the evil in the world, you have to know how to accept and make good use of that portion of pain that life will bring. I am thinking of the magnificent recent book *Filosofia della libertà* (*Philosophy of Freedom*) by Luigi Pareyson. After several pages of high metaphysical tension on the terrible question of whether evil paradoxically lurks in the same sphere as the divine, Pareyson celebrates pain, freely accepted and not ignored, as the means of overcoming evil.

It's not essential to be a practicing Christian to accept this point of view: it permeates Western thought, and the finest writings of poets and philosophers who are nonbelievers, above all Giacomo Leopardi, originate from this ethos. Many Eastern doctrines are wholly extraneous to such an ethos. I would not agree with Cardinal Ratzinger if, based on such assumptions, he wanted to prevent laypeople or non-Christians from practicing whatever forms of religious discipline they choose. Likewise, I wouldn't wish to comment on the assurances of the Catholic clergy who remind the cardinal that sitting in the lotus position doesn't mean forgetting the mystery of the cross. These are internal Church matters. But the debate involves us all to the extent that, as Benedetto Croce said, we cannot *not* call ourselves Christians.

Recently a philosopher declared on a TV chat show that to resolve the crisis in the Western world we have to rediscover Islamic spirituality, using the unfortunate metaphor "sword of Islam," once used by Mussolini. I don't rule out the possibility that some might find the solution to their problems in the totemic rituals of Native American tribes. But, being what we are, our philosophy included, we have been brought up in a Judeo-Christian culture. It may be helpful for repentant terrorists to shed their skin, but philosophers decide their own conversion by looking inside the skin in which they are born.

2005

Relativism?

Perhaps it's not so much the fault of media crassness as of those obsessed with how the media will report them, but certain debates even between people not lacking in common sense now take place with the clash of cudgels, with a lack of finesse, using words as subtly as boulders. A typical example in Italy is the debate between so-called theocons, who accuse secular thinkers of "relativism," and representatives of secular thought, who accuse their opponents of "fundamentalism."

What does "relativism" mean in philosophy? That our representations of the world's complexity are not exhaustive, but are always views from differing perspectives, each of which contain a grain of truth? There have been, and still are, Christian philosophers who support this view. That these representations are not to be judged in terms of truth, but in terms of historical or cultural needs? Richard Rorty supports this in his version of "pragmatism." The proposition that whatever we know is relative to the way in which the subject knows it? This comes from Kant. That every proposition is true only within a given paradigm? This is called "holism." That ethical values are relative to cultures? This was discovered in the 1600s. That there are no facts but only interpretations? This is what Nietzsche said. What about the concept that if there's no God, then all is permissible? That is Dostoyevskian nihilism. What about the theory of relativity? Come on, let's be serious.

But it ought to be clear that if someone is a relativist in the Kantian sense, he cannot be one in the Dostoyevskian sense. Kant believed in God and duty. Nietzschean relativism has little to do with cultural anthropology, since the former doesn't believe in facts and the latter doesn't doubt them. "Holism," as interpreted by Quine, is firmly anchored in sane empiricism, which places much reliance on the stimuli we receive from the environment, and so forth.

In short, it seems that the term "relativism" can refer to forms of modern thought often in mutual conflict. Sometimes thinkers firmly anchored in a profound realism are regarded as relativists, and "relativism" is used with the polemical ardor with which nineteenth-century Jesuits spoke of "Kantian poison."

But if all of the above is relativism, then there are only two philosophies that completely withstand this accusation, and they are radical Neo-Thomism and the theory of consciousness in Lenin's *Materialism and Empirio-Criticism*. A strange alliance.

2005

Chance and Intelligent Design

Last week in *La Repubblica,* Eugenio Scalfari wrote about a story that seemed dead and buried, or rather, a story limited to the American Bible Belt, isolated from the world, clinging to its fierce fundamentalism. The arguments over Darwinism have resurfaced, and have even affected plans for the reform of our school system, by which I mean the Italian Catholic school system.

I emphasize the word "Catholic" because Christian fundamentalism comes from Protestant circles and is characterized by a determination to interpret the scriptures literally. But for the scriptures to be interpreted literally, they must be freely interpreted by the believer, and this is typical of Protestantism. There should be no Catholic fundamentalism, since for Catholics the interpretation of the scriptures is mediated by the Church.

Back in the time of the Church fathers, and earlier with Philo of

Alexandria, there was a softer hermeneutic approach, such as that of Saint Augustine, who was ready to admit that the Bible often spoke using metaphors and allegories, and it was therefore quite possible that the seven days of the creation were seven thousand years. And the Church accepted this hermeneutic position.

Once it is conceded that the seven days of the creation are a poetical account that can be interpreted beyond the letter, Genesis suggests that Darwin is right: first there is the Big Bang with the explosion of light, then the planets take form, and on Earth there are great geological upheavals as the lands are separated from the seas. Plants, fruits, and seeds appear, and the waters begin to teem with living creatures as life starts to emerge from the water. Birds rise up in flight, and only later do mammals appear. The genealogical position of reptiles is unclear, but we can't expect too much of Genesis. Only at the culmination of this process, and, I suppose, after the great anthropomorphous monkeys, does man appear. Man, who, lest we forget, is not created from nothing, but from mud—in other words, from previous material. More evolutionist than this, though without excluding the presence of a Creator, is hardly possible.

What has Catholic theology always claimed so as not to identify itself with materialistic evolutionism? Not just that all of this is the work of God, but that there is a qualitative leap in the evolutionary ladder when God introduced an immortal rational soul into a living organism. The battle between materialism and spiritualism is based on this point alone.

One interesting aspect of the debate taking place in the United States for its inclusion in school curriculums, alongside the Darwinian "hypothesis" (don't forget that Galileo escaped conviction in his trial by admitting that his was a hypothesis and not a discovery), is that, so as not to make it sound like a conflict between religious belief and scientific theory, the discussion focuses not so much on divine creation as Intelligent Design. In other words, we don't want to impose on you the embarrassing presence of a bearded and anthropomorphous Yahweh, but you have to accept that if there was an evolutionary development, this didn't happen by chance but in pursuance of a plan, and this plan can only come from some form of Mind, which means that the concept of Intelligent Design could allow a pantheistic God in place of a transcendental God.

What I find curious is that no one has considered that Intelligent Design doesn't rule out a casual process such as Darwin's, which occurs, so to speak, by trial and error, so that the only creatures to survive are those that best adapt to the environment. Let us think of the noblest concept we have of "intelligent design," namely, artistic creation. It was Michelangelo who told us in his famous sonnet that the artist, when he finds himself in front of a block of marble, cannot at first picture the statue that will emerge, but he proceeds by trying, testing the resistance of the material, getting rid of the "surplus" in order gradually to let the statue emerge from the waste matter that imprisoned it. But the artist discovers what the statue is, and whether it is Moses or a slave, only at the end of the process of continually trying.

Intelligent Design can also be seen through a series of acceptances and rejections offered by chance. First, of course, it needs to be decided whether there is a Designer capable of accepting and rejecting, or whether it is Chance that, in accepting and rejecting, shows itself to be the only form of Intelligence—in other words, that it is Chance that makes itself God. And this is no small question. Clearly it's rather more philosophically complex than the fundamentalists suggest.

2005

The reindeer and the camel

In these weeks before Christmas the controversy over nativity scenes rages. On the one hand, several large stores have stopped selling nativity figures for Christmas crèches because, they say, they're no longer in demand. This has aroused the ire of many pious souls who, rather than railing against their fellow citizens for having lost interest in the tradition, have attacked the storekeepers, even a chain store that, it later transpired, had never sold nativity figures in the first place. On the other hand, it has been argued that the loss of interest in the Christmas crib is due to excessive political correctness, the example being cited of schools that have stopped making them to avoid offending the sensibilities of children who belong to other religions.

As regards schools, even if it were a limited phenomenon, this would be a bad sign. A school must not erase traditions but should instead respect them all. If it wants children from different ethnic backgrounds to live together in peace, it must allow each child to understand the other's traditions. So the nativity scene should be there at Christmas, and the symbols and ritual implements of other religions or ethnic groups should be displayed on occasions that are important to them. Children would learn in this way about the plurality of traditions and beliefs, each would take part to some extent in the festivities of the others, a Christian child would find out about Ramadan, and a Muslim child would learn about the birth of Jesus.

As for the news that figurines are no longer for sale, I have the feeling this is journalistic hype. In the San Gregorio Armeno district of Naples, the sale of the most remarkable figures and models continues. Two years ago, I went through the whole floor of a Milan department store devoted to nativity scenes; it was packed with customers. A weekly magazine conducted a survey among politicians showing that the more left wing or rabidly anticlerical they are, the more they like nativity scenes. This makes me wonder whether the Christmas nativity scene is a symbol more dear to nonbelievers, now that churchgoers have been converted to the Christmas tree, putting Father Christmas in the place of Baby Jesus or the Magi, who in my time used to bring the presents, which is why children joyfully celebrated the King who came down from the heavens with their toys.

But the question is ever more confusing. We think that the tree and Father Christmas represent a Protestant tradition but forget that Santa Claus was a Catholic saint, Saint Nicholas. His name originates from a distortion of Nicholas or Nikolaus. And the evergreen tree is a pagan legacy, since it recalls the Yule, a pre-Christian festival of the winter solstice: the Church had established Christmas on the very same day so as to absorb tradition and take the place of previous celebrations. The final ambiguity is that neopagan consumerism has entirely secularized the tree, which has become a piece of seasonal ornament, like the Christmas lights in city streets. Children and parents enjoy decorating it with colored balls, but I certainly found more enjoyment helping my father build the Christmas crib at the beginning of December, and it was a joy to see gushing fountains and waterfalls operated by hidden virtue of an enema pump.

The practice of building the nativity scene is being lost because it requires work and inventive skill. All Christmas trees look much alike, whereas every nativity scene is different. Those who spend their evenings so preoccupied are in danger of missing television shows important for the preservation of the family, as we are forever warned that parents must be present while their children watch naked women and brains being smashed to pulp.

Remembering that my father, who was so devoted to the Christmas crèche, was a middle-of-the-road socialist, mildly deist, and moderately anticlerical, I feel that to ignore the tradition of the crib is also bad for nonbelievers, and maybe even more so for them. Indeed, the invention of the crib required a character like Saint Francis, who expressed his religiosity above all by talking to wolves and birds: the crib is the most human and least transcendent thing that could be invented to remember the birth of Jesus. In that sacred diorama, apart from the star of Bethlehem and two angels that hover over the cattle stall, there is no reference to theological niceties, and the more populated the cattle shed, the more it celebrates everyday life, helping children to understand what daily life used to be, and perhaps feel nostalgia for a nature that was still uncontaminated.

While the secular and consumerist tradition of the tree evokes superstitions that are even, dare one say, somewhat national socialist, superstitions that are lost in the darkness of time, the religious tradition of the crèche celebrates a secular and natural environment, with its hillside cottages, sheep, hens, blacksmiths and carpenters, women carrying water, the ox, the donkey, and the camel, which will easily pass through the eye of a needle, while those who leave super-expensive presents beneath the tree will not enter the kingdom of heaven.

2006

Watch it, loudmouth . . .

Fifteen years must have gone by since I wrote that in a few decades Europe would become a continent of mixed races, but that the process would cost blood and tears. I wasn't a prophet, just someone with common sense who often looks at history, convinced that by learning about what took place in the past we can often understand what might happen in the future. Terrorist attacks aside, I need only see what's on people's minds these days. A schoolteacher in France writes critically of Islam and runs the risk of being killed. In Berlin a production of Mozart's *Idomeneo* is canceled because it shows the decapitated heads not only of Jesus and Buddha but also of Muhammad. I won't dwell on the words of Pope Benedict, who at his age ought to have known that there's quite a difference between a university lecture given by a professor and a pontiff's speech broadcast by every television station, and that perhaps he should have been a little more cautious. Yet those who have used a historical reference as a pretext for attempting to stir up a new religious war are certainly not the kind I'd like to have dinner with.

Bernard-Henri Lévy has written a fine article about the case of the French schoolteacher: we may totally disagree with what he thinks, but we have to defend his right to express a free opinion on questions of religion. Sergio Romano has written about the case of *Idomeneo* in *Corriere della Sera,* which I'll try to sum up in my own words: if a director desperate for novelty stages an opera by Mozart and introduces the decapitated heads of religious founders, when such an idea had never crossed Mozart's mind, the least we can do is give him a good thrashing, but for aesthetic and philological reasons, in the same way directors who stage *Oedipus Rex* with characters in double-breasted pinstripe suits should be flogged. Yet on the same day, in *La Repubblica,* a musician as illustrious as Daniel Barenboim, though wisely asking whether it really was in the spirit of Mozart to attempt such a production, claims that it's the prerogative of art.

I think my friend Daniel would regret the tendency years ago to condemn, or ban, Shakespeare's *The Merchant of Venice.* It's a play inspired by an anti-Semitism common at the time and even earlier, from Chaucer onward, but shows Shylock in a human and poignant light. Yet this is what we are faced with: the fear of speaking out. We must remember that these taboos cannot all be traced back to Muslim fundamentalists, who can be rather touchy, but started with political correctness, inspired by a spirit of respect toward others, and which now makes it impossible, at least in America, to tell jokes not only about Jews, Muslims, and disabled people, but also about Scottish, Genoese, Belgians, policemen, firemen, garbage collectors, and Eskimos, who shouldn't be called that, but if you call them as they'd like to be called, then no one would understand whom you're talking about.

Twenty years ago I was teaching in New York, and to demonstrate how to analyze a text, I chose, almost at random, a story in which, on a single line, a foulmouthed sailor described the vulva of a prostitute as "large as the mercy of . . ."—and here I put dots in place of the name of a divinity. At the end of the class I was approached by a student, evidently Muslim, who respectfully reproached me for lack of respect for his religion. I of course replied that I was only quoting someone else's vulgarity, but that in any case I apologized. The following day, I introduced into my discussion a not very respectful, though playful, reference to an illustrious figure in the Christian pantheon. Everyone laughed, and the Muslim student joined in the general hilarity. At the end of the lesson I took him under the arm and asked why he had showed a lack of respect for my religion. Then I sought to explain the difference between making a witty remark, taking God's name in vain, and swearing, and I invited him to be more tolerant. He apologized, and I feel sure he understood. What he may not have properly understood is the extreme tolerance of the Catholic world. In a "culture" of swearing, in which a God-fearing believer can describe the Supreme Being using adjectives that do not bear repeating, then who could be scandalized any longer by anything?

Not all educational relationships, however, can be as peaceful and civilized as the one I had with my student. In other circumstances it is better to keep quiet. But what will happen in a culture in which, for fear of making a gaffe, not even academics will dare refer to an Arab philosopher? It would cause a *damnatio memoriae*, the elimination of a diverse and worthy culture through silence. And it would not be good for mutual knowledge and understanding.

2006

Idolatry and iconoclasm lite

Are we living in a world of images in which the culture of the word is lost, or is the word returning in triumph with the Internet? Where do we place television, DVDs, video games? The human relationship with images has always been a difficult one, as Maria Bettetini recalls in her book *Contro le immagini: Le radici dell'iconoclastia* (*Against Images: The Roots of Iconoclasm*). It's only 160 pages long, but I don't wish to mislead anyone: it's a dense book aimed at readers who know something about philosophy and theology. Since its density makes it difficult to summarize, I'll make only a few general observations on the human ability, unknown to animals, of fashioning "simulacra."

For Plato, if objects are imperfect reproductions of ideal models, images are imperfect imitations of objects, and therefore pale secondhand imitations. But in Neo-Platonism images become a direct imitation of ideal models, and the word *agalma* means statue as well as image, but also splendor, dignity, and therefore beauty.

The ambiguity was present in the Hebrew world, where it was forbidden to make images of God or to utter his true name. Yet God had created humankind in his own image, and if we read biblical descriptions of the Temple of Solomon, we see that there were depictions not only of plants and animals of every kind, but also of cherubs. And since the same prohibition on portraying heavenly things applied in the Muslim world, places of worship used abstract calligraphic forms, though the Muslim culture has furnished us with splendid and highly imaginative miniatures.

With Christianity, not only had God assumed a "visible" body, but this divine body had left images of its face on veils and bloodstained handkerchiefs. Christianity needed images too, Hegel would later explain, to represent not just the glory of the heavens, but also the disfigured face of Christ in pain and the cruelty of his persecutors.

At this point, the matter becomes ever more complicated, since Neo-Platonists like Pseudo-Dionysius the Areopagite tell us that divine things can be spoken about only in the negative, so that if it's necessary to refer to God, it's better to use the most outrageously dissimilar imagery, such as a bear or a panther. Yet people who had read Pseudo-Dionysius had formed the idea that every earthly thing was none other than the image of a celestial thing, and every creature of the world is almost a "picture" of things that would otherwise escape our senses, so that it was right and proper to produce pictures of these pictures.

But for uneducated people it was easy to pass from the fascination of the figure to identifying it with the thing it represented, and to slip from the cult of images into idolatry, the return of the Golden Calf. Which led to iconoclasm and the famous Byzantine campaign against images.

Conversely, the Church of Rome didn't relinquish the use of visual representations, since, as would often be repeated, *Pictura est laicorum literatura,* and illiterate people can be taught through images alone. And yet there was debate over what power was exerted by this multitude of figures that populated abbeys and cathedrals, and a cautious theory was developed in the time of Charlemagne that images were good, but only to stimulate the memory, and that it would in the end be difficult to decide if a female image represents a Virgin to be venerated or a pagan Venus to be abhorred unless it had a *titulus,* or label. It's as though the Carolingians had read Roland Barthes, who theorized about the verbal anchoring of images, not for the celebration of God but for the sale of new commercial idols, and who had anticipated the theory of a verbal-visual culture, such as today's, in which television—image plus word—has simply replaced the cathedral. And it is, I suggest, on television screens that the pope is venerated, and at times idolized, by people who no longer go to church.

This prompts other reflections that bring Maria Bettetini's slim but disturbing book to its conclusion. She fears that the beauty of images, including sacred images, makes people forget God (this had already worried Saint Bernard), and complains laically that in new images there is a "loss of aura." But she also feels that contemporary art first destroys or disfigures traditional images, as with Picasso or informalism, then plays around by multiplying them, as with Warhol, and finally substitutes, jettisons, recycles, re-creates them, in a sort of permanent "iconoclasm lite."

So the times in which we live are still more complicated than those that worried Plato.

2007

The cocaine of the people

A recent debate on the semiotics of religion ended in a discussion of an idea that goes from Machiavelli to Rousseau and beyond: the Roman concept of a "civil religion," meaning a body of beliefs and obligations capable of holding society together. It was believed that this notion, in itself virtuous, is just a short step away from the idea of religion as an *instrumentum regni,* an expedient that a political power, perhaps represented by unbelievers, uses to maintain control over its subjects.

The idea goes back to writers who had experienced the civil religion of the Romans. For example, in book VI of *The Histories,* Polybius wrote in relation to Roman rituals that "in a nation formed by wise men alone, resorting to means such as this would be pointless, but since the multitude is by its nature voluble and subject to passions of every sort, from immoderate greed to violent anger, the only alternative is to entertain them with such contrivances and with mysterious fears. I am therefore of the view, not that the Ancients had no reason to introduce religious faith and superstitions about Hades among the multitudes, but rather that those who seek to get rid of them today are foolish ... The Romans, while handling much larger sums of money in public offices and embassies, remain honest only out of respect for their oath; among other peoples it is rare to find those who do not touch public money, whereas among the Romans it is rare to find someone who taints himself with such guilt."

Although the Romans behaved so virtuously during the republican period, clearly at some point this stopped. And we can witness this because, centuries later in his *Tractatus Theologico-Politicus,* Spinoza gave another interpretation to the *instrumentum regni,* and to its splendid and captivating ceremonies: "But if, in despotic statecraft, the supreme and essential mystery be to hoodwink the subjects, and to mask the fear, which keeps them down, with the specious garb of religion, so that men may fight as bravely for slavery as for safety ... yet in a free state no more mischievous expedient could be planned or attempted."

From here it is not hard to arrive at Karl Marx's famous definition of religion as the opium of the people.

But do religions always have this *virtus dormitiva*? A very different opinion has been expressed, for example, by José Saramago, who has repeatedly attacked religions as the instigators of conflict: "Religions, all of them, without exception, will never serve to bring harmony and reconciliation among people; on the contrary, they have been and continue to be the cause of unspeakable acts of suffering, slaughter, monstrous physical and spiritual violence which constitute one of the darkest chapters in man's miserable history" (*La Repubblica*, September 20, 2001).

Saramago concluded elsewhere that "if all of us were atheists we would live in a more peaceful society." I am not sure he is right. Pope Benedict responded to the statement indirectly in his recent encyclical *Spe salvi*, in which he says that, on the contrary, nineteenth- and twentieth-century atheism, despite being presented as a protest against the injustices of the world and of world history, has led to "the greatest forms of cruelty and violations of justice."

My sense is that the pope was thinking of such godless folk as Lenin and Stalin, but was forgetting that the Nazi flag was inscribed *Gott mit uns* ("God with us"); that phalanxes of military chaplains blessed the Fascist pennants; that the Spanish butcher Francisco Franco was inspired by devoutly religious principles and supported by Warriors of Christ the King; that the people of the Vendée were devoutly religious in their fight against republicans, who themselves had invented a goddess Reason (an *instrumentum regni*); that Catholics and Protestants have happily slaughtered each other for years and years; that both the crusaders and their enemies were spurred on by religious motives; that Christians were fed to the lions to defend the Roman religion; that people were burned at the stake for religious motives; that Muslim fundamentalists—the attackers of the Twin Towers, Osama bin Laden, and the Taliban who bombed the Buddhas of Bamiyan and who for religious motives oppose India and Pakistan—were all devoutly religious; and finally, that it was with the words "God bless America" that Bush invaded Iraq.

So it occurred to me that perhaps, if religion is or has sometimes been the opium of the people, more often than not it has been its cocaine.

2007

The crucifix, almost a secular symbol

I don't remember the details, but there was a controversy over the display of crucifixes in schools some six years ago. After all this time, the question still lingers, except that there is now a conflict between the Italian government and the Church on one side and the European Union on the other.

The Republic of France prohibits the display of religious symbols in state schools, yet some of the great trends in modern Catholicism have emerged in republican France, on both the right and the left, from Charles Péguy and Léon Bloy to Jacques Maritain and Emmanuel Mounier, as well as worker priests—and although Our Lady of Fátima is in Portugal, Lourdes is in France. Evidently, removing religious symbols from schools doesn't affect the vitality of religious feelings. In Italian university lecture halls there are no crucifixes, but many students belong to the Catholic "Communion and Liberation" movement. Conversely, at least two generations of Italians spent their childhood in schoolrooms that displayed a crucifix between portraits of the king and the Duce, and some of the thirty pupils in each class would become atheists, others anti-Fascists, and others still, I imagine the majority, voted in favor of the Italian republic.

But while it was a mistake to refer only to the Christian tradition in the European Constitution, since Europe has also been influenced by pagan Greek culture and by Judaic traditions (what indeed is the Bible?), it is also true that Christian beliefs and symbols have played a significant role in the history of its nations. Likewise, crosses appear on the official banners of many Italian cities that may well have been governed for decades by Communists, as well as on noble crests and national flags (British, Swedish, Norwegian, Danish, Swiss, Icelandic, Maltese, and so on), in a way that has stripped the symbol of any religious significance. Not only that, but a sensitive Christian ought to feel offended by the sight of gold crosses nestling in the chest hairs of Italian Lotharios lying in wait for female German tourists, and around the necks of women of easy virtue. We note how a certain eighteenth-century cardinal by the name of Lambertini, on seeing a cross on the ample bosom of an attractive lady, made salacious comments on the sweetness of that Calvary. Crosses and chains are worn by young girls who go about with bare navels and skirts around their groins. If I were the pope, I'd demand that a symbol so desecrated should be removed from school classrooms out of respect.

Since the crucifix, except when it appears in church, has become a secular symbol, or in any event neutral, is the Church being more pious for wanting to keep it, or is the European Union more pious for wanting to remove it?

In much the same way, the Islamic half moon appears on the flags of Algeria, Libya, Malaysia, the Maldives, Mauritania, Pakistan, Singapore, Tunisia, and Turkey, yet there's talk of a country like Turkey entering Europe. And if a Catholic cardinal is invited to a conference in a Muslim country, he knows that he'll be speaking in a room decorated with verses from the Koran.

What do we say to non-Christians who now live in large numbers in Europe? That in this world certain customs and practices exist, more deeply rooted than faiths or the rejection of any faith, and that such customs and practices are to be respected. So when I visit a mosque I remove my shoes or else I don't go in. For the same reason, atheists who visit a Christian church should dress fittingly or stick to museums. The cross is part of cultural anthropology, and its outline has become rooted in a shared sensibility. People who come to live in Europe must also familiarize themselves with the aspects of shared sensibility. I know that alcohol consumption is forbidden in Muslim countries, except in permitted places such as hotels for foreigners, and I don't go around infuriating the local inhabitants by swigging from whiskey bottles in front of a mosque.

In a Europe increasingly populated with non-Europeans, integration has to be based on mutual tolerance. I don't think Muslim children would feel unsettled by a crucifix in a schoolroom, provided that their own beliefs are respected, and especially if the hour of religious instruction is transformed into an hour of religious history, including discussion about their own beliefs.

Of course, if the problem is to be overcome, a simple bare cross should be placed in the schoolroom, of the kind found even in an archbishop's study, so as to avoid the overly explicit reference to a specific religion. But I assume such a reasonable solution would be regarded as a surrender. We therefore carry on arguing.

2009

Those strangers, the Three Kings

Over the past few days I happened to witness two scenes, almost by chance: one of a girl of fifteen leafing with great interest through reproductions of paintings in an art book, and the other of two fifteen-year-olds fascinated by their visit to the Louvre. All three were born and educated in thoroughly secular countries and in non-Christian families. This meant that on seeing *The Raft of the Medusa* they understood that some unfortunate people have escaped from a shipwreck, or the two figures in Francesco Hayez's *The Kiss,* on show at Brera Art Gallery, were lovers, but what they couldn't understand was why Fra Angelico had painted a young girl in conversation with a winged youth, or why an unkempt old man was leaping down a mountain carrying two heavy tablets of stone and emitting rays of light from two horns.

The teens naturally recognized something in a nativity or crucifixion scene, since they had already seen similar images, but if there were three lords in the cattle stall with cloaks and crowns, they likely wouldn't know who they were or where they had come from.

It's virtually impossible for people to understand, let us say, three quarters of Western art unless they are familiar with the Old and New Testaments and the lives of the saints. Who is the girl with her eyes on a plate? Does she come from *Night of the Living Dead*? And is a soldier who slashes a piece of clothing in two involved in a protest against Armani?

Children from many cultural backgrounds learn at school about the death of Hector but not about Saint Sebastian; they will perhaps know about the marriage of Cadmus and Harmony but not about the marriage at Cana. In some countries there's a strong tradition of reading the Bible, and children know all about the Golden Calf but nothing about Saint Francis and the Wolf. Other places are steeped in the Stations of the Cross, but kept in the dark about the *mulier amicta solis,* the "woman clothed with the sun," in the book of Revelation.

But it is obviously worse when Westerners, and not just fifteen-year-olds, have to deal with representations of other cultures, a phenomenon all the more apparent today when people travel to exotic countries and the inhabitants of those countries come to Europe. I'm not talking about the puzzled reactions of Westerners in front of an African mask, or their amusement at the sight of Buddhas weighed down by cellulite, though, when asked, they might reply that Buddha is the god of Easterners, in the same way they might say that Muhammad is the god of Muslims. There again, many of our neighbors would be tempted to think the façade of an Indian temple had been designed by Communists to depict what was going on at Berlusconi's summer residence, or would shake their heads when they see a crouching figure with the head of an elephant being taken seriously by Indians, though they'd find nothing odd about a divinity represented as a dove.

And so, regardless of any religious consideration, and from a strictly secular point of view, schoolchildren need basic instruction in the ideas and traditions of different religions. To think this unnecessary is much the same as saying there's no need to teach us about Jupiter or Minerva because these were fairy tales for the old folk of Piraeus.

It's culturally dangerous to reduce religious education to the teaching of a single religion, such as the Catholic religion in Italy, since non-Catholic pupils or the children of non-Catholics cannot be forced to attend the class, thus losing even a minimum of cultural basics. School education then loses all reference to other religious traditions. What is more, even Catholic religious classes could be used for moral discussions on our duties to our peers or on the nature of faith, leaving aside those elements that enable us to distinguish Raphael's *Fornarina* from a penitent Mary Magdalene.

It's true that my own generation learned much about Homer and nothing about the Pentateuch, and art history was taught badly. Likewise, we learned all about Burchiello and nothing about Shakespeare, though we managed to get by despite this, since there was evidently something in the environment that provided us with stimulus and information. But those three fifteen-year-olds I mentioned earlier who didn't recognize the Three Kings make me think that the environment is now transmitting less and less useful information, and more and more that is entirely useless.

2009

Mad about Hypatia

With all the publicity and discussion around Alejandro Amenábar's film *Agora*, there's unlikely to be anyone who hasn't at least heard the name Hypatia. But for those who haven't, Hypatia lived in Egypt in the early years of the fifth century AD, in an empire that by then was ruled by a Christian. Her home city, Alexandria, was torn by a conflict between three forces: the pagan aristocracy, the new religious power represented by its bishop, Cyril, and a large Jewish community. She was a teacher and Neo-Platonist philosopher, a mathematician and astronomer, and was said to have been most beautiful and idolized by her pupils. A group of Parabalani, who were a sort of Christian Taliban of the time and Bishop Cyril's personal militia, attacked Hypatia and literally tore her to pieces.

No works by Hypatia have survived (Cyril may have had them destroyed), and there is little evidence, Christian or pagan, about her. More or less everyone accepts that Cyril was to some extent responsible for her death. Hypatia lay forgotten until the seventeenth century, when she was reappraised, in particular by Enlightenment philosophers, as a martyr of free thought, and celebrated by Gibbon, Voltaire, Diderot, Nerval, Leopardi, up to Proust and Mario Luzi, until she became a feminist icon.

The film certainly isn't kind to Christians or to Cyril, though it doesn't conceal the violence of pagans and Jews, and when word spread that dark reactionary forces were intending to stop its screening in Italy, a petition was circulated that collected thousands of signatures. As far as I understand, the Italian distributors were rather hesitant about releasing a film that might stir strong Catholic opposition, thus jeopardizing its screening, but the petition persuaded them to go ahead. What I want to talk about, however, is not the film, which is well made despite some glaring anachronisms, but the conspiracy theory that it set off.

Surfing the Internet, I found attacks by Catholics who protested against the presentation of only the violent side of religion. The director has repeatedly said that his argument was against fundamentalism of every kind, but no one has tried to deny that Cyril, who was not only a man of the Church but also a political figure, was tough on Jews and pagans alike. It's no coincidence that he was made a saint and doctor of the Church almost 1,500 years later by Leo XIII, a pope obsessed with the new paganism of Freemasonry and the anticlerical liberals who held power in Rome at that time. It was embarrassing to witness the commemoration of Cyril on October 3, 2007, by Pope Benedict, who praised "the great energy" of his rule without a word to lift the shadow that history has placed over him.

Cyril puts everyone in difficulty. On the Internet I found one Italian journalist who relied on Eusebius of Caesarea as a guarantor of his innocence. An excellent witness, except that Eusebius died seventy-five years before the execution of Hypatia and so couldn't have witnessed anything. If anyone feels the need to spark off a religious war, they should at least check Wikipedia.

But back to the conspiracy. On the Internet there are numerous reports of censorship (by whom?) to cover up the Hypatia scandal. For example, it has been stated that volume 8 of *Storia della filosofia greca e romana* (*History of Greek and Roman Philosophy*) by Giovanni Reale—dedicated to Neo-Platonism, with information about Hypatia —has mysteriously disappeared from bookshops. A telephone call to the publisher clarified that, of the ten-volume series, only volumes 7 and 8 are out of stock and will be reprinted, no doubt because they touch on arguments such as the *Corpus Hermeticum* and certain aspects of Neo-Platonism that not only interest students of philosophy but excite all those who dabble in real or occult sciences. But then I found a copy of this infamous volume 8 on my bookshelves and saw that Giovanni Reale—a historian of philosophy whose writings can all be read, whereas nothing of Hypatia's survives—devotes seven lines, yes, seven lines, to Hypatia, where he limits himself to saying what little is known. So why censor it?

But the conspiracy theory goes further, and on the Internet they say that all books on Neo-Platonism have disappeared from the bookshops, a nonsense that would make any first-year philosophy student laugh. In short, if you want to find out something about Hypatia, there are additional references on Wikipedia, or you'll find all you wish, uncensored, in *Roman Women* by Silvia Ronchey, in a chapter called "Hypatia the Intellectual."

2010

Halloween, relativism, and Celts

During this year's feast of All Saints there was much Catholic condemnation of Halloween, a feast when candles are placed inside pumpkins and children dressed as little witches and vampires demand treats from adults. Since the feast of Halloween, which seeks to exorcize the idea of death, is seen as an alternative to the celebration of All Saints' and All Souls' Day, the custom, criticized also for being a second-rate Americanism, has been branded a form of "relativism."

I'm not sure in what respect Halloween is relativist, but the word "relativism" is now being used the way the word "Fascist" was used in 1968, when a Fascist was anyone who didn't think as you did. I ought to say that I'm not exactly a Halloween enthusiast, except that I love Charlie Brown. I object, however, to the suggestion that it's a second-rate American import. It is, rather, an import on its way back, since Halloween originated as a pagan festival in Celtic Europe and in certain parts of northern Europe where it was Christianized to some degree.

What happened to Halloween is not unlike what happened to Santa Claus, a saint born in Turkey. It seems that the name Santa Claus came from the Dutch feast of Sinterklaas, celebrated on the saint's birthday. Then Father Christmas merged with Odin, who in German mythology brought gifts for children, hence the close link between a pagan ritual and the Christian feast.

Personally I have a bone to pick with Father Christmas, since it was Baby Jesus and the Three Kings who used to bring my Christmas presents, which was why I went recently to Cologne Cathedral to make sure that the remains of the Three Kings were still there after Rainald of Dassel and Frederick Barbarossa stole them from the basilica of St. Eustorgio in Milan. As a child I was upset by other children who gave credit not to the Three Kings but to the Befana, a figure herself of pagan origin similar to Halloween witches; the Church hierarchy doesn't find her upsetting because she was in some way Christianized, adopting her name from the Epiphany. Thus, after the 1929 Lateran Treaty between the Vatican and the Italian state, even the feast of the Fascist Befana was deemed acceptable.

One lone voice in the recent Halloween controversy was that of Roberto Beretta, writing in the Catholic newspaper *Avvenire,* who cautioned prudence when hurling anathemas and calling for pastoral crusades, for with Halloween "the Church is being paid back in its own coin. That's right. Indeed, from at least the fourth century, the wisdom of the Church fathers . . . preferred to mediate rather than eliminate, to superimpose and transform rather than annul, annihilate, bury, censor. In other words: our ancestors knew how to 'Christianize' pagan festivals."

Bear in mind that no gospel suggests Jesus was born on December 25, and indeed, according to astronomical calculations, the star must have appeared in the autumn. Christmas Day was fixed to coincide with the pagan customs and Germanic and Celtic traditions that celebrated Yule, the feast of the winter solstice. I myself prefer the traditional nativity scene, as it requires more imagination, whereas the Christmas tree can be decorated by any suitably trained ape.

The answer, therefore, instead of getting upset, is to Christianize Halloween, as Beretta suggests: "If Halloween, which literally means 'All Hallows' Eve,' returned to its Celtic guise, whether actual or supposed, or cloaked itself instead in consumerist frills or even hid itself beneath more or less 'satanic' rituals, then all it would be doing is reappropriating a territory formerly its own; and we would be left pondering how and why we haven't had the cultural or spiritual strength to repeat what our forefathers did."

2011

Damned philosophy

La Repubblica recently published an extract of a forthcoming translation of *The Grand Design* by Stephen Hawking and Leonard Mlodinow, with a subtitle from a passage in the book: "Philosophy is dead, physicists alone can explain the cosmos." The death of philosophy has been announced a number of times, so it's no surprise, but it seemed to me that Hawking was talking nonsense. To be sure that *La Repubblica* hadn't given an inaccurate summary, I bought the book, and my suspicions were confirmed.

The book cover describes Mlodinow as a first-rate popularizer and screenwriter of several episodes of *Star Trek*, and this is evident from the magnificent illustrations, which seem designed for a children's encyclopedia of yesteryear, colorful and fascinating, but explaining precisely nothing about the complex physical-mathematical-cosmological theorems they should be illustrating. Perhaps it wasn't the best idea to entrust the fate of philosophy to people with pointy ears.

The book opens with the peremptory statement that philosophy now has nothing more to say and that only physics can tell us (i) how to understand the world we live in, (ii) what the nature of reality is, (iii) whether the universe has need of a creator, (iv) why there is something instead of nothing, (v) why we exist, and (vi) why this particular set of laws exists and not another. As we can see, these are standard philosophical questions, and the book shows how physics can respond in some way to the last four, which seem the most philosophical of all.

To attempt to answer the last four questions, answers are required for the first two questions—in other words, what does it mean that something is real, and do we know the world exactly as it is? When they are taught philosophy, Italian schoolchildren start off with questions such as: Do we learn by adjusting the mind to the thing? Is there something outside us? Or are we the kind of beings envisaged by Berkeley, or, as Putnam says, brains in a vat?

The answers that this book offers are essentially philosophical, and if it weren't for those philosophical answers, then not even physics could say why it knows and what it knows. Indeed, the authors talk about a "model-dependent realism"—that is, they assume that "there is no picture- or theory-independent concept of reality." And so "different theories can describe the same phenomenon in a satisfactory way through disparate conceptual structures," and all we can perceive, know, and say about reality depends on the interaction between our models and that something which exists outside, but which we know only thanks to the form of our perceptual organs and our brains.

More wary readers might recognize the ghost of Kant, but certainly the two authors are proposing what is known in philosophy as holism, which some philosophers call internal realism and others constructivism.

As we can see, this book is not about physical discoveries but about philosophical notions that support and justify the physicist's research —and competent physicists cannot avoid asking questions about the philosophical foundations of their own methods. This is something we already knew, just as we already knew something about the extraordinary revelation, thanks to Mlodinow and the *Star Trek* crew, that "in ancient times people instinctively attributed violent acts of nature to an Olympus of spiteful and malicious gods." By heavens and by Jove!

2011

Evasion and secret redress

There are tax evaders in every country: the reluctance to pay taxes is deeply human. But it is believed that Italians are more prone to this vice than others. Why?

For an answer I have to go back in time, and to the figure of an old Capuchin friar of great humanity, learning, and kindness, of whom I was very fond. Now, this amiable old man, while instructing me and other young people in the principles of ethics, explained to us that smuggling and tax evasion, if they are sins, can be forgiven, since they contravene no divine law but only laws of the state.

He ought to have reminded us of Christ's recommendation to render unto Caesar that which is Caesar's, as well as Paul's advice to the Romans: "Pay to all what is owed to them: taxes to whom taxes are owed, revenue to whom revenue is owed." Perhaps, though, he knew that some theologians, in centuries past, had claimed that tax laws bring no obligation in terms of conscience, but only by force of sanction. Reporting today on this opinion, Luigi Lorenzetti, the director of *Rivista di Teologia Morale,* comments: "We do a disservice to those theologians, however, if we ignore the social and economic context that caused them to come up with such a theory. The organization of society was by no means democratic; the iniquitous tax system and exorbitant taxes oppressed the poor."

Indeed, my Capuchin friar quoted another case, that of secret redress. To explain it in the simplest terms, workers who feel badly underpaid commit no sin if they quietly take the extra amount to which they are entitled. But only if their wage is clearly unjust and they are denied the possibility of appealing to labor laws. On such an argument, however, Saint Thomas Aquinas (in *Summa Theologiae*) had his doubts. On the one hand: "If the need be so manifest and urgent . . . then it is lawful for a man to succor his own need by means of another's property, by taking it either openly or secretly: nor is this properly speaking theft or robbery." On the other hand: "He who, by stealth, takes his own property, if this be unjustly detained by another, he sins indeed; yet not because he burdens the retainer, and so he is not bound to restitution or compensation: but he sins against general justice by disregarding the order of justice and usurping judgment concerning his own property." Saint Thomas's ideas about the general justice were clear and strict, and he wouldn't have agreed with Berlusconi's observation that it was understandable if citizens evaded a tax that was exorbitant. For Thomas, the law was the law.

Nevertheless, the Thomist conception of the right of ownership was universally more "social," in that property was to be considered "in terms of possession" but not "in terms of use": if I have a loaf of bread, honestly acquired, then I have the right to be recognized as its owner, but if there's a down-and-out person near me who's dying of hunger, then I ought to give half of it to him. To what extent, then, can evasion be regarded as hidden redress?

On a Catholic website I found a *Treatise on Moral Theology*, which, while it advises people to respect the law and observes that "the more healthy part of the population" pays taxes and doesn't get involved in smuggling, it nevertheless concedes that "evasion is not regarded as an act detrimental to honor, the law itself regards it as an administrative and not a criminal offence, even though it creates a sense of moral discomfort." So our prime minister, Mario Monti, is wrong when he says that tax evaders are thieves: they are simply people who ought to feel moral discomfort.

But the friar I mentioned earlier didn't trouble himself with such casuistic subtleties, and limited himself to saying that tax evasion and smuggling are not mortal sins because they are "only" against the laws of the state. His position seems to reflect something he had been taught as a child, before the Lateran Treaty, that the state was bad and that no notice should be taken of it. It seems something of these old ideas has survived in the Italian DNA.

2012

The holy experiment

Pope Francis, though a Jesuit, takes a Franciscan name, lives in Franciscan simplicity lacking only sandals and a cowl, chases cardinals who drive Mercedes-Benzes out of the temple, and goes alone to the island of Lampedusa to show solidarity with refugees fished out of the Mediterranean as though the draconian laws of the Italian state did not exist. Is he really the only person who can still be described as left wing by what he says and does? At first there were rumors about his excessive prudence toward Argentinean generals, and some recalled his opposition to liberation theologians, and that it wasn't clear where he stood on abortion, on stem cells, on homosexuals, on whether a pope should go around doling out condoms to the poor. Who is Jorge Mario Bergoglio?

I think it's a mistake to consider him an Argentinean Jesuit: he's a Paraguayan Jesuit. It's impossible for someone with his training not to have been influenced by the "holy experiment" of the Jesuits of Paraguay. What little people know about these Jesuits comes from the film *The Mission*, which condensed, with much license, a hundred and fifty years of history into two hours of entertainment.

In brief, the Spanish conquistadores had committed unspeakable massacres from Mexico to Peru, supported by clergy who claimed the

Indios were bestial, orangutans to a man. Only one brave Dominican priest, Bartolomé de las Casas, was prepared to stand up against the cruelty of people like Cortés and Pizarro, showing the native people in quite another light. In the early seventeenth century the Jesuit missionaries decided to acknowledge the rights of the natives—particularly the Guaraní, who lived in very primitive conditions—and organized them into "reductions," which were independent, self-supporting communities. The Jesuits didn't round them up to make them work for the colonizers, but they taught them to look after themselves, free from slavery, sharing all the commodities they produced. The structure of the villages and the methods of this "communism" remind us of Thomas More's *Utopia* or Tommaso Campanella's *The City of the Sun*, and Benedetto Croce writes of "so-called Campanellian communism," but the Jesuits were inspired more by early Christian communities. They set up elected councils consisting only of natives, though the fathers administered justice, and they taught their subjects architecture, agriculture and sheep farming, music and the arts, reading and writing, and sometimes produced talented artists and writers. The Jesuits had established a strict paternalistic regime, not least because civilizing the Guaraní meant rescuing them from promiscuity, indolence, ritual drunkenness, and sometimes cannibalism. And so, as with every ideal city, we are all ready to admire their organizational perfection, but we wouldn't want to live there.

Their rejection of slavery and the attacks of the *bandeirantes,* or slave hunters, led to the setting up of a popular militia, which bravely fought against the slave traders and colonialists. In the course of the eighteenth century, the Jesuits, who were seen as troublemakers and dangerous enemies of the state, were first banished from Spain and Portugal and then suppressed, bringing an end to the "holy experiment."

Many Enlightenment thinkers attacked this theocratic government as the most monstrous and tyrannical regime the world had ever seen. But others, such as Ludovico Muratori, spoke of "voluntary communism of high religious inspiration," while Montesquieu said that the Company of Jesus had begun to heal the wound of slavery, Gabriel de Mably compared the reductions to the government of Lycurgus of Sparta, and Paul Lafargue would later speak of the "first socialist state ever."

Before attempting to interpret Pope Francis's actions, we should bear in mind that four centuries have passed and that the notion of democratic freedom is now shared even by Catholic hardliners. The pope doesn't go to Lampedusa to carry out holy or secular experiments, and it would be for the best if he got rid of the Vatican Bank. But it's no bad thing, every now and then, to see the glimmer of history in what is happening today.

2013

Monotheisms and polytheisms

There is a threat of war in the air, no small local war but a conflict that could involve several continents. The threat now comes from a fundamentalist notion that seeks to Islamize the known world as far, it is said, as Rome, though no one has as yet threatened to take their camels to drink from the holy water stoops of St. Peter's.

All of this leads to the thought that the great transcontinental threats always come from monotheistic religions. Greeks and Romans didn't seek to conquer Persia or Carthage in order to impose their own gods. They had territorial and economic concerns, but from the religious point of view, as soon as they came across new gods in exotic countries, they welcomed them into their pantheon. You're Hermes?

Fine, I'll call you Mercury and you can become one of us. Did the Phoenicians worship Astarte? Well, the Egyptians translated her into Isis, and for the Greeks she became Aphrodite or Venus. No one ever invaded any land in order to stamp out the cult of Astarte.

The first Christians were martyred not because they recognized the god of Israel—that was their own business—but because they denied the legitimacy of other gods.

No polytheism has ever instigated a large-scale war to impose its own gods. That doesn't mean that polytheistic peoples haven't fought wars, but these were tribal conflicts that had nothing to do with religion. The barbarians of the north invaded Europe, and the Mongols invaded the lands of Islam, but not to impose their gods—in fact, they soon converted to the local religions. It's curious that the barbarians of the north, having converted to Christianity, and having established a Christian empire, then set off on crusades to force their god on Islamic peoples, even if in the end, monotheism for monotheism, it amounted to the same god.

The two monotheisms that have fought wars to impose one sole god have been Islam and Christianity. Among the wars of conquest I would include colonialism, which, economic interests aside, has always justified its conquests through the virtuous plan of Christianizing the conquered peoples, beginning with the Aztecs and the Incas, up to Italy's own "civilizing" of Ethiopia in the 1930s, conveniently forgetting that the Ethiopians were already Christians.

Jewish monotheism is a case in point. By its nature, it has never proselytized, and the wars described in the Bible were intended to secure a land for the chosen people, not to convert other populations to Judaism. Nor have the Jewish people ever incorporated other cults and beliefs.

With all this I don't want to suggest that it's more civilized to believe in the Great Spirit of the Prairie or the gods of the Yoruba than in the Holy Trinity or the Only God of whom Muhammad is the prophet. All I'm saying is that no one has ever tried to conquer the world in the name of the Great Spirit or of one of the gods in the Brazilian Candomblé ceremonies—nor has the voodoo Baron Samedi sought to urge his followers beyond the narrow bounds of the Caribbean.

One could say that only a monotheistic belief enables the formation of large territorial areas, which then tend to expand. The Indian subcontinent has never sought to export its own divinities. The Chinese empire covered a vast area yet had no belief in a single entity that had created the world, and so far it has never sought to expand into Europe or America. Perhaps China is doing that now, but through economic means, not religion. It is engaged in acquiring industries and stocks in the West, regardless of whether people there believe in Jesus, or in Allah, or in Yahweh.

Perhaps we can find an equivalent to the classic monotheisms in secular ideologies, such as Nazism, though its inspiration was pagan, and Soviet atheist Marxism. But with no military god to galvanize their followers, their war of conquest came to naught.

2014

A Good Education

Who gets cited most?

When we discuss the standards of Italian universities, the talk is about criteria used in other countries. One of these is to look at the number of times the works of a lecturer or candidate for a post have been cited in the academic press. Some institutions provide detailed figures, and this kind of check seems at first sight a good idea. But like all quantitative measures, it has its limits. It's rather like the idea that has also been proposed, and sometimes applied, of establishing the efficiency of a university on the basis of the number of graduates. A university that churns out a lot of graduates gives the appearance of being efficient, but it's easy to see the limitation of such statistics. You might have a very poor university that attracts many students by giving free credits and not being too strict about the quality of its theses, so a numbers criterion would then be of negative value. What about a university that has exacting standards and prefers to produce fewer, better graduates? A more reliable criterion, though also open to criticism, would be to compare the number of graduates with the number of students who enroll at the start of the course of study. A university that has only a hundred enrollees but produces fifty graduates would seem more efficient and exacting than another that has ten thousand enrollees and two thousand graduates.

So criteria that are merely quantitative have their shortcomings. Let's go back to the question of checking the number of citations. First let me say that this criterion may apply more to hard-science publications (mathematics, physics, medicine, etc.) than to those in the soft sciences, like the so-called social sciences. For example: I publish a book in which I show that Jesus was the true founder of Freemasonry —note that for a substantial sum, to be donated to charity, I could also provide an appropriate, up-to-date bibliography, though it would contain works that haven't been taken particularly seriously. If, however, I manage to find some apparently reliable supporting documentation, it would cause pandemonium in the field of historical and religious studies, and hundreds of essays would appear citing my work. Let's also assume that most of these essays cite my book in order to dispute it. Is there any quantitative control that discriminates between positive and negative citations?

What then can be said about a solid and well-argued book that has nevertheless stirred controversy and criticism, such as Eric Hobsbawm's book on the short twentieth century, and what criteria could be used to remove all citations by those who discuss it critically? And then, would we refuse Darwin a teaching post simply by demonstrating that over fifty percent of those who cited him, and who still cite him, did so and still do so in order to say he was wrong?

If the criterion is purely quantitative, we would have to accept that among the authors most cited over recent decades are Michael Baigent, Richard Leigh, and Henry Lincoln, who have written a book on the Holy Grail that became a bestseller. They have written a pile of rubbish, but they have been, and will be, frequently cited. If the criterion was quantity alone, a university that offered them a post in the history of religions ought to leap to the top of the charts.

Such doubts in relation to the soft sciences ought to be raised in many cases for the hard sciences. Stanley Pons and colleagues shook the world of science a few years ago with a much-criticized and probably false theory on cold fusion. They have been cited endlessly, almost always to refute them. If the criterion is only quantitative, we have to take them into serious consideration. Some people might argue that in such cases the quantitative criterion should apply only to journals of serious scientific value. But leaving aside that this itself would be a qualitative criterion, what do we do if these serious journals refute what the academics have said? Qualitative criteria would have to be introduced once again. I'd like, however, to see how much criticism Einstein received when he announced his general theory of relativity, and there again, let's take one of the most debated questions, whether what is known as the Big Bang actually happened. We know that eminent scholars have conflicting views. If a new theory appears that rejects the Big Bang, do we have to cross out all negative citations by those who still support this idea?

I say these things not because I have a ready-made solution, but to highlight how difficult it is to establish criteria of excellence on quantitative bases and how dangerous it is to introduce qualitative elements, which in the end were those used by Stalinist official culture to expel from the scientific community those who didn't subscribe to the principles of dialectical materialism or didn't take seriously the theories of Lysenko. Nor do I want to claim that no criteria exist. I wish only to point out how difficult it is to formulate them, and what a sensitive subject it is.

2003

Political correctness

Political correctness is a movement of ideas that grew out of the American universities, inspired by liberal, radical, and left-wing values, aimed at recognizing multiculturalism and reducing certain deep-rooted linguistic vices that led to forms of discrimination against minorities. The usage changed from "Negroes" to "blacks" and then "African Americans," and from the thousand pejorative words used against homosexuals to "gays." This campaign for the purification of the language inevitably produced its own brand of fundamentalism, including the more glaring cases of feminists who proposed that "history" should become "herstory," clearly ignoring the Greco-Latin etymology of the word, which makes no reference to gender.

The trend has also developed a neoconservative or openly reactionary complexion. If the decision is no longer to call people in wheelchairs "handicapped" or "disabled" but "differently abled," and no access ramps to public buildings are built, it simply means that the word has been removed but not the problem. There is also talk of replacing "unemployed" with "indefinitely jobless," or describing someone who has been sacked as "in programmed transition between employments." Who knows why a banker doesn't feel embarrassed by his title and insist on being called a "savings operative." If the name is changed it may well be because there is something wrong with what that name denotes.

Edoardo Crisafulli deals with this and countless other problems in his book *Il politicamente corretto e la libertà linguistica* (*Political Correctness and Linguistic Freedom*), which examines the contradictions and the arguments for and against this trend, and what's more, it's most entertaining. Reading it made me think of the curious situation in our own country. While there's been a rapid explosion of political correctness elsewhere, in Italy there has always been far greater interest in political incorrectness. If, once upon a time, our politicians, reading from a piece of paper, had said, "It emerges that there is a generally agreed preference, not for a policy of parallel convergence, but for one that follows an asymptotic option that also eliminates individual points of interchange," today they would say, "Dialogue? Fuck those filthy sons of bitches!" It's true that at one time, in the first Communist social clubs, the adversary was branded as a "freeloader," and in parliament, during heated exchanges, the choice of language would be more unrestrained than a dockworker's, but these were instances when a certain form of behavior was accepted, as happened, too, in houses of ill repute, where the women were no more verbally restrained than a politician. Today, however, the insult is transmitted on television—a sign of Italy's unswerving faith in the values of democracy.

2004

Thoughts in fair copy

Ten days ago, Maria Novella De Luca and Stefano Bartezzaghi took up three pages of *La Repubblica* to reflect on the decline of handwriting. It's now clear that our children, with computers and text messages, no longer know how to write by hand except in awkward capitals. One teacher, when interviewed, said they also make many spelling errors, but that's a separate issue. Doctors know how to spell but write badly, and you can be an expert calligrapher and still not know how to spell accomodation.

I know children who attend good schools and have decent handwriting, but the articles I'm referring to mention fifty percent of children, and evidently I happen to know the other fifty percent. Curiously, the same thing applies to me in politics.

But the problem is that things began to go wrong long before the computer and the cell phone. My parents used to write with a slightly sloping hand, holding the paper at an angle, and their letters were minor works of art, at least by today's standards. It's very true that there was a general belief, probably promoted by those who wrote badly, that fine calligraphy was the art of simpletons, and it's clear that having a fine hand isn't necessarily a sign of great intelligence. Nevertheless, it was nice to read a note or document written as God used to intend.

My generation was taught to write neatly, and during our first months at elementary school we had to form our letters on rows of vertical sticks, an exercise that was later regarded as dull and repressive, though it taught us to keep our wrists firm in forming loops that were plump and round on one side and fine on the other, using delicate nibs manufactured by Perry & Co. But not always, since the pen often came out of the inkwell caked in a sticky goo that messed up our desks, exercise books, fingers, clothing—and took ages to clean up.

The problem began after World War II with the advent of the ballpoint pen. It's true that the first ones also made a great deal of mess, and the writing would smudge if you ran your finger over the last words you'd written, but there wasn't the same urge to write neatly. Even when it wrote cleanly, a ballpoint pen didn't have the same feel, style, or personality as the nib pen.

Why should we mourn the loss of fine calligraphy? Writing well and fast on a keyboard encourages swiftness of thought; the automatic spell checker generally, though not always, underlines errors; and using the cell phone encourages younger generations to write "HAND" instead of "have a nice day." Let's not forget that our forefathers would have been appalled to see us write "bus" instead of "omnibus," or "best" instead of "yours sincerely," and Cicero would have turned pale if he'd known that medieval theologians would one day write "*respondeo dicendum quod.*"

The art of calligraphy, it is said, teaches hand control and coordination between wrist and brain. Writing by hand means that each phrase has to be formed in the mind before it is written down, but in any event, handwriting, with the resistance of pen and paper, requires a slowing down of thought. Many writers, even when accustomed to writing with a computer, know that sometimes they'd prefer to carve like the Sumerians on a tablet of clay so as to think in peace.

Children will write more and more on their computers and cell phones. Yet those pursuits that civilization no longer sees as necessities are being rediscovered by humanity as sporting exercises and aesthetic pleasures. People don't need to get around by horse, but they still go to riding school; aircraft now exist, but many enjoy sailing like Phoenicians of three thousand years ago; there are tunnels and railways, but people still find pleasure clambering over alpine passes; in the age of email there are still collectors of postage stamps; people go to war with Kalashnikovs but enjoy the peaceful pursuit of fencing.

It would be a good thing for parents to send children to schools that teach fine calligraphy, and not only for them to learn something beautiful but also to advance their fine motor skills. Such schools exist —just search "calligraphy classes" on the Internet. And it's a skill that might provide good opportunities for someone without a steady job.

2009

Meeting face-to-face

Each autumn there's a proliferation of literary and philosophy festivals in Italy. Every city, it seems, wants a festival of its own, emulating the original success of the Mantua Literature Festival; each vies for the best minds, some of which move from festival to festival, but all in all the quality of speakers is fairly high. Newspapers and magazines are now beginning to get excited, not so much that such festivals are being held, but that they attract crowds large enough to fill a stadium, mostly young people from other cities who have come to spend a day or two listening to writers and thinkers. What's more, to run such events requires teams of young volunteers, who give their time in the same way their parents did in 1966 when they rescued books from the mud after the flooding of Florence.

I think it's therefore superficial and foolish of certain moralists to view these events as a sort of intellectual McDonald's and take culture seriously only when it's pursued by a select few. It's an interesting phenomenon, and we ought to ask ourselves why young people go to festivals rather than clubbing. Let no one say it amounts to the same thing, as I have never heard of a carful of kids on ecstasy crashing at two in the morning on their way back from a literary festival.

There is nothing new here, though there's been an explosion of interest in recent years. Back in the 1980s, Cattolica's town library, on the Adriatic coast, organized evenings with the title *Che cosa fanno oggi i filosofi* (*What Philosophers Are Doing Today*), and the audience came in droves from a radius of at least a hundred kilometers. Then, too, people were wondering what was going on.

Nor do I think this can be compared with the *cafés philosophiques* that thrive around Place de la Bastille in Paris, where people go on Sunday mornings to sip Pernod and indulge in simple and therapeutic philosophy, a less costly form of psychoanalysis. No, in the gatherings we are talking about here, people spend hours listening to academic discussions: they go, they stay, they come back.

There are only two kinds of explanation. One was discussed during those early gatherings at Cattolica: many young people are tired of lightweight entertainment, of journalistic reviews reduced, with a few honorable exceptions, to half a column or ten lines, of television stations that discuss books only after midnight, if at all. And so they welcome more serious initiatives. Those who go to festivals number in the hundreds, even thousands, but they still make up a small percentage of their generation. They are an elite, but they are a mass elite, whatever an elite might mean in a world of seven billion inhabitants. It is the least that a society can demand in the balance between those who determine their own lives and those who allow their lives to be determined by others.

Such cultural gatherings also show that new ways of virtual socialization are not enough. You can have thousands of Facebook contacts, but in the end, unless you're completely stoned, you realize there is no real human contact online, so you look for opportunities to share experiences and be face-to-face with people who think like you.

2013

The pleasure of lingering

When I gave the Norton Lectures at Harvard University some twenty years ago, I recalled that eight years previously they were to have been given by Italo Calvino, who died before he could write the sixth and final lecture. The texts were later published in English as *Six Memos for the Next Millennium*. As a tribute to Calvino I used his lecture in praise of quickness as a starting point, noting, however, that his enthusiasm for speed didn't negate the pleasures of lingering. So I devoted one of my lectures to the pleasures of lingering.

Lingering was something a certain Monsieur Humblot didn't approve of when he rejected Proust's *À la recherche du temps perdu* for the publisher Ollendorff: "I may be slow on the uptake," he wrote, "but I just can't believe that someone can take thirty pages to describe how you toss and turn in bed before falling asleep." A denial of the pleasures of lingering would thus prevent us from reading Proust. But apart from Proust, I mentioned a typical case of lingering in *The Betrothed* by Alessandro Manzoni.

Don Abbondio is on his way home, reciting his breviary, and he sees something he didn't want to see, namely, two bravoes waiting for him. Another writer would immediately have satisfied the reader's impatience and told us what happens. But Manzoni takes several pages here to explain who bravoes were, and having done so, he lingers on to describe how Don Abbondio fingers his collar and looks behind him to see whether anyone might come to his aid. And finally the author asks, anticipating Chernyshevsky: "What is to be done?"

Did Manzoni have to introduce those pages of historical detail? He knew perfectly well that the reader would be tempted to skip them, and every reader of *The Betrothed* has done just that, at least on a first reading. And yet, even the time required to turn the pages forms part of a narrative strategy. The delay increases the torment, not only of Don Abbondio but also of his readers, and makes the drama more memorable. And isn't *The Divine Comedy* also a story that lingers? The journey in Dante's dream might last a single night, but to reach the final apotheosis we have to work our way through a hundred cantos.

Anna Lisa Buzzola's book *Letteratura lenta nel tempo della fretta* (*Slow Reading in Hurried Times*) is about slow reading, but she doesn't just hope for the return to a more leisurely approach to reading. She links the problem to the question of speed in modern life and to recent anthropological studies, placing her subject at the center of a series of healthy practices that include the "slow food" movement.

When it comes to literature, the author examines the theories of Gérard Genette, Viktor Shklovsky, and others, and gives a full analysis of the works of Javier Marías, Ian McEwan, Gesualdo Bufalino, Erri De Luca, José Saramago, Milan Kundera, Philippe Delerm, Paolo Rumiz, and Alessandro Baricco. Honesty requires me to reveal that she also kindly refers to me and the pleasure of lingering over the infinity of lists in my books.

This analysis gives rise to a phenomenology of techniques in the art of lingering that makes the reader want to read more slowly, even if you have to linger over thirty pages to understand how someone can toss and turn in bed before falling asleep.

2014

On Books, Etc.

Is Harry Potter bad for adults?

I wrote an article about Harry Potter nearly two years ago, at a time when the first three novels had been published, and the English-speaking world was arguing over whether children might be morally harmed by such tales of magic, and might be tempted to take occult mumbo jumbo seriously. Now that the film version has transformed Harry Potter into a global phenomenon, I watched an Italian chat show a few weeks ago whose guests included a well-known wizard and a Catholic priest and exorcist. The wizard, dressed in a sorcerer's garb that not even Ed Wood would have used in one of his horror films, was very happy about this promotion of people like him, while the priest felt the Potter stories transmitted satanic ideas. Most of the panelists were levelheaded, and considered magic, black or white, to be drivel, though they felt that those who believe in it should be taken seriously, while the exorcist thought that every form of magic, black, white, or spotted, should be taken seriously, as the work of the devil.

If this is what we have come to, I think it's time to speak out for Harry Potter. It's true that these are stories about wizards and witches, and they have clearly been a success because children have always loved fairies, dwarfs, dragons, and sorcerers, yet no one has ever thought Snow White was the product of a satanic plot. The stories have become a success because their author, by clever calculation or astounding instinct, has managed to reproduce certain truly archetypal narrative situations.

Harry Potter is the son of two good and kind magicians murdered by the forces of evil, although at first he didn't know this. He has been brought up as an orphan in the house of a mean and tyrannical uncle and aunt, then discovers his true nature and vocation, and is sent to a school for young wizards and witches, where he has remarkable adventures. And here is the first classic plot structure: take a young and tender child, subject him to all manner of suffering, let him discover his noble background, his great destiny, and here you have not just the Ugly Duckling and Cinderella, but also Oliver Twist, and Rémi in Hector Malot's novel *Sans Famille*. Hogwarts School of Witchcraft and Wizardry, where Harry learns to make magic potions, mirrors British boarding schools where pupils play one of those Anglo-Saxon sports that fascinate readers on that side of the Channel because they can guess the rules, and fascinate continental readers because they can't. But another archetypal situation is that of Ferenc Molnár's novel *The Paul Street Boys*. There's also something of Vamba's novel *Il giornalino di Gian Burrasca*, with schoolchildren who join forces against eccentric, even wicked, teachers. What's more, the pupils play games on flying broomsticks, and here we also see Mary Poppins and Peter Pan. Finally, Hogwarts looks like one of those mysterious castles we read about in children's books where a group of boys in short trousers and girls with long golden hair manage to unmask the dealings of a dishonest official, a corrupt uncle, or a band of villains, and discover in the end a treasure, a lost document, a chamber of secrets.

While in Harry Potter books there are fearsome spells and gruesome animals (their stories aimed at youngsters brought up on cinema monsters and Japanese cartoons), those children nevertheless fight for good causes like so many Boy Scouts, and listen to virtuous teachers, producing much the same feel-good effect as Edmondo De Amicis's incomparable nineteenth-century children's classic, *Heart*.

Do we really imagine that children who read stories about magic will turn into adults who believe in witches, which was what our chat-show wizard and exorcist both thought, though from opposing poles? We all used to have a healthy fear of ogres and werewolves, but once we grew up we learned to fear the hole in the ozone layer rather than the poisoned apple. And when we were children we believed that babies were delivered by storks, but this hasn't prevented us, as adults, from finding a more convenient and agreeable way of producing them.

The real problem is not children brought up believing in Pinocchio's Fox and Cat who then have to learn about other, less fanciful villains. More worrying are those adults, perhaps the ones who didn't read stories of magic when they were children, who are persuaded by TV channels to visit readers of tea leaves or tarot cards, or attend black masses, or seek out crystal gazers, healers, table tilters, fake conjurers of ectoplasm, revealers of the mystery of Tutankhamen. And then, by believing in magicians, they trust even the Fox and the Cat.

2001

How to protect yourself from the Templars

I've just received two books about the Knights Templar. The first is a fat volume of three hundred pages, the other a mere sixty pages, neither of which is complete mumbo jumbo. This would be a strange way of introducing a biography of Julius Caesar or a history of the Pilgrim Fathers, but with the Knights Templar you have to be careful from the very start.

If you're a publisher who wants to make some money, get a hack writer to produce a book on the Templars. The more historically improbable the facts you put together, the more mystery-starved readers you'll find to buy it. But if you want to know whether a particular book on the Templars is to be trusted, look at the contents page. If it starts with the First Crusade and ends with the burning of the Templars at the stake in 1314, with no more than an appendix recounting later legends with a certain degree of skepticism, then the book is probably serious. If it confidently arrives at the Knights Templar of today, then it's a canard.

Unless, that is, the writer wants to give a historical account of how the myth began and was developed. The best documented work on this subject is still *La Franc-Maçonnerie templière et occultiste au XVIIIe et XIXe siècle* by René Le Forestier. Those who wish to follow the development of the myth in the tangled forest of contemporary occultism, among gnostic sects, satanic fraternities, spiritualists, Pythagorean and Rosicrucian orders, Illuminati, Freemasons, and UFO hunters, can read Massimo Introvigne's *Il cappello del mago* (*The Magician's Hat*). But if you want a good historical, balanced, and reliable summary, from the trial up to modern times, search out Franco Cardini's *I segreti del tempio: Esoterismo e Templari,* a supplement to *Storia e Dossier.* In any event, for the true history of the "real" Knights Templar, you'll also find it useful to read *Philippe le Bel* by Jean Favier, *Vie et mort de l'ordre du Temple, 1120–1314* by Alain Demurger, and *The Knights Templar and Their Myth* by Peter Partner.

Why have the Knights Templar inspired so many legends? Because their history is the stuff of serial fiction. Create an order of monastic knights, get them to carry out extraordinary warlike feats, make them vastly wealthy, find a king who wants to get rid of what has become a state within a state and who finds inquisitors ready to gather rumors here and there, some true and some false, and fit them into a terrible mosaic of conspiracy, foul crimes, unspeakable heresies, witchcraft, and a good dose of homosexuality. Then arrest and torture the suspects, let them know that the life of anyone who confesses will be spared, while those who declare their innocence will be burned at the stake. The victims themselves will be the first to justify your inquisitorial construction, and the legend that follows it.

The history of the order ends tragically at that point, and marks the beginning of other political and ideological trials that would follow, up to the present day. But after such brutal repression, inevitable questions arise: What happened to the Knights Templar who escaped execution? Did they end their days in some monastery trying to forget the whole terrible business? Or, being distrustful like all turncoats, did they reestablish themselves in a secret society that became more and more secretive and ramified through the centuries? The second hypothesis has no historical support, but can prompt endless games of historical fantasy.

On the Internet you'll find many modern orders of Knights Templar still active. There's no law to stop anyone appropriating a legend. Anyone can call themselves high priest of Isis and Osiris—after all, there are no longer any pharaohs to challenge them. So if you want historical fantasy, go to the sensationalist pseudo-historiography of Louis Charpentier's *The Mysteries of Chartres Cathedral,* or *Dante* by Robert L. John, which claims that Dante was a Knight Templar, and where you'll find such examples of argumentative style as: "Beatrice's 'limbs scattered in earth' ... are (we repeat) the numerous limbs, scattered throughout Italy, of the spiritual Knights Templar associations that the Most Noble Lady indicates with that plainly gnostic name."

But if this is what you're looking for, go straight to *The Holy Blood and the Holy Grail* by Michael Baigent, Richard Leigh, and Henry Lincoln for the most brazen example of historical fantasy. Their fanciful dishonesty is so evident that inoculated readers can amuse themselves in a game of bluff.

2001

The whiff of books

I've spoken twice in recent weeks about book collecting, and the audience on both occasions included many young people. It's difficult to talk about a personal passion for books. Once, in a radio interview, I said it's rather like being a pervert who makes love with goats. If you say you've spent a night with Naomi Campbell or with the beautiful girl next door, they follow you with interest, envy, or roguish delight. If you talk about the pleasurable experience of having intercourse with a goat, people become embarrassed and try to change the subject. Anyone visiting the home of a person who collects Renaissance paintings or Chinese porcelain is thrilled by such wonders. If he shows them a seventeenth-century book in duodecimo with reddened pages and says that you can count those who own a copy on the fingers of one hand, the visitor will look anxiously for an excuse to leave.

A bibliophile loves books, but not necessarily their contents. If you're interested in content, you can go to a library, whereas the bibliophile, though aware of the content, wants the object, and ideally he wants it to be the first off the printer's press. To such an extent that there are some bibliophiles—I don't agree, but I understand them—who won't cut the pages when they find an uncut book, so as not to violate it. Cutting the pages of a rare book would for them be like a collector of watches breaking open the case to look at the mechanism.

A bibliophile doesn't love *The Divine Comedy*; he loves a particular edition and a particular copy of *The Divine Comedy*. He wants to touch it, turn its pages, run his hands over the binding. In this sense he "converses" with the book as an object, for what the book has to say about its origins, its history, the countless hands through which it has passed. At times the book recounts its history through thumb-prints, marginal notes, underlinings, an autograph on the front page, even wormholes. And it has an ever finer history to tell when, after five hundred years, its virgin white pages still crackle between the fingers.

A book as object can tell a good story even when it's been around for only fifty years. I have a copy of *La philosophie au Moyen Âge* by Étienne Gilson, published in the 1950s, which I've owned since the days of my university thesis. The paper at that time was of poor qual-ity, and the book now falls apart each time I turn the pages. If it were simply a tool of my profession, I'd have no option but to look for a new edition, which can be found cheaply. But I want that copy, with its fragile antiquity, with its underlinings and notes in various colors marking the times I've reread it. Holding it reminds me of my years as a student and beyond, and therefore forms part of my memory.

Young people need to know this, since book collecting is generally considered a passion only for the rich. There are of course old books that cost millions (a first edition incunabulum of *The Divine Comedy* recently fetched 1.5 million euros), but those who love books are in-terested not just in antique tomes but in more recent books, which might be a first edition volume of modern poetry. Some readers col-lect complete sets of children's books. Three years ago I found a first edition of Giovanni Papini's 1931 satirical novel *Gog*, rebound but with its original cover, for 10 euros. It's true that ten years ago I saw a 1914 first edition of Dino Campana's *Canti orfici* in a catalog for 13 million lire (the equivalent of 6,500 euros)—evidently the poor man could afford to print only a few copies—but it's possible to build an im-pressive collection of twentieth-century literature for no more than a few meals at a restaurant. One of my students used to prowl the bookstalls collecting nothing but tourist guides from different periods. At first I thought it a bizarre idea, but using those booklets of faded photographs, he produced a magnificent thesis showing how the look of a particular city could change over the years. There again, a cash-strapped youngster can still browse the bookstalls of a city like Milan and find sixteenth- and seventeenth-century 16mo editions for the price of a good pair of sneakers, and, though not rare, they can still give something of the flavor of the time.

Book collecting is like stamp collecting. The great collector has items worth a fortune, but as a child I bought assorted packs of ten or twenty stamps from the newsstand and spent many evenings dreaming about Madagascar or the islands of Fiji, gazing at multicolored rectangles that were wonderful, though not rare. Ah, what nostalgia.

2004

Here's the right angle

It's generally believed that things are known by the way they are defined. In certain cases this is true, as with chemical formulas. Knowing that something is NaCl helps anyone who understands chemistry to see that it is composed of chlorine and sodium, and to conclude, even though the definition doesn't expressly say so, that it is salt. But the chemical definition doesn't tell us all we need to know about salt: that it is used for preserving and flavoring food, that it increases blood pressure, that it is extracted from the sea or from salt mines, and that it was more expensive and precious in ancient times than it is today. To discover all we know about salt, or all we need to know (leaving aside other details), we have to listen not so much to definitions, but to stories. Stories that, for those who really want to know everything about salt, also become marvelous tales of adventure, with caravans trailing along the salt road through the desert between the Mali Empire and the sea, or stories of the first doctors who bathed wounds in salt solution. In other words, our knowledge of science is just as interwoven with stories as any other knowledge.

A child has two ways of getting to know the world. One is called ostensive learning. He asks his mother what a dog is, and she points to a dachshund. The amazing thing is that the next day he can identify a greyhound as a dog, perhaps later going too far and including the first sheep he sees as a dog, though it is unlikely he'll fail to recognize another dog as a dog. The second way is not by definitions such as "the dog is a placental, carnivorous, fissiped, canine mammal," which, though taxonomically correct, means nothing to a child, but by some form of story: "You remember the day we went into Grandma's garden and there was an animal with . . ."

Children in fact don't ask what a dog or a tree is. They generally see them and somebody then explains what they are called. And that's when the question "Why?" emerges. It's not so difficult to understand that a beech and an oak are both trees, but the real curiosity arises with these questions: Why are they there? Where do they come from? How do they grow? What are they for? Why do they lose their leaves? This is where stories come in. Knowledge is spread through stories: a seed is planted, it germinates, and so on.

And the real "thing" that children want to know, namely, where babies come from, can only be told in the form of a story, whether it's about the birds and the bees, or about Daddy who gives a seed to Mommy.

I'm among those who believe that scientific knowledge should take the form of stories, and I always refer my students to a fine passage by Charles Sanders Peirce. In defining lithium, he describes in twenty lines the process for its extraction in the laboratory, which I think of as a purely poetic description. One day I witnessed this wonderful process and felt as if I were in an alchemist's lair, and yet it was true chemistry.

At a conference on Aristotle, my friend Franco Lo Piparo pointed out that Euclid, the father of geometry, doesn't define a right angle as an angle of ninety degrees. If we think about it, that definition is correct, but of course it's useless for anyone who doesn't know what an angle is, or doesn't know what degrees are, and I hope that no parents will ever undermine their children by telling them that angles are right angles if they are at ninety degrees.

This is how Euclid explains it: "When a straight line standing on a straight line makes the adjacent angles equal to one another, each of the equal angles is right, and the straight line standing on the other is called a perpendicular to that on which it stands."

Got it? You want to know what a right angle is? I'll tell you how to make one, or rather, I'll tell you the story of what steps you take to arrive at it. Then you'll understand. Besides, you can learn what steps to take later, after you've constructed that marvelous intersection between two straight lines.

To me this seems both instructive and highly poetic. It brings us closer to the universe of imagination, where to create stories we imagine worlds, and to the universe of reality, where to understand the world we create stories.

Why have I told you all this? Because in my very first column, back in 1985, I told you I'd be talking about everything that came into my head, and this is what came into my head today.

2005

Journey to the center of Jules Verne

As children, we divided into two groups: supporters of Emilio Salgari and those who supported Jules Verne. I admit that I supported Salgari, and history makes it imperative for me to reassess the opinions I once held. It seems that Salgari, though an author who is still read, quoted from memory, and adored by all the Italians who read him when they were young, no longer attracts the younger generation. And in truth, even adults, when they reread him, either do so with a hint of nostalgia and wry amusement, or find him hard going and the excess of mangroves and babirusas tiresome.

Now, in 2005, we are celebrating the centenary of the death of Jules Verne, and newspapers, magazines, and conferences, not just in France, are reappraising him, demonstrating how often his imaginings anticipated reality. A glance at publishers' catalogs in Italy suggests that Verne is republished more frequently than Salgari, which is also the case in France, where there is an antiquarian book trade devoted to him, due no doubt to the old Hetzel bindings of Verne that are of great beauty. In Paris, there are two shops on the Right Bank alone devoted to these splendid volumes bound in red and gold, which fetch prohibitive prices.

Whatever merit we must concede to Salgari, the creator of the pirate Sandokan didn't have a great sense of humor, nor did his characters, with the exception of Yanez, whereas Verne's stories are full of humor. Suffice it to recall the splendid pages of *Michael Strogoff; or, The Courier of the Czar*, where, after the battle of Kolyvan, the *Daily Telegraph* correspondent Harry Blount, to prevent his rival Alcide Jolivet from sending his dispatch to Paris, keeps the telegraph office busy by dictating verses of the Bible at a cost of several thousand rubles, until Jolivet manages to steal his position at the telegraph counter, transmitting songs by Pierre-Jean de Béranger. Verne's story continues: "'Hallo!' said Harry Blount. 'Just so,' answered Alcide Jolivet." Tell me this isn't style.

Many stories that anticipate the future, when read after a space of time, perhaps when the future they had forecast has already arrived, are somewhat disappointing, since the events that have actually occurred, the real inventions, are infinitely more amazing than what the writer had once imagined. Not with Verne. No atomic submarine will ever be as technologically amazing as the *Nautilus*, and no airship or jumbo jet will ever have the fascination of Robur the Conqueror's majestic propeller ship.

A third merit, for which author and publisher share equal credit, are the engravings that accompany the stories. We followers of Salgari fondly recall the marvelous illustrations by artists like Alberto Della Valle, Pipein Gamba, and Gennaro Amato, but they were paintings, and it was like seeing a Raphael in black and white. Verne's engravings are far more mysterious and intriguing, and they make you want to examine them through a magnifying glass.

Captain Nemo, who sees the giant octopus from the large porthole of the *Nautilus*; Robur's airship bristling with high-tech masts; the balloon that crashes down on the Mysterious Island ("Are we rising again?" "No. On the contrary." "Are we descending?" "Worse than that, captain! We are falling!"); the enormous projectile that points toward the Moon; the caves at the center of the Earth—all are images that emerge from a dark background, outlines with thin black strokes alternating with whitish gashes, a universe without areas of uniform color, a vision scratched and scored, reflections that dazzle for lack of any strokes, a world seen by an animal with a retina all its own, as seen perhaps by oxen or dogs or lizards, a world glimpsed at night through the thin slats of a venetian blind, a territory always rather nocturnal and almost subaqueous, even in full daylight, made with the dots and abrasions that generate light only where the engraver's tool has dug or left the surface in relief.

If you don't have the money to buy Hetzel antiquarian editions, and you're not convinced by the modern republished versions, go to http:// jv.gilead.org.il/. Someone by the name of Zvi Har'El has collected all there is about Verne, with a complete bibliography, an anthology of essays, 488 incredible images of Jules Verne postage stamps from various countries, Hebrew translations (Mr. Har'El is Israeli, and fondly dedicates the site to his son, who died at the age of nineteen), but above all a "Virtual Library" where you'll find Verne's complete works in numerous languages, with all the engravings, at least from the original French editions, which you can save and enlarge as you wish, so that, though somewhat grainy, they become even more fascinating.

2005

Corkscrew space

Some might think it bad form for me to review a book for which I've written the preface. But while a review is expected to be objective and not tainted by personal interests, these fortnightly articles are by definition an expression of my personal interests, curiosity, and preferences. If I've written the preface for a book, it means I like it, and so I'm going to talk about it. The book is called *Elementare, Wittgenstein!* (*Elementary, Dear Wittgenstein!*) by Renato Giovannoli, which, despite its jaunty title, is both serious and demanding.

Giovannoli has also written one of the most fascinating "scientific" books, *La scienza della fantascienza* (*The Science in Science Fiction*), a thorough survey of the many fictional scientific ideas that circulate in mainstream science-fiction stories (the laws of robotics, the nature of aliens and mutants, hyperspace and the fourth dimension, time travel and temporal paradoxes, parallel universes, and so forth). These ideas display unexpected consistency, as though they constituted a system, equal in its uniformity and implications to that of science. This is no surprise: first, because science-fiction writers read each other's books, and certain themes move from story to story, and various precepts have been created that run parallel to official science; second, because storytellers don't develop their fictional tales in opposition to the solutions of science, but take science to its furthest conclusions; and finally, because some of the notions aired by science fiction, from Jules Verne onward, have later become scientific realities.

Giovannoli now applies the same criteria to the archipelago of crime literature, and suggests that the methods used by detectives in fictional narratives are similar to those of philosophers and scientists. The idea itself is not new, but the novelty here lies in the extent and rigor with which it is developed, so that we might wonder, in the end, what Giovannoli is doing—whether his book is a philosophy of detective fiction or whether it's a philosophy manual that uses examples of reasoning found in detective fiction. As I'm not sure whether to recommend it to those wanting to understand crime fiction or those wanting to understand philosophy, I'll play it safe and recommend it to both.

We can see, therefore, that not only do crime writers know about problems in philosophy and science (see the pages on the relationship between Dashiell Hammett, topology, and the theory of relativity), but also that certain thinkers may not have thought as they did if they hadn't read detective stories. We can see what benefit Wittgenstein's later ideas had gained from his reading hard-boiled novels.

I don't know whether philosophy comes before the detective novel —after all, *Oedipus Rex* is the story of a crime investigation. But certainly, from the Gothic novel and Edgar Allan Poe onward, crime fiction has perhaps influenced academic thinkers more than we realize. Giovannoli demonstrates with logical formulas and diagrams that the evolution of the crime story from crime investigation to crime action is similar to the evolution from Wittgenstein's *Tractatus Logico-Philosophicus* to his *Philosophical Investigations:* the transition from a paradigm of deduction (which envisages an ordered world, a Great Chain of Being that can be explained in terms of almost fixed relationships between causes and effects and ruled by a sort of preestablished harmony for which the order and association of ideas in the detective's mind reflect the order and associations governing reality) to a "pragmatist" paradigm in which the detective, rather than going back to the causes, provokes the effects.

The investigative crime story is certainly a small-scale model of metaphysical research, since both end up with the question "Who did this?," which is the philosophical version of the whodunit. G. K. Chesterton described the detective story as a symbol of higher mysteries, and Gilles Deleuze maintained that a book on philosophy ought to be a kind of detective story. What are Saint Thomas Aquinas's five ways to demonstrate the existence of God if not a model of investigation, following the tracks left by Someone? But there's also an implicit philosophy in the hard-boiled novel. Look at Pascal and his wager: let's try shuffling the cards, then see what happens. The stuff of Philip Marlowe or Sam Spade.

I'd like to mention the paragraphs that discuss the possible relationships between Agatha Christie and Heidegger. Giovannoli is not suggesting that *And Then There Were None* (1939) had influenced *Being and Time* (1927), even though Agatha Christie's earlier use of time paradoxes could have inclined him in that direction. But I certainly think the suggestion that Christie's writing contains an idea of "being-toward-death," drawn from medieval sources, is a masterstroke. A final recommendation: read the pages on Hammett and corkscrew-shaped space.

2007

On unread books

I recall, though my recollection may be faulty, a magnificent article by Giorgio Manganelli explaining how a sophisticated reader can know whether a book is worth reading even before he opens it. He wasn't referring to the capacity often required of a professional reader, or a keen and discerning reader, to judge from an opening line, from two pages glanced at random, from the index, or often from the bibliography, whether or not a book is worth reading. This, I say, is simply experience. No, Manganelli was talking about a kind of illumination, a gift that he was evidently and paradoxically claiming to have.

How to Talk About Books You Haven't Read, by Pierre Bayard, a psychoanalyst and professor of literature, is not about how you might know not to read a book, but how you can happily talk about a book you haven't read, even to your students, even when it's a book of extraordinary importance. His calculation is scientific. Good libraries hold several million books; even if we read a book a day, we would read only 365 a year, around 3,600 in ten years, and between the ages of ten and eighty we'll have read only 25,200. A trifle. On the other hand, Italians who've had a good secondary education know perfectly well that they can participate in a discussion—let's say on Matteo Bandello, Francesco Guicciardini, or Matteo Boiardo, on the tragedies of Vittorio Alfieri, or on Ippolito Nievo's *Confessions of an Italian*—knowing only the name and something about the critical context, but without ever having read a word.

And critical context is Bayard's crucial point. He declares without shame that he has never read James Joyce's *Ulysses*, but that he can talk about it by alluding to the fact that it's a retelling of the *Odyssey* (which he also admits never having read in its entirety), that it is based on an internal monologue, that the action unfolds in Dublin during a single day, etc. "As a result," he writes, "I often find myself alluding to Joyce without the slightest anxiety." Knowing a book's relationship to other books often means you know more about it than you do on actually reading it.

Bayard shows how, when you read certain neglected books, you realize you're familiar with their contents because they have been read by others who have talked about them, quoted from them, or have moved in the same current of ideas. He makes some extremely amusing observations on a number of literary texts that refer to books never read, including ones by Robert Musil, Graham Greene, Paul Valéry, Anatole France, and David Lodge. And he does me the honor of devoting a whole chapter to my *The Name of the Rose*, in which William of Baskerville demonstrates a familiarity with the second book of Aristotle's *Poetics* while holding it in his hands for the first time. He does so for the simple reason that he infers what it says from some other pages of Aristotle. I'm not citing this passage out of mere vanity, though, as we shall see at the end of this article.

An intriguing aspect of this book, which is less paradoxical than it might seem, is that we also forget a large percentage of the books we have actually read, and indeed we build a sort of virtual picture of them which consists not so much of what they say, but what they have conjured up in our mind. So that if someone who hasn't read a book then cites nonexistent passages or situations from it, we are ready to believe that they are in the book.

Bayard is not interested so much in people reading other people's books as in the idea—and here is the voice of the psychoanalyst rather than the professor of literature—that every reading, or nonreading, or imperfect reading, must have a creative aspect, and that, to put it simply, readers have to do their own bit. And he looks forward to the prospect of a school where students "invent" books they don't have to read, since talking about unread books is a means to self-awareness.

Except that Bayard demonstrates how, when someone talks about a book he or she hasn't read, even those who have read it don't realize what he or she has said about it is wrong. Toward the end of his book he admits he has introduced three false pieces of information in his summaries of *The Name of the Rose*, Graham Greene's *The Third Man*, and David Lodge's *Changing Places*. The amusing thing is that, when I read them, I immediately noticed the error regarding Graham Greene, was doubtful about David Lodge, but didn't notice the error in my own book. This probably means that I didn't read Bayard's book properly, or alternatively, and both he and my readers would be entitled to suspect this, that I merely skimmed through it. But the most interesting thing is that Bayard has failed to notice that, in admitting his three intentional errors, he implicitly assumes that one way of reading is more correct than others, so that he carries out a meticulous study of the books he quotes in order to support his theory about not reading them. The contradiction is so apparent that it makes one wonder whether Bayard has actually read the book he's written.

2007

On the obsolescence of digital media

Last Sunday, at a conference in Venice, there was a discussion about the transient nature of digital media. The Egyptian stele, the clay tablet, papyrus, parchment, and of course the printed book have all been media for information. The last of these, the book, has managed to survive well for five hundred years, though only when made with rag paper. From the mid-nineteenth century there was a move toward wood pulp paper, which seems to have a maximum life of seventy years—try handling newspapers or books produced shortly after World War II and you'll discover how many of them disintegrate as soon as you turn the page. For some time, therefore, conferences and researchers have been looking for ways to save the books that cram our libraries. One of the most popular ways, though it's almost impossible for every book in existence, is to scan and transfer each page onto electronic media.

But this raises another problem. Every medium used for transferring and conserving information, whether the film reel, the disk, or the USB memory stick we use with our computers, is less durable than the book. We know about some of these: the old audiocassette tapes would unravel after a while and we'd try rewinding them, often unsuccessfully, by sticking a pencil in the hole; videocassettes easily lost their color and definition, and soon got damaged if they were wound back and forth. We had long enough to find out how well a vinyl record would fare before it became scratched, though we didn't have time to find out how long a CD would last. Having been welcomed as an invention that would replace the book, the CD disappeared as soon as the same content became available more cheaply online. We don't know how long a film will last on DVD; we know only that it sometimes starts skipping when we use it too many times. Likewise, we didn't have enough time to discover how long floppy disks would last: before we could find out, they were replaced by rigid diskettes, and then by rewritable disks, and then by USB memory sticks. The disappearance of these media has led to the disappearance of the computers that can read them. I don't suppose anyone has a computer at home with a slot for a floppy disk, and unless all files on the previous support have been transferred to the later support, and this every two or three years, presumably forever, then the information is irretrievably lost, unless we keep a dozen or so computers in the attic, one for each obsolete file-storage method.

This means that all mechanical, electrical, and electronic media have either been shown to deteriorate rapidly, or we don't know and will probably never know how long they would have lasted.

Finally, it only requires a power surge, lightning, or some other trivial incident to demagnetize a memory card. During a fairly prolonged blackout I would be prevented from using any electronic memory. Though I have all of *Don Quixote* in my electronic memory, I would not be able to read it by candlelight, in a hammock, on a boat, in the bath, or on a swing, whereas I can read a book in the most adverse conditions. If I drop my computer or e-book from the fifth floor, I would certainly lose everything, but if I drop a book, at worst it would fall apart.

Modern media seem to be aimed more at the broadcasting of information than its conservation. Yet the book was a prime instrument not just for broadcasting information—think of the role played by the printed Bible in the Protestant Reformation—but also for conserving it. It's just possible that in a few centuries' time, once all electronic media have become demagnetized, a fine incunabulum will be the only way of finding out about the past. And the modern books that survive will be those that are printed on the best quality acid-free paper.

I'm no traditionalist. On a 250-gigabyte portable hard disk I've recorded the greatest masterpieces of world literature and the history of philosophy; there it's much easier and quicker to find a quote from Dante or the *Summa Theologiae* than to go to a top shelf and take down a heavy volume. But I'm happy those books are still there on my shelves, useful backups for the time when electronic instruments eventually pack up.

2009

Festschrift

In academic jargon a Festschrift is a volume of learned contributions prepared by friends and students to celebrate a scholar's birthday. This volume can be a collection of specific studies about the person in question, in which case, if a great effort is required from those taking part, there's a danger that the contributions will be from faithful students rather than eminent colleagues, who have little time or inclination to carry out such a demanding task. Alternatively, in order to attract famous names, the essays may be on any topic, and the volume will not be "about Joe Bloggs" but "in honor of Joe Bloggs."

In practical terms it's easy to imagine how an essay written for a Festschrift gets lost, especially in the latter case, since no one will know that you've written on the specific topic in a publication of that kind. In any event, it's a sacrifice that contributors may willingly make, perhaps hoping they can recycle what they've written elsewhere. Except that the Festschrift used to be presented when the subject reached sixty, a reasonably good age, and if all went well he'd die before seventy. Today, thanks to medical advances, the subject is in danger of living to ninety, and his students will have to write a Festschrift for him when he reaches sixty, seventy, eighty, and ninety.

Moreover, since international links have been strengthened over the past half century and each academic has many more close colleagues than used to be the case, the average academic receives at least twenty or thirty requests a year for volumes celebrating colleagues throughout the world who have happily reached ages of biblical proportions. If we bear in mind that a paper written for a Festschrift, if it's not to look too mean, must be at least twenty pages long, each academic would be writing an average of six hundred pages a year, every page ideally original, to celebrate those long-lived and much-loved friends. The demands are clearly impossible, yet a refusal might be mistaken for lack of respect.

There are two ways of avoiding this quandary. Establish that a commemorative volume is produced only for those who have reached eighty and beyond, or alternatively, do as I do and send the same essay for every Festschrift, altering the first ten lines and the conclusion. No one has ever noticed.

2010

The Catcher in the Rye fifty years on

After the recent death of J. D. Salinger, I read numerous reminiscences on *The Catcher in the Rye* and noticed that they fell into two categories: the first were fond accounts of how reading the novel had been a marvelous adolescent experience, and the second were critical reflections by those who, being too young or too old, had read it as you might read any other novel. Those latter readers were puzzled, and questioned whether *The Catcher in the Rye* would remain part of literary history or would represent a phenomenon attached to a single period and generation. Yet no one raised such issues on rereading *Herzog* when Saul Bellow died, or *The Naked and the Dead* on the death of Norman Mailer. Why then *The Catcher in the Rye*?

I think I'm an ideal guinea pig when it comes to answering this question. The novel came out in 1951, and was published in Italian the following year with the none-too-encouraging title *Vita da uomo* (*A Man's Life*). It went unnoticed and achieved success only in 1961, when it was published under the title *Il giovane Holden* (*The Young Holden*). It's therefore the Proustian madeleine for Italian adolescents of the 1960s. By that time I was thirty, reading James Joyce, and Salinger passed me by. I eventually read it some ten years ago, almost out of professional duty, and was left unmoved. Why?

First, because it didn't bring back to me any adolescent passion. Second, the youthful language Salinger had used with such originality was now obsolete—youth-speak, as we know, changes from month to month—and therefore it had a false ring. Finally, the "Salinger style" had had such a success since the 1960s, and reappeared in so many other novels, that it was bound to seem mannered, and neither original nor provocative. The novel had lost its interest because of its success.

This leads me to wonder just how much the "success" of a work depends on the circumstances, the historical context in which it appears, and on its relevance to the reader's own life. Here's an example on another level: I don't belong to the *Tex* generation, and I'm always surprised when I hear people say that they grew up with the Tex Willer legend. The explanation for this is simple: *Tex* first appeared in 1948, and at that time I was already in secondary school and had stopped reading comics. When I went back to reading them, around the age of thirty, it was the time of Charlie Brown, when classics such as *Dick Tracy* and *Krazy Kat* were being rediscovered, and the beginning of the great Italian comic book tradition, with artists like Guido Crepax and Hugo Pratt. Similarly, I remember the early comics of Benito Jacovitti, such as *Pippo, Pertica e Palla* of the 1940s, and not *Cocco Bill,* which came much later.

But we must be careful not to reduce everything to a personal level. Someone might loathe *The Divine Comedy* because at the time they were studying it they were desperately disappointed in love, but this could happen just as well with a Totò film. We mustn't indulge, however, in the pseudo-deconstructionist vice of thinking that a text has no meaning and it all depends on the way the reader interprets it. We might feel sad recalling *Totò, Peppino, and the Hussy* because our girl-friend left us the same day we went to see it, but this doesn't prevent us from reaching the objective conclusion that the scene in which Totò and Peppino write the letter to Marisa is a masterpiece of comic timing and effect.

If, then, the artistic value of a work can be assessed independently of the way in which we ourselves receive it, there remains the question of why it became successful or unsuccessful at a particular moment in time. To what extent can the success of a book be linked to the period and cultural context in which it appears? Why did *The Catcher in the Rye* fascinate young Americans in the early 1950s but have no effect at the time on young Italians, who came to discover it only ten years later? It's not enough to suggest that its Italian publisher the second time around had greater prestige and editorial power than the first.

I could name many works that achieved vast popular success and critical acclaim that they wouldn't have enjoyed had they been published ten years before or after. Certain works have to arrive at the right moment. And as we've known since the times of Greek philoso-phy, "the right moment," or *kairòs*, is a serious issue. To state that a work appears or doesn't appear at the right moment doesn't mean we can explain why a particular moment is right. It's one of those intrac-table problems, like predicting where a ping-pong ball thrown into the sea on Monday will fetch up on Wednesday.

2010

Aristotle and the pirates

The Invisible Hook: The Hidden Economics of Pirates, a curious book by Peter Leeson, has just been published in Italian. The author, an American historian of capitalism, explains the fundamental prin-ciples of economics and modern democracy by taking as his model the crews of seventeenth-century pirate ships, like "the Black Corsair" or François l'Olonnese, with skull-and-crossbones flags, from which came the name *Jolie rouge,* which the English then mangled into Jolly Roger.

The author shows how buccaneering, with its iron laws that every decent pirate respected, was an "enlightened," democratic, egalitarian setup open to diversity. In short, it was a perfect model for capitalist society.

Giulio Giorello also develops these themes in his introduction to the Italian translation. What I propose to discuss, however, is not so much Leeson's book but a few ideas that it brought to mind. Of course, the person who drew a parallel between pirates and merchants, free traders, the models for future capitalism, was Aristotle, though he could have known nothing about capitalism.

Aristotle is credited as the first to define metaphor—he did so in

Poetics as well as in *Rhetoric*—and in those first definitions he claimed that metaphor is not pure ornament but a form of knowledge. This seems no small thing, considering that over the following centuries the metaphor was long seen as merely a way of embellishing discourse without changing its substance. And some people still think so today.

In *Poetics* he said that to understand good metaphors implies "an eye for resemblances." The verb he used was *theoreîn,* which means to discern, investigate, compare, judge. Aristotle returned to this cognitive function of the metaphor more extensively in *Rhetoric,* where he maintains that what stirs admiration is pleasant because it allows us to discover an unexpected analogy. In other words, something is "brought before our eyes" that we had never noticed, so that we are prompted to say, "Look, that's exactly how it is, and I just hadn't realized."

We can see that Aristotle attributed an almost scientific function to good metaphors, though it was a science that didn't involve discovering something that was already there, but rather making it appear there for the first time by pointing to a new way of looking at things.

What was one of the most convincing examples of metaphor that brings something before our eyes for the first time? A metaphor—I've no idea where Aristotle came across it—in which pirates were called "purveyors" or "suppliers." As for other metaphors, Aristotle suggested that at least one shared property be identified for two apparently different and irreconcilable things, then the two different things would be seen as species of that same kind.

Even though merchants were generally regarded as good people who went to sea to lawfully transport and sell their goods, whereas pirates were scoundrels who attacked and robbed the ships of those same merchants, the metaphor suggested that pirates and merchants had a shared interest in the passage of goods from source to consumer. There is no doubt that, having robbed their victims, the pirates went off to sell the captured goods, and were therefore transporters, purveyors, and suppliers of goods, even if their customers could have been accused of receiving stolen property. In any event, that instant similarity between merchants and predators created a whole series of suspicions, causing the reader to think, "That's how it was, and previously I was wrong."

The metaphor required a reconsideration of the role of the pirate in the Mediterranean economy, but at the same time it led to suspicion about the role and methods of merchants. In short, that metaphor, in Aristotle's view, anticipated what Brecht would say later, that the real crime is not robbing a bank but owning one, and of course the good man from Stagira couldn't have known that Brecht's apparent jest would seem deeply disturbing in the light of what has happened recently in international finance.

We shouldn't imagine that Aristotle, councilor to a monarch, thought like Karl Marx, but you'll understand why this story about pirates amused me.

2010

Lies and make-believe

I've discussed lying in some of my recent articles because I was preparing to take part in the Milanesiana literary festival, whose theme this year was "lies and truth," and where I spoke about narrative make-believe. Is a novel a lie? On the face of it, when Alessandro Manzoni, in *The Betrothed,* tells us that Don Abbondio met two bravoes on the outskirts of Lecco, he was telling a lie because he knew perfectly well it was an invention. But Manzoni had no intention of lying: he was pretending that what he was recounting had actually happened and was asking us to participate in his pretense, in the way a child who grabs a stick pretends it's a sword.

Narrative make-believe dictates, of course, that the make-believe is signaled from the word "novel" on the book cover, and from opening sentences such as "Once upon a time . . . ," but it often starts with a false indication of truth. An example: "Mr. Lemuel Gulliver . . . three years ago . . . growing weary of the concourse of curious people coming to him at his house in Redriff, made a small purchase of land, with a convenient house, near Newark . . . Before he quitted Redriff, he left the custody of the following papers in my hands . . . I have carefully perused them three times . . . There is an air of truth apparent through the whole; and indeed the author was so distinguished for his veracity, that it became a sort of proverb among his neighbours at Redriff, when any one affirmed a thing, to say, it was as true as if Mr. Gulliver had spoken it."

Look at the title page of the first edition of *Gulliver's Travels*. The name that appears there is not that of Jonathan Swift, author of a fictional story, but Gulliver's as author of a true autobiography. Perhaps readers are not deceived. Ever since Lucian's *True History*, exaggerated claims of truth tend to indicate fiction, but a story often mixes fantastical details with references to the real world in such a way that many readers lose their bearings.

They then take novels seriously, as if they were describing what really happened, and they assume the opinions of the characters are those of the author. I can assure you, as a novelist, that once sales have risen, let's say, above ten thousand copies, one moves from a readership used to reading narrative fiction to one that is indiscriminate and treats the novel as a sequence of true statements.

2011

Credulity and identification

Last week I noted that a large number of people, when they read novels, find it difficult to distinguish between reality and fiction, and tend to assume that the characters' feelings and thoughts are those of their author. As confirmation, I've found a website that records the thoughts of a number of authors, and among "the phrases of Umberto Eco" I find the following: "The Italian is an untrustworthy, lying, contemptible traitor, finds himself more at ease with a dagger than a sword, better with poison than medicine, a slippery bargainer, consistent only in changing sides with the wind." It's not that there's no truth to it, but it's one of those centuries-old commonplaces promoted by foreign writers, and appears in my novel *The Prague Cemetery*, written by a man who has expressed every kind of racist impulse using the most hackneyed clichés. I try to make sure my characters are never banal, otherwise I'd end up being attributed with such trite propositions as "You only have one mother."

Now Eugenio Scalfari, commenting in *L'Espresso* on a recent article of mine, raises a new issue. Scalfari accepts that some people confuse narrative fiction with reality, but thinks, and correctly thinks that I think, that narrative fiction can be more real than the truth, that it can inspire a sense of identification with and perception of historical phenomena, that it can create new ways of feeling, and so on. It's a point of view with which one can hardly disagree.

Narrative fiction, moreover, produces aesthetic effects. A reader can be perfectly aware that Madame Bovary never existed and still enjoy the way in which Flaubert constructs his character. But the aesthetic aspect takes us back to the "alethic" aspect—in other words, that notion of truth shared by logicians, by scientists, or by judges who have to decide whether or not a witness in court has given a correct version of events. They are two different aspects: woe betide a judge who is moved by a guilty man's lying in an aesthetically appealing manner; I was referring to the alethic aspect, since my line of reasoning started off from a discussion about falsity and lies. Is it false to say that a television conjurer can make your hair grow back? It's false. Is it false to say that Don Abbondio encounters two bravoes? From the alethic point of view, yes, but Manzoni isn't trying to tell us what he's narrating is true. He's pretending it's true and asks us to pretend too. He is asking us, as Coleridge suggested, to "suspend disbelief."

Scalfari quotes Werther, and we know how many young romantics killed themselves having identified with Goethe's protagonist. Did they perhaps believe the story was true? Not necessarily. We know that Emma Bovary never existed, and yet we are moved to tears by her fate. We recognize fiction as fiction, and yet we identify with the character.

Madame Bovary never existed, though we feel that many women like her have existed, and that we are also perhaps a little like her, and we learn something about life in general and about ourselves. The ancient Greeks believed that what happened to Oedipus was true, and used it as an opportunity to reflect upon fate. Freud knew well that Oedipus never existed, but he interpreted his story as a way of understanding how the unconscious works.

What happens to those readers who are totally incapable of distinguishing between fiction and reality? Their response produces no aesthetic effects, because they are so busy taking the story seriously they don't ask whether it's told well or badly, they make no attempt to learn from it, and they fail to identify with the characters. They simply exhibit what I would call a fictional deficit; they are unable to suspend disbelief. Since there are more such readers than we might imagine, this bears thinking about, because we know that all other aesthetic and moral questions elude them.

2011

Who's afraid of paper tigers?

In the early 1960s, Marshall McLuhan had forecast various drastic changes in our way of thinking and communicating. One of his intuitions was that we were entering the era of the global village, and many of his predictions have certainly come true in the world of the Internet. But, having examined the influence of printing on the evolution of culture and our own individual sensibility in *The Gutenberg Galaxy*, McLuhan went on, in *Understanding Media* and other works, to predict the decline of alphabetic linearity and the rise to dominance of the image—in the simplest terms, what the mass media translated as "You no longer read. You watch television or the strobe images in a nightclub."

McLuhan died in 1980, when personal computers were being introduced into everyday life. The first models made little more than an experimental appearance in the late 1970s, but the mass market opened up in 1981 with IBM computers, and if he'd lived a few more years, he'd have had to admit that, in a world apparently dominated by the image, a new alphabetic culture was establishing itself. You can't do much with a personal computer unless you can read and write. It's true that young children can use an iPad these days even at preschool age, but all the information we receive via the Web, emails, and text messages is based on alphabetic knowledge. The computer fulfilled what had been predicted in Victor Hugo's *The Hunchback of Notre-Dame* by Archdeacon Frollo, who pointed first to a printed book, then to the cathedral decorated with images and other symbols that could be seen through the window, and said: "This will kill that." The computer has shown itself to be a global instrument with its multimedia links, and is capable also of bringing to life "that" image of the Gothic cathedral, but it is based fundamentally on principles that postdate *The Gutenberg Galaxy.*

With a return to the written word, the invention of e-books has also meant that texts can be read on a screen rather than on a printed page, prompting new forecasts about the disappearance of books and newspapers, suggested in part by a decline in sales. Every hack journalist's favorite sport for years has been to ask writers how they view the disappearance of printed paper. And it's not enough to claim that the book is still vitally important for moving and storing information, that we have scientific evidence that books printed five hundred years ago have survived remarkably well, whereas we have no scientific evidence to show that magnetic media currently in use can survive more than ten years, nor can we find out, given that today's computers can no longer read a 1980s floppy disk.

But the newspapers are now reporting disturbing developments whose significance and consequences we have yet to understand. Jeff Bezos, the head of Amazon, recently bought the *Washington Post,* and while the decline of the printed newspaper has been proclaimed, Warren Buffett recently acquired sixty-three local papers. As Federico Rampini observed in *La Repubblica,* Buffett is a giant of the old economy, and no innovator, but he has a rare acumen for investment opportunities. And other Silicon Valley wheeler-dealers appear to be moving into the newspaper trade.

Rampini wonders whether Bill Gates or Mark Zuckerberg might inflict the final blow by buying the *New York Times.* Even if this doesn't happen, it's clear that the digital world is rediscovering paper. Is all this commercial calculation, or political speculation, or a desire to preserve the press as a bastion of democracy? I don't feel I can yet attempt any interpretation of what's happening. But I think it's interesting that we are witnessing another reversal of prophecies. Perhaps Mao was wrong: beware of paper tigers.

2013

From Stupidity to Folly

No, it's not pollution, it's impurities in the air

With the winds of war blowing, we are in the hands of the most powerful man in the world, George W. Bush. Now, no one is claiming, as Plato did, that states should be governed by philosophers, but it would be good for them to be in the hands of someone with clear ideas. It's instructive to look at some sites on the Internet that have collected Bush's famous sayings. Among those sayings that have no date or place, I've found: "If we don't succeed, we run the risk of failure," "It's time for the human race to enter the solar system," "It isn't pollution that's harming the environment, it's the impurities in our air and water that are doing it."

To journalists: "I would have to ask the questioner. I haven't had a chance to ask the questioners the question they've been questioning" (Austin, Texas, January 8, 2001). "I think if you know what you believe, it makes it a lot easier to answer questions. I can't answer your question" (Reynoldsburg, Ohio, October 4, 2000). "The woman who knew that I had dyslexia—I never interviewed her" (Orange County, California, September 15, 2000).

Politics: "Illegitimacy is something we should talk about in terms of not having it" (May 20, 1996). "I believe we are on an irreversible trend toward more freedom and democracy—but that could change" (May 22, 1998). "I am mindful not only of preserving executive powers for myself, but for predecessors as well" (Washington, January 29, 2001). "We are ready to work with both parties to reduce the level of terror to a level acceptable to both sides" (Washington, October 2,

2001). "I know there is a lot of ambition in Washington, obviously. But I hope the ambitious realize that they are more likely to succeed with success as opposed to failure" (Associated Press interview, January 18, 2001). "The great thing about America is that everyone should vote" (Austin, December 8, 2000). "We want anybody who can find work to be able to find work" (*60 Minutes II*, CBS, December 5, 2000). "One of the common denominators I have found is that expectations rise above that which is expected" (Los Angeles, September 27, 2000). "It's very important for folks to understand that when there's more trade, there's more commerce" (Summit of the Americas, Quebec City, April 21, 2001).

Education: "Quite frankly, teachers are the only profession that teach our children" (September 18, 1995). "We're going to have the best educated American people in the world" (September 21, 1997). "I want it to be said that the Bush administration was a results-oriented administration, because I believe the results of focusing our attention and energy on teaching children to read and having an education system that's responsive to the child and to the parents, as opposed to mired in a system that refuses to change, will make America what we want it to be—a literate country and a hopefuller country" (Washington, January 11, 2001). "The public education system in America is one of the most important foundations of our democracy. After all, it is where children from all over America learn to be responsible citizens, and learn to have the skills necessary to take advantage of our fantastic opportunistic system" (May 1, 2002).

Science: "Mars is essentially in the same orbit . . . Mars is somewhat the same distance from the Sun, which is very important. We have seen pictures where there are canals, we believe, and water. If there is water, that means there is oxygen. If oxygen, that means we can breathe" (November 8, 1994). "For NASA, space is still a high priority" (September 5, 1993). "Natural gas is hemispheric. I like to call it hemispheric in nature because it is a product that we can find in our neighborhoods" (Austin, December 20, 2000). "I know the human being and fish can coexist peacefully" (Saginaw, Michigan, September 29, 2000).

Foreign countries: "We spent a lot of time talking about Africa, as we should. Africa is a nation that suffers from incredible disease" (press conference, June 14, 2001). "I [spoke] recently with Vicente Fox, the newly elected president in Mexico. He's a man I know from Mexico. I talked about how best to expedite the exploration of natural gas in Mexico and transport it up to the United States, so we become less dependent on foreign sources of crude oil" (first presidential debate, October 3, 2000). "The problem with the French is that they don't have a word for 'entrepreneur'" (discussion with Prime Minister Tony Blair). "Do you have blacks too?" (to President Fernando Cardoso of Brazil, April 28, 2002). "After all, a week ago, there were—Yasser Arafat was boarded up in his building in Ramallah, a building full of, evidently, German peace protesters and all kinds of people. They're now out. He's now free to show leadership, to lead the world" (Washington, May 2, 2002). "More and more of our imports come from overseas" (Beaverton, Oregon, September 25, 2000). "I understand that unrest in the Middle East creates unrest throughout the region" (Washington, March 13, 2002). "My trip to Asia begins here in Japan for an important reason. It begins here because for a century and a half now, America and Japan have formed one of the great and enduring alliances of modern times. From that alliance has come an era of peace in the Pacific" (Tokyo, February 18, 2002).

2002

How to get rich on other people's suffering

If you feel you're not making enough money and want to change jobs, clairvoyance is one of the best paid occupations and, despite what you might think, one of the easiest. All you need is a certain charm, a minimum understanding of others, and a certain amount of chutzpah. But even without such qualities, probability still works in your favor.

Try this experiment. Approach someone at random, though it's helpful if the person is well disposed toward your paranormal qualities. Look him or her in the eye and say: "I feel there's someone thinking of you very much, someone you haven't seen for many years, but who once loved you, and suffered because you hadn't reciprocated . . . and now that someone realizes how much you have suffered, and is sorry, though perhaps it's too late . . ." Is there anyone in the world, apart from a young child, who hasn't had an unhappy experience in love, or at least in love inadequately reciprocated? And so your subject will be the first to run to you for help, and cooperate, telling you that he or she knows exactly whom you've captured so clearly in your mind.

You can say: "There's a person who underestimates you, and speaks badly of you, but does so out of envy." It's most unlikely your subject will reply that he or she is admired by all and sundry and has absolutely no idea who this person could be. He is more likely to identify the person right away and admire your skill in extrasensory perception.

Alternatively, say that you can see a dear departed loved one standing beside your subject. Go up to someone of a certain age and tell him you see the shadow of an elderly person who has died of a heart ailment. Every living being has had two parents and four grandparents, and if you're lucky, several uncles and aunts and a beloved godparent as well. If your subject is of a certain age, it's likely these people will be gone, and probable that out of at least six dead relatives, one has died of heart failure. If you're unlucky, and since you've had the foresight to approach your subject in the company of others equally attracted by your paranormal gifts, you can say you're perhaps mistaken, that the person you see is not a relative of the person you're talking to, but of someone standing nearby. You can bet that one of those present will say that it's his or her father or mother, and at that point you're home and dry, you can talk of the warmth this shadow radiates, of the love it feels for that person, now ready for your enticement . . .

Discerning readers will have identified the techniques of the charismatic personalities who appear on television shows. Nothing is easier than to convince a parent who has just lost a child, or someone who's still grieving the death of a parent or spouse, that this good soul has not vanished into thin air and is still sending messages from the other side. I repeat, being a psychic is easy: other people's suffering and credulity work in your favor.

That is, of course, unless you're dealing with someone belonging to CICAP (the Italian Committee for the Investigation of Claims of the Pseudosciences). CICAP researchers investigate phenomena claimed to be paranormal (poltergeists, levitation, psychic phenomena, crop circles, UFOs, water divining, not to mention ghosts, premonitions, spoon bending, card reading, weeping Virgin Marys, and so forth), and they demonstrate how it's done, reveal the trick, explain scientifically what appears to be miraculous, often repeating the experiment to show, once the trick is understood, how we can all become magicians. Two CICAP sleuths, Massimo Polidoro and Luigi Garlaschelli, have published some of the results in a book, which makes for amusing reading.

But I hesitate to talk about amusement. The fact that CICAP has its work cut out means that gullibility is more widespread than we might think, and the book will in the end sell a few thousand copies, whereas someone like Rosemary Altea, when she appears on television, playing on people's suffering, has a following of millions.

2002

Miss World, fundamentalists, and lepers

Most readers, by the time they read this, may have forgotten about the Miss World riots in Nigeria, which have left more than two hundred people dead. And this would be reason enough not to let the matter drop. Or the situation may have deteriorated, even now that the Miss World contest has been moved to London, since it has become clear that the arrival of the contestants in Nigeria was merely a pretext for stirring up trouble or cultivating subversive plans of quite a different kind—indeed, it's hard to understand why anyone protesting against a beauty contest had to murder Christians and burn down churches, as the bishops could hardly be blamed for the initiative. But if things had gone ahead, it would have been all the more important to think about the pretext that led to the hideous fundamentalist reaction.

Wole Soyinka, the Nigerian Nobel Prize winner who suffered imprisonment for his attempt to defend the basic freedoms of his unfortunate country, has written an article, published in *La Repubblica,* in which, along with illuminating reflections on the troubles in Nigeria, he said that he felt no liking for the national and global beauty contests, but when faced with the anger of Muslim fundamentalists, he felt he had to defend the rights of women over their bodies and their beauty. I believe that if I were Nigerian I'd think like him, but it so happens I'm not, and I'd like to look at what took place from my own point of view.

To protest against a contest of young women in swimsuits by zealously killing over two hundred people who have nothing to do with it cannot be justified. Put this way, it's clear we're all on the side of the girls. I feel, though, that the organizers of Miss World, in deciding to hold the contest in Nigeria, have behaved appallingly. Not because they could or should have anticipated such protests, but because to hold a vanity fair, at a cost that would feed many tribes for a month, in a deprived country like Nigeria, where children are dying of hunger and women are stoned for adultery, is like publicizing porno films in a home for the blind, or handing out beauty products in a leper colony and publicizing them with photographs of Naomi Campbell. And don't tell me a beauty contest is a way of changing traditional customs and practices, since such encouragement comes, where appropriate, in homeopathic doses and not through blatant provocation.

The whole business, aside from the observation that it was an appalling decision clearly made for publicity purposes and with absolute cynicism, is of direct interest to us, especially now, since it relates to the issues surrounding globalization. I'm one of those who thinks that five out of ten aspects of globalization can be beneficial, but one negative aspect is the violent imposition of Western models on developing countries in order to encourage consumption and expectations that these countries cannot meet. In short, if I present you with a line of girls in swimsuits, it's to encourage you to buy Western swimsuits, perhaps sewn by starving children in Hong Kong—swimsuits that can also be bought in Nigeria by those who are not dying of hunger but have money to spend because they're making it on the backs of those who are dying of hunger, by those who are collaborating with Western-ers to exploit such people and hold them in a precolonial state.

So I wouldn't have been too sorry if, during the contest in Nigeria, the more aggressive antiglobal lobbies had arranged a gathering of the *Tute Bianche* and Black Bloc movements. The *Tute Bianche* could have peacefully, though firmly, seized the contest organizers, stripped them to their underwear like their contestants, smeared them with honey, covered them with feathers from ostriches and other local birds, and paraded them through the streets, making fun of them as appropri-ate. And the Black Bloc would have had to deal with the local fun-damentalists—accomplices of Western colonialism who are perfectly happy for their countries to remain underdeveloped—and could have used all their fighting skills to prevent them from carrying out their massacres, and perhaps we would all have applauded such warriors of peace (for once, and only once), not least because if you are violent, then you need to have the courage to pit your strength against worthy adversaries.

And the aspiring Miss Worlds? Perhaps, having been persuaded to join the more moderate ranks of the antiglobal movement, they might have been retrained to waggle their well-clothed buttocks once in a while around the village square, handing out cans of meat and bars of soap, along with antibiotics and cartons of milk. We'd have pro-nounced them to be truly magnificent.

2002

Return to sender

An old saying had it that war is too serious to be left to the mili-tary. These days it needs bringing up to date: the world has become too complex to be left to those who used to run it. As though the Manhattan Project for the atomic bomb were to be left to the engineers who had dug the Mont Blanc tunnel. I was thinking about such matters in Washington two weeks ago at the very instant a sniper was blithely shooting people who had stopped at a gas station or were leaving a restaurant. He was perched high up, with rifle and telescopic sight, working away on a highway intersection or a quiet hillside. The police turned up, closed the streets for two or three hours, but failed to find anyone, since the sniper had moved on. So people couldn't leave their homes or send their children to school for days afterward.

Some say this is happening because of the open sale of firearms, but the gun lobbies see it differently. It's not about possessing weapons but using them properly. As though shooting to kill were not a proper use of arms.

The Washington sniper was eventually caught. He had left his tracks everywhere. In the end people only want to get into the newspapers. But anyone not wanting to be caught could have carried on until he had killed more people than were massacred in the Twin Towers. This is why America was, and still is, in such a state of nerves: if a terrorist organization, rather than wasting time hijacking airplanes, let thirty or so snipers loose to wander about the whole country, it could paralyze the nation. And not only that: it would spark off a copycat contest among those who are not terrorists but would happily join the party.

What do those who are no longer able to run the world propose? To manufacture weapons that automatically "sign" the bullet and the cartridge case, so that the projectile removed from the body practically contains the assassin's address. It doesn't seem to have occurred to anyone that if I am intent on murder, I won't use my own gun, but one I've stolen. And if I'm a terrorist, I'll know people who are able to get hold of a gun stolen or manufactured outside America.

But that's not all. I read recently in *La Repubblica* that at the Federal Reserve they are worried about deflation: people are not spending as much, prices are falling, a crisis worse than in times of inflation. So they propose a perishable dollar—in other words, a banknote with a magnetic strip that gradually loses value, and also loses value if you keep it in the bank.

How would Mr. Smith, who works hard to earn a hundred dollars a day, respond? He would become less productive. Why should he flog himself working to earn something that gradually becomes worthless, and which he can't even put into his savings account toward the cost of a small house? He'll work hard enough to earn thirty dollars a day to buy himself a beer and a steak. Or he could invest his hundred dollars a day on useless items—T-shirts, pots of jam, pencils—that he could then use as barter: three pots of jam for a T-shirt. In the end, people would have to hoard a mass of useless stuff at home, while money would almost stop circulating. Or Mr. Smith could buy a small house, and pay for it in installments each time he has a hundred dollars to spare. Not only would the house, with interest and everything else, cost him ten times the price, but why would the current owner want to sell, since he would end up without a house and with lots of dollars that he has to spend fast? And so the construction industry would come to a standstill. And since the currency depreciates even when saved, who will put money in the bank?

All in all, the initiatives that are being taken, including the war in Iraq, to hold back the thousands of potential fundamentalist snipers, fall into the category of "the world has become too complex to be left to those who used to run it."

2002

Give us a few more deaths

La Repubblica recently carried the news that the French government had introduced a point system on driver's licenses, as has now been done in Italy, and in the course of one year the number of accidents had fallen, with fewer fatalities. Excellent news. But the president of the Groupement National des Carrossiers Réparateurs, an association of mechanics, having said that as a citizen he was of course pleased about the fall in the death rate, nevertheless, as a mechanic, he had to report that it was causing hardship to his members. Fewer accidents, fewer repairs. And it appears that as a result of this major economic blight, not only are mechanics in distress and asking for state assistance, but some are even urging less strenuous controls. In short, if the report is accurate, they're asking for fewer fines so that more cars get damaged.

I'm not suggesting for one moment that they are after more deaths, since those killed in road accidents don't, as a rule, take their cars to be repaired, and the next of kin ship them straight to the junkyard. Yet a few good collisions with no fatalities and limited injuries, and the car not being transformed into a coffin and written off, wouldn't be a bad thing.

Such reports shouldn't surprise us. Technological innovation, progress, has always produced unemployment, and it all began with the eighteenth-century weavers who smashed mechanical looms for fear of ending up without work. The advent of the taxi must have been disastrous for coachmen. When I was a child, I remember old Pietro being called with his buggy to take my family and our baggage to the railroad station. Public autos arrived a few years later, and he was too old to get a license and take up a new job as a taxi driver. But the pace of innovation at that time was fairly slow, and Pietro would have been close to retirement when he found himself jobless.

Today things are more hurried. I suppose longer life expectancy has caused difficulties for funeral directors and cemetery staff, except that the process has been gradual, and by the time they realized there were fewer sixty-year-olds to bury, they must already have been burying eighty-year-olds who hadn't died at seventy. Jobs in this line of work—thanks to that mother of all syllogisms, "All men are mortal" —should never be in short supply. If tomorrow scientists discover, perhaps not the secret of immortality but a drug that could suddenly extend the average life to 120 years, we might see funeral directors on the streets demanding financial assistance from the government.

The problem is that in an ever-increasing number of cases the acceleration of innovation will bring ruin to whole categories of labor. Just think of the 1980s crisis of typewriter repairers. Either they were youngsters bright enough to become computer experts, or they found themselves without work.

The challenge is therefore to provide professional training to ensure rapid reemployment. When mechanical looms were introduced, a weaver couldn't become a mechanical loom maker overnight. But machines today are more or less universal; their physical structure is far less important than the software programs that make them work; so a specialist capable of creating the program that operates a washing machine could fairly easily retrain to work on the program that regulates the dashboard of a car.

To deal with the prospect of accelerated reemployment, a large part of professional training will have to be intellectual development: learning about software more than about the machine's hardware, its structure, its physical components.

And so, rather than thinking about schooling that offers only two options, university or work, there ought to be an education system that ends just with qualifications in the humanities or sciences, because whoever ends up becoming, for example, a sanitation worker will need the intellectual training necessary to plan and program his or her own reemployment.

This is not an abstract democratic and egalitarian ideal. It's the same logic as that of working in a computerized society, which requires the same education for all and is modeled on the highest, not the lowest, standard. Otherwise, innovation will always and only produce unemployment.

2003

Speaking with license

Early in 1991 I wrote an article about the Gulf War in which I explained that "friendly fire" is "the bomb mistakenly tossed at you by some shit wearing the same uniform." After the recent case of Nicola Calipari, the Italian military intelligence officer killed by American soldiers, readers are perhaps more aware that people die from friendly fire. But in response to my article there was a great deal of protest not about the immorality of friendly fire but the immorality of the word "shit." As well as many letters from readers, I was also criticized by other newspapers so severely that I had to write another article about how many eminent writers had used words of a similar kind.

Practices change over time, and publishers can now print without fuss a translation of *On Bullshit* by Harry G. Frankfurt, an emeritus professor of philosophy at Princeton University.

"Bullshit" is generally applied to something claimed, said, communicated: "What you've said is bullshit," "That film is real bullshit."

Frankfurt considers the eminently semiotic interpretation of "bullshit" by starting off with a definition that another philosopher, Max Black, had given to "humbug": "deceptive misrepresentation, short of lying, especially by pretentious word or deed, of someone's thoughts, feelings, or attitudes."

American philosophers are generally sensitive to the problem of the truth of what we say, so they question whether it's true or false to say that Ulysses went back to Ithaca, even if Ulysses never existed. Frankfurt therefore sets out to determine, first, in what way bullshit is stronger than humbug and, second, what it means to provide a "deceptive misrepresentation" of something short of lying.

The only way of dealing with the second problem is to examine thoroughly all the authorities on the question, from Saint Augustine until today. Anyone who lies knows that what he's saying isn't true, and says it to deceive. Anyone who says something untrue without knowing it's untrue is not lying, poor thing, but is simply mistaken or mad. Let's say that someone claims, and believes, that the Sun goes around the Earth. We'd say he's talking humbug, or even bullshit. But according to Black's definition, anyone who talks humbug does so to provide a deceptive misrepresentation not only of external reality but also of his own thoughts, feelings, or attitudes.

This also happens to those who lie. If someone says he has a hundred euros in his pocket and it's not true, he is doing so not just to make us believe he has a hundred euros in his pocket, but also to persuade us that he believes it. But Frankfurt explains that the main purpose of a humbug, unlike a lie, is not to create a false belief in relation to the state of things, but rather to create a false impression about what is going on in the speaker's mind. Since this is the purpose of a humbug, it never reaches the level of a lie. To use an example given by

Professor Frankfurt: a president of the United States can use bombastic expressions about the Founding Fathers being guided by God, and he does so not to spread beliefs that he knows to be false, but to give the impression of being a pious man who loves his country.

The chief characteristic of bullshit, as opposed to humbug, is that it's a false statement proffered to make us believe something, but the speaker has no interest in whether what he's saying is true or untrue. "The fact about himself that the bullshitter hides . . . is that the truth-values of his statements are of no central interest." Our ears immediately prick up at statements such as this, and indeed Frankfurt confirms our worst suspicions: "The realms of advertising and of public relations, and the nowadays closely related realm of politics, are replete with instances of bullshit so unmitigated that they can serve among the most indisputable and classic paradigms of the concept." The aim of bullshit isn't even to misrepresent states of affairs; it's to create an impact on listeners barely capable of distinguishing between true and false, or those who have no interest in such subtleties. I think those who talk bullshit also rely on the poor memory of their listeners, which allows them to talk a continual and contradictory stream of bullshit: "However studiously and conscientiously the bullshitter proceeds . . . he is also trying to get away with something."

2005

Conciliatory oxymorons

Only a few years ago, when using the word "oxymoron" one had to explain what it meant. People would cite well-known examples such as "parallel convergences," and explain that an oxymoron is created when two contradictory words are put together, such as "strong weakness," "desperate hope," "gentle violence," "senseless meaning," and in Latin, *formosa deformitas, concordia discors,* and *festina lente.*

Now oxymorons are all the rage. They're often found in the press, and I've heard politicians talk about them on television. Either everyone's been reading treatises on rhetoric or there's something oxymoronic going around. It could be argued that this is not symptomatic of anything. Linguistic fashions are continually developing through laziness and imitation. Some last a morning, others survive longer. Young people in the 1950s used to say "beastly," and more recently "absurd," without referring in any way to zoology or Ionesco. "Wait a minute" became "wait a sec," though not because time had actually shortened; or people would say "exactly" rather than "I do" (even when they got married in church), not through any concern for mathematical accuracy but from the influence of television quiz shows.

I suspect, though, that the oxymoron has become more popular because we live in a world that has seen the disappearance of ideologies that sought, at times ineptly, to reduce contradiction and impose an unambiguous view of things. Debates are held from contradictory positions. If you want a glaring example, we have Virtual Reality, which is rather like Concrete Nothing. Then there are Intelligent Bombs, which appears not to be an oxymoron, though it is when we consider that a bomb, by its very nature, is stupid and ought to fall where it's thrown —otherwise, if it does what it pleases, it risks becoming Friendly Fire, a magnificent oxymoron, if by fire we mean something brought about to harm someone who is not a friend. The Exportation of Freedom seems fairly oxymoronic, if freedom is by definition something that a population or a group earns through personal determination and not through imposition by others. If we think about it, there's also an implicit oxymoron in Conflict of Interests, since it can be interpreted as

Private Interest Pursued for the Public Good, or Common Interest Pursued for Particular Personal Advantage.

I'd like to point out that the Global Mobilization of the Antiglobal Movement is oxymoronic, as are the Peace Army and Humanitarian Intervention, if intervention means, as it does, a series of warlike activities in someone else's country. I see more of them closer to home, judging from the electoral program of a Fascist Left, and I think Clerical Atheists are fairly oxymoronic. I wouldn't exclude expressions that we've become quite familiar with, such as Artificial Intelligence and Electronic Brain, if the brain is something soft within our skull, and don't forget Embryos with Souls. Likewise, to remain bipartisan, I think a proposal put forward by the center-left for Compulsory Community Service Volunteers is just as oxymoronic.

In short, when people can no longer make sense of ideas that are incompatible, they resort to Conciliatory Oxymorons to give the impression that what cannot coexist coexists—the peace mission in Iraq, the Italian laws against the judiciary, politics on television and farces in the chambers of parliament, the banning of unauthorized satire, retrospective prophecies such as the third secret of Fátima, Arab kamikazes, former student activists of the 1960s who work for Berlusconi, liberal populism. And lastly, same-sex marriage virtuously opposed by cohabiting divorcées.

2006

The human thirst for prefaces

What I'm going to talk about happens not just to me, but to all who have published books or articles and enjoy a certain authority in their field. And you don't have to think only of great poets, Nobel Prize winners, or emeritus professors. I believe, indeed I know, that the same is true of head teachers of provincial secondary schools, who may never have published anything but have a reputation in the local community for being learned, respectable, and reliable. It also happens to those who are thought of as neither learned nor reliable, nor perhaps even respectable, but have become celebrities, perhaps for having appeared in their underpants on a talk show.

All end up being asked to write the preface to someone else's book. To this kind of request each reacts in his own way, and some regard it as a welcome act of recognition. Others, like me, receive a dozen requests a month on subjects of all kinds, and from all sorts of people: the worthy colleague, the poetaster paying to be published, the first-time novelist, the inventor of a new perpetual motion machine.

Apart from finding it impossible to read every manuscript, and not wishing to sound like one of those prefacers who charges by the line, I now reply that, having said no to many close friends, it would seem offensive if I said yes to an outsider. And the matter usually ends there. But when it's a friend who asks, I take the time to write a more detailed letter explaining what I have learned from many decades of experience in the book world. I explain that the motive for my refusal is to save him or her from a publishing disaster.

There are only two instances in which a preface is not a bad thing. One is when the person being prefaced is among the dead: a young scholar might introduce a new publication of the *Iliad*, and Homer will not be any the worse for it. The other, a famous and venerable author writing the preface for a new young talent. This is an act of paternalism, though the debut author will not worry about that, but will be proud of it, since he or she venerates and admires the matchless prefacer, and is pleased that the success of this first work will be assured.

All other cases—by a living scholar to a living author, and by an adult to an adult—are a death blow to the author.

Generally the author or the publisher, in asking for a preface, imagines that the prefacer might help to sell a few more copies. The effect on a discerning reader is the following: "If this author, about whom I know nothing, needs help from this prefacer, it's an indication that I'm better off knowing nothing about him or her, since he or she is clearly someone of little importance whom the prefacer has helped out for reasons of friendship, pity, political solidarity, or perhaps for money or sexual favors."

If I go into a bookshop and find a book, let's say memoirs in post-Wilhelmine Germany, my first reaction is "Good God, how ignorant I am. I knew nothing about this author. He or she must be a great expert on post-Wilhelmine Germany!" It's a natural feeling. If, at a conference, someone refers to a book by So-and-So, someone I'd never heard of, my first reaction, if I have any sense, is to feel a cultural inadequacy and promise myself that sooner or later I will search this author out. But if I find the work of So-and-So in a bookstore and see it has a preface by some big name, my mind is instantly put at rest: of course I didn't know So-and-So, because clearly he or she needs help to get noticed.

This line of reasoning is, I think, obvious, consistent, and persuasive, and when I explain it to the person who asked me to write a preface, I add that personally I wouldn't wish to be prefaced by anyone—on the contrary, I'm against the practice of the university professor writing a preface for the student, since it's the most lethal way, for all the above reasons, of exposing the youth and immaturity of the author.

And yet my interlocutor often remains unconvinced, and suspects my reasoning is inspired by ill will. And as I get older, many of those I've tried to help by my refusal become hostile.

Unless it happens, and I promise it actually did happen, the person then publishes the book at his own expense using my courteous letter of refusal as a preface. Such is the human thirst for prefaces.

2006

A noncomrade who gets it wrong

A website called *La storia nascosta* (*The Hidden Story*) quotes something I'm supposed to have said in *El País:* "The Red Brigades had the right idea about fighting against multinational companies, but were wrong to believe in terrorism." It implies that I would go along with the formula "comrades who get it wrong," and concede that "one could agree with the ideas, but not with the methods." And it concludes: "If this is all Italian culture has to say thirty years after the assassination of Aldo Moro, it's the same old story. Alas."

But the site also has comments from visitors, including these sensible words from an anonymous person: "I rather doubt that Prof. Eco would have said something so banal. *Foucault's Pendulum* includes, among other things, his own personal assessment of the Red Brigades in the 1960s and '70s, which certainly doesn't glorify the world of terrorism. I would be curious to know his exact words, and not the version that comes from the newspapers." The person who runs the website, on the other hand, has read neither my *Foucault's Pendulum* nor the articles I wrote in *La Repubblica* at the time of Aldo Moro's kidnapping and murder, which were republished in my book *Sette anni di desiderio* (*Seven Years of Desire*). That is his right, which I will defend until my dying day. But I suspect he hasn't read my interview in *El País* either, based on a number of paragraphs in Italian, and which the article summed up in a few lines. To make a deduction from incomplete and false premises is an error of logic.

I will nevertheless respond, out of respect for that cautious anonymous contributor, and for others who, from a visit to this insidious website, might be led astray in all good faith.

What I said in the Spanish interview was the same as I had written thirty years ago. I said that the newspapers described the statements of the Red Brigades as "insane" when they talked about the so-called "Imperialist State of the Multinationals," whereas, though expressed in rather colorful terms, it was the only idea that was not insane—save for the fact that the idea was not theirs but had been borrowed from European and American publications, in particular the *Monthly Review*. Talking at that time about the State of the Multinationals meant believing that world politics was no longer determined by individual governments but by a network of transnational economic powers who could moreover decide on questions of war and peace. In those days the prime example was what became known as the Seven Sisters, the seven oil companies that dominated the world's petroleum industry. But today even children talk about globalization, and globalization means that the lettuce we eat is grown in Burkina Faso, washed and packaged in Hong Kong, and sent to Romania before being distributed to Italy or France. And that is the government of multinationals, and if the example seems banal, think about how large transnational aircraft companies can influence the decisions of the Italian government when it comes to the future of Alitalia.

What was truly insane in the thinking of the Red Brigades and other terrorist groups was the conclusions they drew from it: first, that to fight the multinationals there had to be a revolution in Italy; second, to throw the multinationals into turmoil they had to kill Moro and

many other good people; third, that their actions would lead the proletariat to revolution.

First of all, revolution in a single country would have made little
difference to the multinationals, and in any event international pressure would have quickly restored order; second, the influence of one
Italian politician in this game of interests was entirely irrelevant; and
third, they ought to have realized that, however many people the terrorists killed, the working class would not have been drawn into a
revolution. And to understand this, there was no need to forecast how
events would develop. It sufficed to look at what had happened with
the Tupamaros in Uruguay and similar movements that managed, at
most, to persuade colonels in Argentina to carry out not a revolution
but a coup d'état, while the proletarian masses lifted not a finger.

Now, anyone who draws three wrong conclusions from a premise that is, all in all, quite acceptable can only be wrong. If one of my
school friends had said that because the Sun rises and sets, then it
revolves around the Earth, I would have called him not just wrong, but
an idiot.

2008

Saying sorry

I have spoken previously about the tendency to say sorry, which has
now gone too far, and I used George W. Bush's repentance over Iraq
as an example. To do something that ought not to be done and then
simply to say sorry is not enough. For a start, you have to promise
not to do it again. Bush won't invade Iraq a second time because the
Americans have relieved him of responsibility, but perhaps he would

do it again if he could. Many who throw stones and then hide their hands say sorry precisely so they can do it again. Saying sorry costs nothing.

It's rather like the story of criminals who repent. Once upon a time, people who repented for their wrongdoing first made amends in some way, then they devoted their lives to penance, took refuge in the Thebaid and beat their breast with sharp stones, or cared for lepers in Africa. A person who repents today confines himself to giving evidence against his ex-accomplices, then keeps careful guard over his new identity in a comfortable secret location, or gets early release from prison and writes his memoirs, gives interviews, meets heads of state, and receives romantic love letters from young girls.

On the Internet there's a whole website dedicated to "phrases for saying sorry." The most lapidary is *Sorry, I'm Clearly a Perfect Shit*. Another site, called *The Art of Saying Sorry,* is only for lovers who have been unfaithful, and offers this advice: "The important and universal rule is never to feel yourself a loser when you say sorry. Saying sorry is not synonymous with weakness but with control and strength, it means returning straightway to the side of right, wrong-footing the partner who is forced to listen. Admitting your own errors is also a gesture of liberation: it helps to bring emotions out into the open without repressing them, and to experience them more intensely." As if to say: sorry means summoning the strength to start all over again.

If the person who has done wrong is still alive, he apologizes in person. But if he's dead? Pope John Paul II pointed the way when he said sorry for the trial against Galileo. Even if the wrong had been committed by one of his predecessors, it is the legitimate successor who says sorry. But it's not always clear who the legitimate successor is. For example, who should apologize for the Slaughter of the Innocents?

The wrongdoer was Herod, governor of Jerusalem; therefore his only legitimate successor is the Israeli government. Whereas responsibility for the death of Jesus, contrary to what Saint Paul led us to believe, lies not with the wicked Jews but with the Roman government. Those at the foot of the cross were centurions and not Pharisees. Once the Holy Roman Empire had gone, the sole surviving heir of the Roman government is the Italian state, so our president, Giorgio Napolitano, should be the one to apologize for the crucifixion.

Who says sorry for the Vietnam War? It's unclear whether this should be the next president of the United States or a member of the Kennedy family. For the Russian Revolution and the murder of the Romanovs, there's no doubt, since the only true and legitimate heir of Leninism and Stalinism is Vladimir Putin. And for the St. Bartholomew's Day Massacre? It's the French Republic, as successor to the monarchy, but since the brains behind the whole business was a queen, Catherine de' Medici, the task of saying sorry today ought to be performed by Carla Bruni.

There would then be some rather awkward cases. Who would say sorry for the mess caused by Ptolemy, the man truly responsible for the case against Galileo? If, as some say, he was born at Ptolemais, which is part of modern Libya, the person saying sorry should be Muammar Gaddafi, but if Ptolemy was born in Alexandria, then it should be the Egyptian government. Who says sorry for the extermination camps? The sole heirs of Nazism are the neo-Nazi movements, and they don't look as if they want to say sorry. On the contrary, they'd do it again if they could.

And who in Italy would say sorry for the assassination of socialists like Giacomo Matteotti and the Rosselli brothers during the Fascist period?

2008

The Sun still turns

The geneticist Edoardo Boncinelli recently gave a series of lectures at Bologna University on the theory of evolution, its origins and developments, and I was struck not so much by the now incontrovertible evidence about evolutionism, in its neo-Darwinian form, as by so many naïve and confused ideas, not just among those who oppose it but those who agree. For example, take the idea that according to Darwinism man is descended from the apes. (One is perhaps tempted, given instances of racism in our time, to respond as Dumas did to an impudent Parisian who made an ironic remark about his mixed blood: "I may perhaps be descended from the apes, but you, sir, are reverting to one.")

Science always has to deal with public opinion, which is less evolved than one imagines. As educated people, we know that the Earth revolves around the Sun and not vice versa, and yet in our daily life we display a naïveté of perception and happily say that the Sun rises, is high in the sky, sets. But how many "educated" people are there? A survey carried out in 1982 by the magazine *Science et Vie* showed that one in three French people thought the Sun went around the Earth.

I take this news from *Les Cahiers de l'Institut* (2009), the publication of a national institute for studying and investigating *fous littéraires*, namely, all those more or less crackpot authors who put forward improbable theories. France leads the field, and I have considered the literature on the subject in two previous articles, as well as on the death of its leading expert, André Blavier. But in this issue of *Les Cahiers de l'Institut*, Olivier Justafré looks at those who deny the terrestrial movement and spherical form of our planet.

That the Copernican theory was still being denied at the end of the

1600s, even by eminent scholars, comes as no surprise, but the number of studies published in the nineteenth and twentieth centuries is quite remarkable. Justafré limits himself to French publications, but these are more than enough, from Abbé Matalène, who demonstrated in 1842 that the Sun was only thirty-two centimeters in diameter, an idea put forward by Epicurus twenty-two centuries earlier, to Victor Marcucci, according to whom the Earth was flat, with Corsica at its center.

We might make allowances for the nineteenth century, but *Essai de rationalisation de la science expérimentale,* by Léon Max, was printed in 1907 by a reputable scientific publishing house, and *La terre ne tourne pas* was published in 1936, written by one Bojo Raïovitch, according to whom the Sun is smaller than the Earth but larger than the Moon, though Abbé Bouheret in 1815 had claimed the opposite. In 1935, Gustave Plaisant, who describes himself as an *ancien polytechnicien,* published a work with the dramatic title *Tourne-t-elle? (Does It Turn?),* and as late as 1965 there was a book by Maurice Ollivier, another *ancien élève* of the École Polytechnique, arguing once again that the Earth is fixed in place.

Outside France, Justafré's article refers only to the work of Samuel Birley Rowbotham, which shows that the Earth is a disk with the North Pole at its center, 650 kilometers away from the Sun. Rowbotham's work was published in 1849 with the title *Zetetic Astronomy: Earth Is Not a Globe,* but over a period of thirty years his book expanded to 430 pages and led to the creation of a Universal Zetetic Society, which remained in existence until World War I.

In 1956, a member of the Royal Astronomical Society, Samuel Shenton, founded the Flat Earth Society to continue the legacy of the Universal Zetetic Society. NASA photographed the Earth from space in the 1960s, and at that point no one could continue to deny that it was spherical. Shenton, however, claimed that such photographs could only delude an untutored eye: the entire space program was a sham, and the Moon landing a cinematic illusion aimed at deceiving the public with the false idea of a spherical Earth. Shenton's successor, Charles Kenneth Johnson, continued to denounce the plot against Flat Earthers, writing in 1980 that the idea of a revolving globe was a conspiracy against which Moses and Columbus had fought. One of Johnson's arguments was that if the Earth were a sphere, the surface of a great mass of water would have to be curved, whereas he had tested the surfaces of Lake Tahoe and the Salton Sea and had found no curvature.

Is it any surprise, then, that there are still antievolutionists around?

2010

What you mustn't do

Should anyone ever express an insulting opinion about your literary or artistic work, don't sue, even if their words cross that often narrow boundary between ruthless critical judgment and insult. In 1958, Beniamino Dal Fabbro, a spirited and controversial music critic, wrote an article in *Il Giorno* in which he tore into a performance by Maria Callas, a diva for whom he had no love. I don't remember exactly what he had said, but I remember the epigram that this amiable and sarcastic figure circulated among his friends at Bar Giamaica, in the Brera district of Milan: "*La cantante d'Epidauro—meritava un pomidauro*" ("The singer from Epidaurus—deserved a tomautus").

Callas, not an easy character herself, was furious, and sued. I remember Dal Fabbro describing it at Bar Giamaica: he arrived at the trial dressed in black on the day his lawyer was to speak, so when the lawyer pointed to him, he would appear as a severe and incorruptible man of learning; but on the day it was the turn of Callas's lawyer (who, according to Dal Fabbro, might have brought out some malicious stories that portrayed him as a Jonah), he turned up in a light linen suit and straw-colored Panama hat.

Naturally the court acquitted Dal Fabbro, recognizing his right to criticize. But the amusing aspect of the story was that the general public, following the case in the newspapers, had some misconceptions about the law and a person's constitutional right to freely express his beliefs. So they interpreted the court's judgment not as an acknowledgment of the critic's freedom of expression, but as a confirmation of what he had said: that Callas sang poorly. And so Callas emerged from the case unjustly labeled as a bad singer by an Italian court of law.

So what do you do with those who have insulted you? Leave well alone. If you are involved in literature or the arts, you have to accept the fact that you will be criticized, and that is part of the job, and you must hope that millions of future readers will prove your enemy wrong. History has dealt justice to Louis Spohr for his description of Beethoven's Fifth Symphony as "an orgy of noise and vulgarity," and to Thomas Bailey Aldrich, who wrote of Emily Dickinson: "The incoherence and formlessness of her—versicles are fatal." And to the executive at Metro-Goldwyn-Mayer who, after screen-testing Fred Astaire, commented, "Can't act, can't sing. Balding. Can dance a little."

2012

The miraculous Mortacc

My doctor has prescribed a drug to treat my arthritic pains. To avoid any tedious legal implications, I will give it a fictitious name, Mortacc.

Like any responsible person, before taking it I read the accompany-ing leaflet, which tells you under what circumstances you must not use it—for example, if you've drunk a bottle of vodka, or have to drive an articulated truck from Milan to Sicily, or have leprosy, or are preg-nant with triplets. Now, my leaflet suggests that taking Mortacc can cause allergic reactions, such as swelling of the face, lips, and neck, fatigue and giddiness, and in elderly people, falls, blurring or loss of vision, spinal damage, heart and/or kidney failure, and urinary prob-lems. Some patients have threatened suicide and self-harm, and in such cases the leaflet recommends calling a doctor—presumably as the patient is about to leap from the window (though it might be pref-erable to call the fire department). Naturally, Mortacc can result in constipation, paralyzed intestine, convulsions, and, if taken with other medicines, breathing difficulties or coma.

Driving a motor vehicle is out of the question, as is operating com-plicated machinery or a machine press while standing on a girder on the fifty-first floor of a skyscraper. If you take more than the prescribed dose of Mortacc, expect to feel confused, drowsy, agitated, and rest-less. If you take less, or suddenly stop the treatment, you may experi-ence uneasy sleep, headaches, nausea, anxiety, convulsions, depres-sion, sweating, and dizziness.

More than one person in ten experiences increased appetite, ner-vous tension, confusion, loss of libido, irritability, attention loss, awk-wardness (*sic*), memory impairment, trembling, speech difficulty, tin-gling sensation, lethargy and insomnia, fatigue, blurred sight, double vision, dizziness and loss of balance, dry mouth, vomiting, flatulence, difficulty getting an erection, swelling, feeling of intoxication, or un-steady movement.

More than one person in a thousand experiences a drop in blood sugar levels, distorted self-perception, depression, mood swings, difficulty in recalling words, loss of memory, hallucinations, troubled dreams, panic attacks, apathy, feeling strange (*sic*), inability to reach an orgasm, delayed ejaculation, difficulty forming ideas, torpor, anomalous eye movement, reduced reflexes, skin sensitivity, loss of taste, burning sensations, trembling, lowered awareness, fainting, increased awareness of noises, dryness and swelling of the eyes, runny eyes, abnormal heartbeat, low blood pressure, high blood pressure, vasomotor instability, breathing difficulty, dry nose, abdominal swelling, increase in salivation, heartburn, loss of sensitivity around the mouth, excessive perspiration, shivering, muscular contractions and cramps, articular pain, backache, pain in the limbs, incontinence, difficulty and pain in urinating, weakness, falling, thirst, tight-chestedness, altered liver function. Let's forget what happens to fewer than one person in a thousand—it's impossible to be so unlucky.

I avoided taking a single pill, as I was sure I'd be struck down immediately with housemaid's knee, as the immortal Jerome K. Jerome had imagined, even if the information sheet made no mention of it. I thought of throwing the pills away, but if I put them in the garbage bin I risked mutating the mouse population with epidemic consequences. I put the pills in a metal box and buried it deep down in a park.

In the meantime, I have to say, my arthritic pains have gone.

2012

Joyce and the Maserati

Looking through the catalogs from auction houses like Christie's or Sotheby's, apart from artworks, antique books, autographs, and assorted relics, you come across what are called memorabilia: the shoes worn by a diva in a particular film, a fountain pen that belonged to

Ronald Reagan, and so on. A distinction has to be made here between collecting bizarre objects and hunting for fetishistic souvenirs. The collector is invariably slightly mad, even when he spends his last cent buying incunabula of *The Divine Comedy,* but his passion is legitimate. In collectors' magazines you discover people who collect sugar packets, Coca-Cola bottle tops, and phone cards. It's more noble, I think, to collect postage stamps than beer caps, but there's no accounting for taste.

It's a different matter wanting at all costs to own the shoes worn by that diva in that film. If you collect all the shoes worn by film stars, from Georges Méliès on, then you're a collector, and your folly makes sense, but what are you going to do with a single pair?

Recently I found two curious news items in *La Repubblica.* The first reports that the Italian government is auctioning off its official cars on eBay. I can understand that someone might take a fancy to a Maserati and decide to buy one at a bargain price, even one with high mileage and the knowledge that he'll have to spend a great deal of money looking after it. But what's the point of competing with thousands to buy a car purchased with public money to ferry government ministers about, at a price two or three times that listed in used-car magazines? Yet that's exactly what is happening. This is outright fetishism, and it's difficult to understand what satisfaction is to be gained from sitting on a leather seat previously warmed by some illustrious figure—not to mention those who offer exorbitant sums to luxuriate where the buttocks of a mere undersecretary or political aide have sat.

But let's move on to something different, which I found in the same newspaper, on a double-page spread. Love letters written by Ian Fleming at the age of twenty-six have been put up for auction, and are expected to fetch up to 66,000 euros. In them, the young agent, not yet so secret, wrote, "I want to kiss you on the mouth, on the breasts, lower down." Now, there's nothing wrong with collecting personal letters, and as letters go, one that's prurient might be considered more entertaining than one that's not. Even a noncollector would be happy to own the letter in which James Joyce writes to Nora: "I am your child as I told you and you must be severe with me . . . I wish you would smack me or flog me even. Not in play, dear, in earnest and on my naked flesh." Or what Oscar Wilde wrote to his beloved Lord Alfred Douglas: "It is a marvel that those red-roseleaf lips of yours should have been made no less for the madness of music and song than for the madness of kisses." They would be excellent conversation pieces about the weaknesses of great men.

What's unreasonable is the value that literary history and literary criticism often place on such artifacts. Does our knowledge that the twenty-six-year-old Fleming was writing letters typical of a randy adolescent make any difference to our enjoyment of the James Bond stories, or to our critical assessment of the author's style? To understand Joyce's eroticism as a literary fact, read *Ulysses*, especially the final chapter, even if the person who wrote it lived a chaste life. With some great men, it was their writing that was salacious and their lives virtuous, but with others their writing was virtuous and their lives salacious. Would our view of Manzoni's *The Betrothed* change if it came to light that the author was a naughty boy in bed and that his two wives died as a result of his sexual excesses?

2014

Napoleon never existed

I have owned for some time a late translation, dated 1914, of a pamphlet by a Jean-Baptiste Pérès entitled *Napoleon Never Existed*. A few days ago, however, I came across the first edition of 1835, which bore the title *Grand Erratum, source d'un nombre infini d'errata* (*Grand Erratum, Source of an Infinite Number of Errata*). The author demonstrates that Napoleon is merely a sun myth, and supports his argument with plenty of evidence, finding analogies with Apollo, the Sun: "Napoleo" is said to mean "true Apollo the destroyer"; both were born on a Mediterranean island; the name of Napoleon's mother, Letizia, is said to mean "dawn," and Letizia is derived from Latona, which is the name of Apollo's mother. Napoleon had three sisters who are evidently the three Graces, four brothers who symbolize the four seasons, and two wives who are the Moon and the Earth. His twelve marshals were the signs of the zodiac, and, like the Sun, Napoleon ruled the south and was overshadowed in the north.

He brought an end to the scourge of the French Revolution, which reminds us of Apollo's killing of Python. The Sun rises in the east and sets in the west, and Napoleon came from Egypt to govern France and died in the western seas, after a reign of twelve years, which are none other than the twelve hours of daylight. "It is therefore proven that the supposed hero of our century is no more than an allegorical character, whose attributes are all loaned out by the Sun."

Pérès knew how to talk nonsense, but he did so to parody *Origine de tous les cultes* (1794) by Charles-François Dupuis, in which it was argued that religions, fables, myths, and mysteries were no more than physical and astronomical allegories.

After Pérès came one Aristarchus Newlight (*Historic Certainties Respecting the Early History of America*, 1851), who used similar arguments to challenge David Strauss's *The Life of Jesus* and his critical rationalist interpretation of the gospels. But before Pérès, Richard Whately had published *Historic Doubts Relative to Napoleon Buonaparte* in 1819, of which I have a first edition. Whately was an English theologian and the archbishop of Dublin, and had written many serious works on religious and philosophical arguments—his book on logic had influenced Charles Sanders Peirce. Whately had set out to refute the rationalist writers, in particular David Hume, who rejected pseudo-historical events, such as those in scripture and the stories of miracles, because there was no empirical evidence to prove them. Whately didn't challenge Hume and others, but carried their arguments to their logical conclusion. Following these principles, he demonstrated that the stories about Napoleon's exploits, which also have something miraculous about them, were not always firsthand accounts, and that not many of Napoleon's contemporaries had actually seen him.

The antiquarian *trouvailles* I have described are by three writers who satirize not so much those who hunt out mysteries as thinkers who seek to debunk mysteries. But their method is interesting: carry the ideas of others to an extreme and they'll be laughed out of existence.

2014

Are we all mad?

Over the past few weeks we have witnessed acts of undoubted madness. The German airline pilot was mad when he crashed his plane into a mountain, killing all the passengers on board. The Milanese businessman was undoubtedly mad when he committed multiple murder in a courtroom. It's also unsettling to read about another pilot who started firing a gun in his own home. I leave aside that he had been accused of causing a road accident while driving intoxicated, something that might happen to anyone, except that driving when drunk might raise concerns about the habits of a man who had recently piloted the Italian president.

The policemen accused of beating up protesters at the Armando Diaz School in Genoa during the G8 meeting in 2001, were they mad? They were regular officers. What frenzy possessed them to run riot, as if oblivious to the fact that someone in the end would find them out?

This reminded me of the words of the nineteenth-century social reformer Robert Owen: "All the world is queer save thee and me, and even thou art a little queer." After all, we live in the belief that wisdom is the normal state and that madness is the exception. At one time the madhouse was the answer. But is it true? Might we not think that madness is the normal condition and that so-called normality is a transitory state? Paradox aside, wouldn't it be prudent to persuade ourselves that every human being has a dose of madness, which remains latent in some throughout their lives, but which in others explodes without warning? It explodes in nonlethal and at times positive forms in those we regard as geniuses, innovators, and visionaries, but it manifests itself in others as actions we condemn as criminally insane.

If this is so, there is a seed of madness in every living person, all seven billion of us, a seed that might suddenly sprout, and only at certain moments. Part of the time, ISIS cutthroats are probably faithful husbands and loving fathers—perhaps they spend several hours a day watching television or take their children to the mosque. Then they get up in the morning, sling a Kalashnikov around their neck, perhaps their wife prepares an omelet sandwich for them, and they go off to behead someone or machine-gun a hundred children. After all, wasn't that how Adolf Eichmann lived? There again, even the most brutal assassin, if you listen to his mother, was an exemplary child until the day before, and at most mildly irritable or gloomy.

If that's the case, we ought to live in a continual state of mistrust, fearing that at any moment our wife or our husband, our son or our daughter, the neighbor we say hello to on the staircase each morning, or our best friend is suddenly going to produce a hatchet and sink it into our skull, or put arsenic in our soup.

But then our life would be impossible. If we could no longer trust anyone—not the loudspeaker at the railroad station that tells us the train for Rome is leaving from platform five, because the announcer might be mad—we'd become permanently paranoid.

To survive, we have to trust someone. But we have to convince ourselves that absolute trust, of the kind that sometimes happens when people fall in love, does not exist—that the only trust is probabilistic. If a best friend has been dependable over the years, we can wager that he is a person to be trusted. It is rather like Pascal's wager: it's more advantageous to believe in eternal life than not to believe in it. Nevertheless, it's a wager. Living on a wager is risky, but living without such a wager, on friendship if not on eternal life, is essential to our mental health.

I go along with Saul Bellow that in an age of madness, to expect to be untouched by madness is itself a form of madness. So don't take the things you have just read as pure gold.

2015

Idiots and the responsible press

I've been much amused by a story on the Web about idiots. For those who haven't been following it, it was reported online and in the press that in a so-called keynote lecture I stated that the Internet is full of idiots. This is not true. The lecture was on an entirely different subject, but it demonstrates how news becomes distorted when it circulates among newspapers and the Internet.

The story about idiots came up at a press conference when, in answer to some question or other, I made a purely commonsense observation. Out of the planet's seven billion inhabitants there's an inevitable number of idiots, many of whom used to communicate their ravings to friends or relatives at a bar, so their opinions were confined to a limited circle. A substantial number of these people now can express their opinions on social networks. Such opinions therefore reach large audiences, and merge with the many other opinions expressed by reasonable people.

Please note that my notion of idiots contained no racist connotations. No one, with a few exceptions, is an idiot by profession, but someone who is an excellent grocer, an excellent surgeon, or an excellent bank clerk can say some silly things about matters he knows nothing about, or has given insufficient thought to. Reactions on the Internet are immediate, with no time for reflection.

It's right that the Internet should allow space for those with nothing sensible to say, but the excess of stupidity is clogging the lines. And certain unseemly reactions I have seen on the Internet confirm my reasonable contention. Indeed, someone reported me as saying that the Internet gives the same prominence to the opinions of a fool and those of a Nobel Prize winner, and suddenly there was a pointless discussion that went viral over whether or not I'd have accepted the Nobel Prize—without anyone going off to check Wikipedia. All of this shows to what degree people are inclined to talk without pausing to think. In any event, the number of idiots can now be quantified: at least 300 million. Wikipedia is reported to have lost 300 million users in recent times. These are all surfers who no longer use the Internet to find information, but prefer to stay online chatting with their peers, and probably without pausing to think.

The normal Internet user ought to be capable of grasping the difference between incoherent and well-articulated ideas, and here the problem of filtering information arises. It doesn't relate just to opinions expressed in blogs or via Twitter, but is an urgent question for all websites, where you can find information that is reliable and useful, but also—and I defy anyone to deny it—ravings of every kind, accounts of nonexistent conspiracies, Holocaust denial, racism, and information that is culturally false, inaccurate, or slipshod.

How do you filter information? Each of us has the capacity to filter information when we look at websites that deal with topics we know about, but I for one would have a hard time telling whether or not a website on string theory is accurate. Not even schools can teach pupils how to filter information, since teachers are in the same position as I am, and those who teach Greek are likely to find themselves defenseless when they look at a site on catastrophe theory or the Thirty Years' War.

There is only one solution. Newspapers are often slaves to the Internet, as that is where they gather news and stories that sometimes turn out to be false, thus giving voice to their major rival—and doing so always later than the Internet. Instead, they ought to devote at least two pages each day to an analysis of websites, in the same way they review books or films, pointing out the sites that are virtuous and reporting those that carry bogus stories and inaccuracies. They'd be providing a valuable public service and might even persuade those many Internet users who are turning away from newspapers to return to them.

To launch an enterprise such as this, a newspaper would need a team of analysts, many of whom would have to come from outside. It would cost money, but would provide a valuable cultural service and give the press a new purpose.

2015